APPROACHES TO *Islam* IN RELIGIOUS STUDIES

APPROACHES TO
Islam
IN RELIGIOUS STUDIES

Richard C. Martin, Editor

THE UNIVERSITY OF ARIZONA PRESS / TUCSON

About the Editor

RICHARD C. MARTIN's interest in Islam as it is understood and practiced throughout the world is longstanding. He is author of a book entitled *Islam: A Cultural Perspective* and of numerous articles on approaches to understanding Islamic religious phenomena. In addition to chairing the Department of Religious Studies at Arizona State University, he is conducting research on the significance of the Qur'ān in local contexts of the Muslim world.

THE UNIVERSITY OF ARIZONA PRESS

This book was set in 11/13 Linotron Janson.
Manufactured in the U.S.A.

Library of Congress Cataloging in Publication Data
Main entry under title:

Approaches to Islam in religious studies.

An international symposium on Islam and the history of religions hosted by the Dept. of Religious Studies at Arizona State University, Tempe, in Jan. 1980.
Bibliography: p.
Includes index.
1. Islam—Study and teaching—Congresses. I. Martin, Richard C. II. Arizona State University. Dept. of Humanities and Religious Studies.
BP42.A67 1985 297'.07 85-1099
ISBN 0-8165-0868-2

Contents

Foreword *by Charles J. Adams* vii

Preface xi

1 Islam and Religious Studies: An Introductory Essay 1
Richard C. Martin

Part One Scripture and Prophet 19

2 *Qur'ān* as Spoken Word: An Islamic Contribution to the Understanding of Scripture 23
William A. Graham

3 The Popular Muḥammad: Models in the Interpretation of an Islamic Paradigm 41
Earle H. Waugh

Part Two Ritual and Community 59

4 Islamic Ritual: Perspectives and Theories 63
Frederick M. Denny

5 Pilgrimage and the History of Religions: Theoretical Approaches to the Hajj 78
William R. Roff

Part Three Religion and Society 87

6 Primitive Mind/Modern Mind: New Approaches to an Old Problem Applied to Islam 91
Marilyn R. Waldman

7 Approaches to the Study of Conversion to Islam in India 106
Richard M. Eaton

Part Four Scholarship and Interpretation 125

8 The Hermeneutics of Henry Corbin 129
Charles J. Adams

9 Literary Analysis of *Qur'ān*, *Tafsīr*, and *Sīra:* The Methodologies of John Wansbrough 151
Andrew Rippin

10 Toward a Hermeneutic of Qur'ānic and Other Narratives of Isma'ili Thought 164
Azim Nanji

Part Five Challenge and Criticism 175

11 Outsiders' Interpretations of Islam: A Muslim's Point of View 179
Muhammad Abdul-Rauf

12 Approaches to Islam in Religious Studies: Review Essay 189
Fazlur Rahman

Part Six Reference Material 203

Notes to the Chapters 205

About the Contributors 235

Index 239

Foreword

CHARLES J. ADAMS

The appearance of a book on approaches to Islam in religious studies should not require much justification, given the dramatic growth of interest in Islam in recent years. Yet, underlying the essays in this book is the issue of the work of historians of religions in relation to scholarship in Middle Eastern studies (or oriental studies) and the relation of both of these to contemporary Muslim scholarship. The conventional wisdom, to which I have added my own voice in the past, has been that historians of religions have failed to advance our knowledge and understanding of Islam as religion and that Islamists have failed to explain adequately Islamic religious phenomena. The third factor—increasing Muslim sensitivity to Islamic studies in the West—far from resolving the issue of how to approach the study of Islam as religion to the satisfaction of either religionists or Islamists has created still more strident divisions. The present work addresses these issues and is all the more important in light of them.

Several years back I contributed an essay on Islam and the History of Religions to the series of volumes published by the University of

Chicago in commemoration of the fiftieth anniversary of its Divinity School. The preceding conference to which the paper was presented, taking place as it did on the premises of the North American institution most noted for its contributions to history of religions as a discipline, afforded the opportunity to reflect aloud in the midst of a distinguished company on the apparent lack of meaningful relationship between the systematic scientific study of religion on the one hand and the work done by Islamists on the other. The substance of the paper was a complaint, or rather a lament, that the central concerns of the developing science of religion seemed of little relevance to students of Islam and that the methods of historians of religions were finding little application as a means of illuminating Islamic material. The analysis of the situation evoked a vigorous defense of directions taken by historians of religions in recent times and of the themes around which their most significant work had revolved, but there was no contradiction of the central thesis of the paper and no convincing demonstration that historians of religions or their methods had contributed significantly to the understanding of Islam. The rather discouraging picture that was sketched at the Chicago conference in the mid-1960s seemed to find confirmation in a subsequent session of the American Academy of Religion in 1973 (again in Chicago) when a group of scholars with Islamic interests met to discuss the problem once again.

The present volume of essays, first inspired by a symposium on Islam and the history of religions held at Arizona State University in January 1980, is testimony to a partial but growing conquest of the gap between the history of religions and Islamics. The agenda of the symposium was not one of considering questions of method and approach to the field of study in the abstract, but of devoting attention to specific aspects of the Islamic tradition and of actually employing some of the theoretical insights and methodological richness of the science of religion to cast light on the area of interest. For the first time in North America a large group of scholars who were trained or have read widely in the history of religions and who identify themselves with the concerns of this "field" have cooperated to share insights into the Islamic tradition. The book goes beyond the achievement of the symposium by providing scholars, students, and the general public with carefully written essays on topics and issues first raised at the symposium.

Thus, in contrast to the strong, indeed almost exclusive, textual and philological orientation of traditional Islamic studies, we have in this volume papers that deal, for example, with such subjects as Islamic worship, popular religious practice, and the many-faceted significance of Qur'ānic recitation in the daily lives of pious Muslims. The emphasis falls upon an exposition of Islam as it is experienced and lived by members of the community. Although the ideal forms of a normative Islam are not lost to sight, the recognition is brought to bear that the reality of religion has its locus in the experience of the devotee and that scholars must, above all else, subject themselves to that experience. There are also other papers that consider Islamic material in the light of significant theoretical and philosophical schemes of topical importance, which have been used by historians of religions with other specializations to illuminate their fields but have seldom been exploited for the insight they might afford into Islam. Although the battle is by no means won—for the scholars in Islamic studies are a notoriously conservative group—there is within the developments represented by these essays at least the beginning of a breakthrough to a wider perspective on the study of Islam and to a more mutually fructifying relation between those occupied with learning about Islam and those who are principally interested in the phenomenon of religion.

The elation that one may feel in observing the growing rapproachment of what were previously two scholarly solitudes is directly related to the growth of Islamic studies in North American institutions. Although as a religious tradition Islam still does not attract the attention given to more "exotic" traditions of India and the Far East, it has come to be more widely and more firmly represented in departments of religion and major university centers for the study of religion than it was a decade ago. The possibility of work on Islam exists where it did not exist before, but more important is the underlying insight that no study of the human religious venture that neglects the wealth of the Islamic tradition can be complete or valid. A further cause of rejoicing is the fact that those who most strongly exhibit the trend to base the study of Islam on a foundation of the history of religions are younger scholars, people who stand at the beginning of the most productive phases of their careers. These scholars, in general, lack nothing of the historical, linguistic, and philological qualifications of their teachers and predecessors, but they have grafted onto this powerful heritage the systematic and phenomenological concerns which they have absorbed at the feet of their mentors in the history of religions. The lamentations of the former years, therefore, now give way to hope and optimism. On the basis of the evidence presented by this volume of essays we may now look forward to a new phase in the evolution of Islamic studies in which the resources developed for the study of religion in other areas will be made to bear fruit also in the Islamic field.

Preface

Events in the Middle East and elsewhere in the Islamic world have encouraged an increasing number of scholars, journalists and other pundits to write a spate of new works for the American public. In many cases, what we stand to learn from these writings is a variety of views about the political and economic ramifications of Islamic world events for Western nations. Scholars in the humanities, particularly religious studies, have been less aggressive in helping us to understand the religion and cultures of Muslim peoples. The present work is a collection of essays prepared by scholars in the human sciences who wish to effect a qualitative improvement in our understanding of Islam at the levels of research, curriculum, and textbook-writing in higher education. This book presents, therefore, a much needed discussion concerning the study of Islamic religion, and it is meant to address teachers and students in religious studies primarily. Because the Islamic religion—as any religion—is fundamental to the society of the people who profess it, this volume should also be of interest to scholars in other fields and to the educated public, who seek a better understanding of the "religious" dimension of Islamic history.

The occasion for bringing together the contents of this work was an international symposium on "Islam and the History of Religions," hosted by the Department of Religious Studies at Arizona State University, Tempe, in January 1980. Most of the essays found in the volume were presented as working papers and discussed by their authors and some fifty registrants at the symposium.

Much of the cost of the symposium and of preparing these papers for publication was paid for by a grant from the Research Division of the National Endowment for the Humanities in 1979–80. Additional financial and administrative assistance was provided by the Office of Grants and Contracts at Arizona State University. The faculty, graduate students, and secretarial staff of the Department of Religious Studies also contributed considerable time and effort to the project. Generous gifts of time and money were given by OASIS (Organization of Arizonans Supporting Islamic Studies), even at an early stage before other funding had been secured. I am extremely grateful to all of these organizations and individuals for their kind, generous, and expert assistance in making the project and book possible.

I am also indebted to those who participated in the symposium and contributed to this book. The need for a rigorous discussion of methodology in the study of Islamic religion has long been recognized by the authors of this volume, and each has contributed to the success of the project far beyond the mere submission of papers. A special debt of gratitude is owed to Elizabeth Gottschalk, my research assistant at the time, who brought uncommon intelligence and industry to numerous aspects of the project. Several people read drafts of the volume and made helpful suggestions. I am particularly indebted to Barbara Metcalf, Bruce Lawrence, and Dale Eickelman. The final draft of the manuscript was prepared by Betty Daniels and Marsha Johnson.

I have edited the book with a view toward a common style of notes and transliteration. The authors' notes have been abbreviated as little as possible to permit readers who are not thoroughly familiar with the bibliography of Islamic studies easy recognition and access to the relevant primary and secondary sources.

Technical terms and phrases from Islamic languages, especially Arabic, have been transliterated in the book according to the system commonly used in English language journals. In cases where terms such as, say, *tafsīr* (commentary) or *ʿulamāʾ* (religious notables) are used frequently in a given chapter, the word is normally printed in roman type (tafsir, Ulama) after it has first appeared in italics with diacritical marks. In some cases, however, where an author's argument depends heavily on the use of technical terms, diacritical marks have been included throughout the chapter. The authors and editor have also sought to provide the first (or infrequent) use of technical terms with indications of their meaning in English.

I should like to acknowledge the following work quoted at length in this volume: Ibn Isḥāq, *The Life of Muhammad*, trans. Alfred Guillaume (by permission of Oxford University Press) and Jack Goody, *The Domestication of the Savage Mind* (by permission of Cambridge University Press, 1977). For use of the map on page 108, I should also like to credit *A Historical Atlas of Southeast Asia*, ed. Joseph E. Schwartzberg (The University of Chicago Press, 1978).

RICHARD C. MARTIN

APPROACHES TO *Islam* IN RELIGIOUS STUDIES

1

Islam and Religious Studies

An Introductory Essay

RICHARD C. MARTIN

The premise of this book, that Islam should receive greater attention in religious studies, rests on more than the current size, growth, and global impact of the world Muslim population. The essays which follow also presume that our understanding of Islam as religion and our understanding of religion in terms of Islam are issues in need of more focused discussion and clarity from scholars in religious studies. The traditional berth of Islamic studies in oriental- and area-studies programs in select graduate centers at North American universities is part of the problem. The failure of religious studies to congeal as a "discipline," despite the appearance of an increasing number of departments of religion or religious studies, is also symptomatic.

With implications for the study of Islam and non–Judeo-Christian religious traditions generally, two of the subfields associated with religious studies today have operated from quite different viewpoints, often in open conflict with one another and to the detriment of a coherent appreciation of the subject matter. Theology has advocated a normative understanding of "other" religions so that they could be judged by the confessional claims of Christianity. History of religions has held to the contrary that scholarly description and analysis of other religions require detachment on the part of the observer.[1] The claims of both approaches in their extreme forms—fideistic subjectivism versus scientific objectivism—are qualified or rejected by the authors of this volume.

Religious studies departments in North American colleges and universities share a common data field—the textual and behavioral expressions of human religiousness. It is in this context that theologians and historians of religions, who in nineteenth-century Europe conducted bitter polemics with one another from considerable institutional distance, now find themselves in twentieth-century North America in the position—if not yet always the mood—to participate in dialogue with one another within departments and programs of religious studies. Thus, while it may be appropriate to speak of religious studies as a "field" in very general terms, a discipline it is not if "discipline" is taken to mean operating with a common set of theoretical assumptions and methodological procedures. As in Women's studies, Afro-American studies, Jewish studies, and other multi-disciplinary newcomers to the humanities in the 1960s, scholars in religious studies have attempted to forge a new field without agreement on discipline—or more accurately, scholars in religious studies have attempted to gerrymander a data field of their own using a plurality of theories, methods, and religion data bases drawn from other disciplines in the human sciences. In short, the organizing principle of religious studies is a presumed subject matter, not a tradition of scholarship, as we find in such traditional humanities disciplines as classics, philology, philosophy, literary criticism, and history.

Scholars in religious studies, nonetheless, have roots in traditional disciplines. First are the traditional humanities just mentioned. Second are the theological disciplines of theology, biblical studies, and church history. Third are the social sciences, particularly anthropology, linguistics, and psychology. Fourth are area studies (formerly oriental studies), primarily Middle Eastern, East Asian, and South and Southeast Asian studies. The religious studies specialist on Islam may well have received doctoral training in Middle Eastern area studies, or have trained in a theological seminary. Such specialists in the religious studies context may, nonetheless, identify their teaching and writing about Islamic religion as history of religions scholarship. Thus, not just the theologian, but also the trained area specialist who migrates to religious studies departments and curricula must be prepared to ask a new set of questions of the religious data she or he has been trained to interpret. How well do history of religions and Islamic studies fit in the field of religious studies, where religion as such is the discursive subject matter among colleagues and students?

Islamic Studies and History of Religions

In an anthology of essays about the history of religions published nearly two decades ago, Charles J. Adams offered a somber assessment of the relationship between history of religions and Islamic studies.[2] Trained as an Islamicist, Adams also studied history of religions with Joachim Wach at the University of Chicago. Adams chose to pursue this duality of disciplines for the purpose of gaining, he said, "the conceptual tools for an ever sharper analysis of the Islamic tradition and for a more lucid understanding of the relationships among its diverse elements as well as of its structural connections with other traditions." As recently as the mid-1960s, however, Adams was reluctantly forced to conclude that it was "difficult to see a direct and fructifying relationship between the activities of Islamicists and those of historians of religions." The reasons were twofold, he believed. "First, there is the fact that historians of religions, as such, have dealt but little with Islamic data and made only a relatively small original contribution to the growing store of knowledge about Islamic peoples and their religious tradition. The burden of the work in this field has been borne by Arabists, Iranists, Indianists, and so on, working as historians and philologists in a relatively restricted area of concern." Second, "the great themes which have dominated the horizon of historians of religions in recent decades have not been such that would throw light on the Islamic experience or speak to the problems occupying Islamics scholarship."[3] Adams's assessment, with which few have disagreed, calls attention to an anomaly of scholarship that has held unfortunate consequences for the academic study of Islam as religion.

Academic studies of religion and of Islam are constituted by communities of scholars that have experienced notorious difficulty in relating to the rest of academe. As heirs to nineteenth-century *Religionswissenschaft*, historians of religions have been benignly neglected by scholars in other disciplines of the humanities and social sciences. Islamicists, standing in the tradition of orientalism, have come under increasing attack in recent years for their academic provincialism and for the distorted images of Islamic peoples and cultures many say they have created. Ambiguous at best, the position of one who wishes to address the question of "how" to study Islam as religion is further complicated by the prevailing trend toward compartmentalization in higher education. Scholars within the same university, studying various aspects of Islamic civilization—languages, history, geography, economics, politics, geology, or sociology—are not likely to give serious consideration to one another's work unless they belong to the same discipline or department. Prevailing conditions for hiring, promotion, and tenure tend to discourage the writing of books and articles for academic consideration outside of established disciplinary boundaries.

Another element of discord in the attempt to orchestrate cross-disciplinary approaches to cross-cultural studies comes from a cluster of problems surrounding the relation of the observer to the observed. Impartiality and detachment have often been noticeably lacking in writings about "other" human cultures, and there is strong evidence to suggest that religions have changed under the impact of academic study.[4] Among those who theorize about this process are scholars who argue that the contents of another person's faith will forever remain undisclosed unless the observer is sympathetic to the faith of the people he or she is studying. The hard line of this approach has it that only Muslims can study (or teach about) Islam with any degree of competent understanding. The softer line insists that "openness" or "empathy" toward the faith and beliefs of others is a necessary precondition to understanding, which seems to imply that only a "religious" person can comprehend Islam as religion. "Professor of Religion" is a doubly nuanced term, as Frederick Denny remarked at the symposium where working drafts of most of the papers in this volume were first discussed.[5]

Still another question of presuppositions concerns the limitations imposed by the *Weltanschauung* of the place and time from which the scholar makes his or her observations and judgments. Studies in hermeneutical philosophy have made us more conscious of how the interpreting subject is conditioned by a horizon of understanding—her or his historicity—which is a necessary ingredient of the process of textual study.[6] Moreover, many believe that the time is now past for limiting the study of Islam to strictly Western, scholarly points of view. Does this imply that the only valid categories and terms available for analyzing Islamic religious phenomena are to be provided by Islam itself? Or are there general "disciplinary" universes of discourse in, say, historical, linguistic, social-scientific, and religious studies for explaining religious phenomena that would find discursive coherence, if not congruence, among Western *and* non-Western scholars?

History of Religions

Like "religion" itself, "history of religions" is an elusive, imprecise designation used throughout this volume in several different ways. Disciplined, specialized study of the religions of humankind is primarily an academic development of the past century. In Europe, Britain, and North America different schools for the study of religions have arisen (and some have fallen) around a variety of articulated goals and methods. In this sense, *Religionswissenschaft*, *allgemeine Religionsgeschichte*, comparative religions, and phenomenology of religions are designations of scholars and movements belonging to specific periods and countries. Developments in historical, anthropological, sociological, psychological, oriental, biblical, and theological studies have also influenced the work of historians of religions, but the one quality that has separated religious studies from other disciplines has been the insistence that religion as such constitutes a coherent field of data that is susceptible to explanation and interpretation. "History of religions" and "religious studies" are terms used in these pages to refer collectively to several established approaches to the study of religions generally. The present attempt to explain and understand better the religious data of the Islamic tradition in the context of religious studies generally requires a brief survey of developments in the disciplines of the history of religions during the past century.

Although several informative "histories" of the history of religions have been written,[7] the function and role of such scholarship from the point of view of sociology of knowledge has yet to be adequately studied (also true of "oriental" or Islamic studies). The second half of the nineteenth century, when the "scientific" study of religions gained independent status in faculties of European and British universities, was the period when historical, anthropological, oriental, and biblical studies were established as independent disciplines. Looking in retrospect at the contributions of Friederich Max Müller and other founding figures of *Religionswissenschaft*, it is difficult to ascertain the extent to which the "scientific study of religions" advanced our knowledge beyond the simultaneous contributions in the social, historical, and philological sciences. Müller was himself an accomplished philologist whose original work on the Rig Veda eventually brought him supervision of the project to translate the *Sacred Books of the East*. Müller shared the general Victorian intellectual climate of the post-Darwin era in which evolutionary history implied the evolution of culture (and religion) from lower and simpler to higher and more complex forms; in short, "progress." If the prevailing assumption was that Christianity was the highest form of religion, there still remained the evolutionary questions of "origins" and of developmental stages, to be discerned in the study of other religions. Implicit in this view of religions was the teleological assumption of historical progress toward a "natural" religion common to all of humankind. Many believed that if the accidents of "cultural" time and place could be winnowed away, common kernels of "natural" religion would remain on the threshing floor of *Religionswissenschaft*. Specialized historico-philological studies in Sanskrit, Arabic, and other sacred and archival languages held out the promise of enabling useful comparative studies.

Allgemeine Religionsgeschichte was studied on the Continent during the second half of the nineteenth century with the goal of removing it as far as possible from the confessional concerns of the church and of theological faculties. This led ineluctably to conflict between ecclesiastical and scholarly figures. Another thrust of the *allgemeine religionsgeschichtliche Schule* was toward the collective efforts of experts rather than truly cross-disciplinary, cross-cultural studies. The promise of advancing knowledge of religions seemed to lie in such cooperative enterprises as the German *Religion in Geschichte und Gegenwart* and the Scottish *Encyclopaedia of Religion and Ethics*, and in the convening of the first of many international congresses of historians of religions in 1893 at Chicago. Both thrusts, toward encyclopedic knowledge and toward scholarly cooperation in bringing together discrete areas of expertise—eventually involving adherents of the religions being studied—were inheritances from the past century that have been heavily reinvested in the second half of this century. Another important aspect came from the field work of anthropologists, adding the insights of the "participant-observer" to the study of religious data not susceptible to historico-philological methods. Until the beginning of the twentieth century, then, the study of religions developed among specialists—historians, philologists, anthropologists, and archaeologists—whose individual works focused on particular aspects of particular traditions. Those who sought to combine the results in order to focus on the study of religion as such relied upon the methods of accumulation and comparison to learn about the evolution of "natural" religion since the dawn of time.

Perhaps the single most important event to bring about a general change of view was the First World War, whose carnage personally affected many of the scholars by then engaged in the study of religions. The idea of cultural evolution and its attending notion of human progress were badly shaken. In the aftermath a need was strongly felt to find approaches that would allow the authentic expressions of "other" religions to speak for themselves without the imposition of scholars' personal values. What was needed was an objective assessment of the role of religion in human life. In Holland and Scandinavia emerged the school known as the "phenomenology of religions."

Inspired (more than philosophically oriented) by the Continental movement in philosophy by the same name, phenomenologists of religion sought to apply to the manifestations of religion in all cultures methods of pure description in which the scholars' judgments about the value and truth of the religious data under investigation were deliberately suspended (*epoché*). The object was to grasp the essence (*eidetic* vision) that lay behind religious phenomena. Phenomenological studies were more amenable to theological studies than the older attempts at *allgemeine Religionsgeschichte* had been, for equally important to scholars' suspensions of judgment was the assumption that the empirical manifestations of religious "phenomena" concealed deeper "noumenal" or sacred realities that could only be grasped in their essence. If nineteenth-century scholars had produced ways of measuring religion and culture by avoiding the supernatural as a presupposition altogether, phenomenology in the twentieth century was willing to posit human religious experiences as responses to deeper realities, however ineffable. Religion, then, was seen not as a stage in evolutionary history but rather as an essential aspect of human life.

The achievement of phenomenology was important for theorizing about the nature of religion generally, but of little long-range consequence for methodology. Many phenomenologists have opted for methodological pluralism, combining whatever approaches in historical, linguistic, and social-scientific studies that would seem to throw light on the religious phenomena under investigation. Especially from the vast collections of field data made by social anthropologists, the diverse expressions of human religious behavior have been culled and refined in search of common patterns—the universals of human religiousness. Phenomenology has continued the comparative and encyclopedic characteristics of nineteenth-century *allgemeine Religionsgeschichte*, seeking more than simple comparisons by offering syntheses of common, cross-cultural meanings. The most important contribution of phenomenology in recent writings has been to focus on the process of understanding that takes place when the subject (religious person, scholar) confronts the object (religious phenomenon, text). The older historico-philological methods sought in textual analysis the "intention" of the historic author of the text; original meanings, in other words. So, too, structuralism aims at explaining a text or ritual per se, but not so much the historical, diachronic meaning as the holistic, synchronic meaning. Phenomenology, it seems, views the process of religion in terms of stimulus/response (sacred or noumenal/religious thought, action) and thus isolates for analysis the religious response or "experience" as a field of research.

Phenomenological scholarship has also insisted upon open, empathetic approaches to the understanding of religious phenomena. One of the important trends of nineteenth-century historiography was the distinction made by Wilhelm Dilthey (1833–1911) and others between the natural sciences and cultural studies (*Geisteswissenschaften*). Cultural or human studies have as their object all the doings and creations of humankind in the historically evolving expressions of artistic, intellectual, social, economic, religious, political (and scientific) forms. For human studies as for phenomenological studies, understanding culture requires broad knowledge, including psychology, history, economics, philology, literary criticism—in short, all the disciplines that study human beings, their intellectual and social activities. The most important methodological component of Dilthey's historiography was *das Verstehen*, a technical term that meant the comprehension of the ideas, intentions, and feelings of people through the empirical manifestations of culture. The *Verstehen* method assumes that human beings in all societies and historical circumstances experience life as meaningful, and they express these meanings in discernible patterns that can be analyzed and understood.

The goal of understanding another person's religion has amounted for some historians of religions to more than cross-cultural knowledge; cross-cultural communication has also been invested with the teleological goal of universal human understanding. International bodies of historians of religions have sought this end by inviting proponents of the various religions to expound their faiths on their own terms. To the same end, departments of religious studies, especially in North American universities, have appointed Muslims, Buddhists, and others to their faculties to achieve "authentic" instruction in world religions. Laudible as this effort may be for ecumenical and cross-cultural conferences, it also indicates the apparent willingness of some religious studies faculties to be more impressed by confessional than academic credentials. Some scholars in religious studies have justified these unusual hiring practices by observing that the evolving condition of increased international travel, communication, and study have held the practical consequence that learning and teaching about the faith of Muslims now involves Muslims in the classroom on both sides of the lecturn.

Under these circumstances has come yet another approach to the history of religions, usually called the "personalist" or "dialogic" approach. Its most eloquent spokesman, Wilfred Cantwell Smith, has taken a nominalist stance against the standard stock of terms and categories into which the components of religions have traditionally been parsed. While not entirely discounting the achievements in oriental studies and history of religions in the past, Smith argues that the object *sine qua non* of scholarly understanding is the faith held by individual Muslims (or Buddhists, Christians, Hindus, and so forth) in real life contexts. That faith is only imperfectly disclosed in the normative textual materials of a tradition such as Islam. Any reading of these materials will fail to grasp the faith of Muslims if it yields explanations and interpretations that are not in accord with what Muslims themselves say they mean.[8]

The scope of Smith's program for the contemporary phase of the history of the history of religions seems to be truly ecumenical, calling for human beings of many faiths to enter into dialogue in order to better understand each other's deepest concerns, and ultimately, their common humanity. The personalist or dialogic approach is frankly suspect if not antagonistic toward scholarly preoccupation with methodology, for most programs of analysis require an attitude of personal detachment between the observer and the observed. Although Smith has often been attacked and perhaps misunderstood by most Islamicists and historians of religions, his influence is, nonetheless, to be seen in some of the contributions to this volume.

Since 1960 the history of religions in North American universities has become increasingly conscious of its identity as a scholarly discipline.[9] Much of the discussion has tried to focus on content through the lenses of method and theory.[10] The structuralist analysis of myth by Claude Levi-Strauss, the study of religion as a cultural symbol system by Clifford Geertz, and the interpretation of the ritual aspects of pilgrimage by Victor Turner, among others, have inspired considerable writing and scholarly colloquia among historians of religions. In this regard it should be noted that the recent renaissance in the study of religions by cultural anthropologists, although not an explicit recognition of the work of historians of religions, is, nonetheless, an affirmation that religion as such forms a coherent field of research. The importance of such work lies in insisting on the logical priority of achieving methodological clarity and verifiable application of method in relation to the data of specific religious communities and traditions. Another important value of more recent trends in history of religions is the promise of new approaches to cross-cultural studies. The historian of religions with special competence in Islamic studies is in a position to facilitate expanded approaches to the study of Islam which, in both its similarities and dissimilarities to other traditions, must necessarily be studied for any comprehensive understanding of religion as an object of scholarly research. Islam is not a purely Arabian or even Middle Eastern phenomenon. It is found in Southeast Asia; China; the Soviet Union; Africa, south of the Sahara; and other parts of the world in impressive strength. The processes of socialization and symbolization by which Islam is perpetuated in local environments, alongside Hinduism, Confucianism, Christianity, tribal shamanism, and secular ideologies, make the study of Islam an important aspect of the study of religions generally.

Islamic Studies

Scholars admire textual work well done, and few have done it better than nineteenth-century European orientalists. Possession of such rigorous standards of excellence has not been the privilege of everyone who has attempted to contribute to scholarship on Islam. Islamists have conserved the standards of their discipline by assailing the mediocrity they have found in the work of mentors, colleagues, and students with whom they disagree. Measures of appreciation and competence are based on simple and severe criteria: unequivocal knowledge of Muslim oriental languages and the mastery of vast repositories of texts. Until recently, Islamicists have judged themselves more or less in isolation from the rest of academe. Even the Mandarins of other disciplines could only stand in awe at the sheer weight of erudition in Islamic studies. What had taken centuries to edit, translate, codify, and interpret in the Greco-Roman and Hebrew classics had been tolerably well imitated by a handful of orientalists in the nineteenth century, the majority of whom first trained as classicists or Semiticists.

In an acerbic essay entitled "The State of Middle Eastern Studies,"[11] Princeton historian Bernard Lewis places today's poor showing in Middle Eastern studies in perspective by first reviewing the history of the Western study of Islam since the Middle Ages. The original impetus for Europeans to study Islam, Lewis summarizes, sprang from two motives. The first was to learn more about the classical heritage that had been preserved in Arabic translations and commentaries; the second was to mount an informed Christian polemic against Islam. As Christendom pulled ahead of the Islamic world in science and political strength toward the end of the Middle Ages, and as it became apparent that the conversion of Muslims could never be accomplished on a large scale, both motives began to fade. Instead, with the Renaissance came new reasons to study Islam. First was the new intellectual curiosity about alien cultures (a curiosity that Lewis, like G. E. von Grunebaum before him, finds unique to Europeans and especially wanting among the Third World intelligentsia). The Renaissance also brought about a revival of interest in classical philology (which became the paradigm for understanding other cultures) and increased travel to oriental lands, largely in the service of European economic interests. And, the Renaissance saw the rise of biblical and Semitic studies, for which many scholars viewed the study of Arabic language and texts as useful tools.

It was in the nineteenth century, however, that oriental studies came of age as a separate discipline in European universities. In France and England the motives were in part political as both countries pursued colonial ambitions in the Middle East. In Germany and Eastern Europe scholarly work on Muslim oriental languages and texts was more classical, especially among Jewish textualists who had, Lewis observes, better cognate language skills and fewer polemical and political interests in the subjugation of Middle Eastern peoples. Throughout Middle Eastern studies generally in the nineteenth century, however, the primary focus was on Islamic religion, history, and literature. The writing of contemporary Middle Eastern history was left to colonial historians.

World War II convinced educators and the United States government that something had to be done about the lack of trained professionals with language skills and knowledge of other cultures. The growth of area studies programs in major universities at mid-century occasioned the rise of many new programs in Middle Eastern studies in this country. There has been some debate about whether Middle Eastern studies is an interdisciplinary program or a discipline unto itself. Leaving this question aside for the moment, most assessments of Middle Eastern studies in the 1970s have concluded that such programs generally have groaned under an undue burden of "tenured mediocrity." By comparison with oriental studies in the nineteenth and early twentieth centuries, area studies on the Middle East have been crippled by faculty incompetence, inadequate curricula (especially in language preparation), and lower admissions standards for students. A critical analysis of Middle Eastern studies by Leonard Binder[12] finds the fault primarily in faculties ill-prepared to teach their subject, and this he documents from the findings of Richard D. Lambert's *Language and Area Studies Review*, published in 1973.[13] Bernard Lewis agrees, but finds other factors as well to explain the present dilemma of Middle Eastern studies. With the rapid growth in opportunity to teach about the Middle East after World War II, deans with too many positions were chasing after too few competent scholars. The resulting recession of scholarship inevitably resolved itself in the academically inflationary practice of hiring native speakers who seldom had the necessary training in history, economics, or linguistics—the disciplines for which they were hired to teach. Not just in Middle Eastern studies, but in many departments and interdisciplinary programs (including religious studies as we have seen), educators have been curiously persuaded by the epistemological mystique that only a Jew can teach Judaism, a black black studies, a Muslim Islamic studies, and so on. As in religious studies, such hiring practices are not suspect per se but only when adequate training in an academic discipline is thereby overlooked.

Binder raises another problem that bears more directly upon the essays in this volume. In a section of his paper entitled "Area Studies Versus the Disciplines," he points out that many disciplines reject the notion that cultures are unique and thus essentially incomparable. At the root of this issue is the question of whether the subject matter (Middle East, Islamic world) is primary and requires methods of study derived from the subject matter itself (thus requiring a distinct discipline called, say, "Middle Eastern studies"); or are academic disciplines (linguistics, historical studies, political science, anthropology, etc.) primary, and thus able to apply generally valid research methods to the study of Middle Eastern data. The epistemological questions in this debate are serious ones for which there are no easy answers. Binder bases his conclusion that methodology is derived from the cultural object of study on the phenomenology of Edmund Husserl—an epistemological stance that has lost most of its support among hermeneutical philosophers in recent times. Historians of religions are caught squarely in the middle of this dilemma, as the papers in this volume demonstrate. Although most religionists would wish to maintain that religion as such forms a field of study, and thus there must be methods, categories, and hence comparative problems and solutions in the study of the religions of humankind, others would argue that the student of a particular religion must be prepared mentally (some say spiritually) to inhabit the subject matter in order to grasp its specific meanings. Practitioners of religious studies, like those of area studies, have yet to agree upon the proper emphasis and relationship between method and subject matter.

The critique of Islamic studies has taken on a new (or renewed an old) dimension in recent years into which any discussion of "Islam and the History of Religions" is necessarily drawn. In another section of his essay, Binder discusses "Orientalism Versus Area Studies," pointing out that the nineteenth-century tradition of oriental studies was based on historical and philological paradigms established by the study of the classics.[14] Orientalism, then, regarded its subject matter historically as primarily a late contemporary of the classical Judeo–Hellenic–Roman–Christian tradition and polemically as an incomplete or aberrant development out of Western Late Antiquity. These orientalists, nonetheless, have bequeathed to the present generation monumental works of scholarship on the Islamic religion, history, and society, without which Middle Eastern and Islamic studies today would be unthinkable. Many scholars would agree with Binder on both counts—that there are religious and political prejudices to be found in Middle Eastern studies, but that a considerable debt is owed to orientalist scholarship. The question is how serious and how pervasive were the prejudices that animated the desire to study the Muslim Orient, and what effect do they continue to have upon those who pursue Middle Eastern studies today?

A provocative answer to this question has been given by Edward W. Said in his book, *Orientalism*,[15] which will be reviewed briefly in order to grasp the sometimes less visible but nonetheless imposing polemical climate in which the papers in this volume were written and then discussed among the authors.

Edward Said's *Orientalism* seeks to illumine the darker side of Western imperialism and colonialism. It seeks to demonstrate that "oriental studies" as a scholarly discipline was materially and intellectually associated with European political and economic ambitions, and thus that orientalism produced a "style of thought based upon an ontological and epistemological distinction between 'the Orient' and, most of the time, 'the Occident.'"[16] Following Michel Foucault, Said argues that Western orientalism has developed ways of "discoursing" about the Orient (by which he means primarily the Muslim Orient, particularly the Arab) that establish and perpetuate a sense of European cultural superiority over that "other," "alien" culture. In Said's own words,

> the Orientalist surveys the Orient from above, with the aim of getting hold of the whole sprawling panorama before him—culture, religion, mind, history, society. To do this he must see every detail through the device of a set of reductive categories (the Semites, the Muslim mind, the Orient, and so forth). Since these categories are primarily schematic and efficient ones, and since it is more or less assumed that no Oriental can know himself the way an Orientalist can, any vision of the Orient ultimately comes to rely for its coherence and force on the person, institution, or discourse whose property it is.[17]

Edward Said has put his finger on something that has bothered a number of thoughtful students of the Middle East and of Islam for some time. He offers an interpretation of the nature and the causes of the many forms of bias that haunt the writings of Western travelers, colonial historians, missionaries, novelists, *and* scholars. The more popular and easily recognized forms of such biases today have to do with media projections of the Arab (which most people equate with "Muslim") as given to lechery, backwardness, irrationality, and so on. Less obvious, perhaps, are the kinds of academic treatment given to

Muslim scholarship in such otherwise impressive works as the *Encyclopaedia of Islam*, where in countless articles traditional and contemporary Muslim views are contrasted with what their sources *really say* (or fail to say) when they are subjected to historical and textual criticism.

Such academic imperialism, however, not only divides Leiden from al-Azhar, but to be fair, it also divided Athens from Jerusalem and, in our own day, the historian from the believer generally. The real problem posed by Said's undisguised "discourse" against orientalism is that the conflict between the historian and the believer in the West has been an *intra*cultural skirmish, whereas the orientalism quagmire is *inter*cultural. However unavoidable and perceptive the issues raised by Edward Said may be, his essay has elicited much righteous indignation on both sides, but has spurred little helpful communication.

Despite the sorry problems that attend any discussion into which the charges of racial and political chauvinism are injected, the essence of the problem raised by Said is an important one to the academic community. An important question to be asked is whether Middle Eastern (Islamic) studies ought any longer to be considered a distinct and separate discipline, with its own standards and stores of knowledge which only it can interpret, or whether the study of the Middle East and Islam more generally ought to be informed by the disciplines of history, anthropology, literary criticism, religious studies, and so on. The study of Islam in departments of religious studies will not be unaffected by the way scholars in the human sciences choose to answer this question. In the latter case, individual scholars (whether American, British, Egyptian, Iranian, or Japanese), without absolute methods and insights, will have to justify the validity of their selection and interpretation of data among colleagues who work within the same disciplines. In the last few pages of *Orientalism*, Said seems to opt for the latter, although on the whole he does not violate his stated intention of describing the problem of orientalism rather than offering solutions. It seems futile to maintain that there is no problem, although Said complicates the issue by offering an interpretation that is more blatantly ethnocentric and politicized than most of the targets of his own criticism. It seems rather more to the point to try to cast discourse about the Middle East (or Islamic world) in the language and methods of *disciplines*, and to coordinate Middle Eastern studies as cross- or multi-disciplinary ventures. The problems presented by

Western faculty incompetence and by the gratuitous mystique of the native speaker can then be judged by the normal criteria of promotion and tenure applied within each discipline.

It is a hopeful sign that historians, social scientists, and historians of religions are exploring the use of one another's methods in recent times to a much greater degree. Thus semiotics, structuralism, functionalism, and phenomenology have produced theories of cultural meaning that cut across the disciplines of linguistics, anthropology, historiography, and history of religions, among others. Multi-disciplinary focus on common subject matters and the creative adaptation and application of methods to select fields of religious data are really what the contributors to this volume have sought to raise for discussion among readers.

Knowing Muslim languages, or being Muslim, or even being extremely empathetic to Islam is no guarantee that one's interpretation of Islam can claim validity in the human sciences. Yet the lack of competent knowledge of languages, history, and the culture of the people being studied can lead methodologists to mere analytical game-playing with artificial fields of data. Research methods are continually subject to adjustment and refinement as scholars consider the application of these to particular fields of data. The desire to study one field rather than another is probably inspired by the subject matter itself as well as something personal with each scholar. *How* to study a data field, or the *discussion* of how to study it, is what we mean by methodology. The contributors to this volume have, for a variety of reasons, been drawn to the study of Islamic religious data. In the context of the problems to which this book is addressed, the intention has been to clarify how these scholars do what they do as students of Islamic manifestations of religion.

Islam Within the Disciplines of Religious Studies

The subtitle of the final section of this introductory essay paraphrases the title of an article by Jacob Neusner, who raises three questions about the "discipline" of religious studies at the graduate level:

> First, has the discipline produced a common curriculum, based on a firm consensus on what we think education in the discipline should accomplish? Do textbooks transmit this second-level tradition of learning?

> Second, does scholarship in the discipline follow a program of inquiry, so that there is perceptible progress in the investigation of long-term questions?
>
> Third, are there criteria by which achievement is recognized and triviality and pretention properly labeled?[18]

That the answer to all three questions must, in the mid-1980s, be an embarrassing negative rests as much or more on the evidence of how Islam is studied as on how Judaism is studied (as in Neusner's example) in departments of religious studies. To quote Neusner again concerning the analysis of religious texts:

> Even though, through philology, we understand every word of a text, and, through history, we know just what happened in the event or time to which the text testifies, we still do not understand that text. A religious text serves not merely the purposes of philology or history. It demands its proper place as a statement of religion. Read as anything but a statement of religion, it is misunderstood. Accordingly, despite the primitive condition of religious studies as presently practiced, the discipline-in-the-making known as religious studies does promise for Jewish learning what has not yet been attained.[19]

The embarrassment of the failure of religious studies to congeal as a discipline but the promise that it might by seeking consensus on curriculum, problem-solving, and criteria of achievement versus triviality, is the broader academic background to the essays in this book. The narrower resources are history of religions scholarship on Islam, and oriental and Islamic area studies. Drawing necessarily from the narrower academic contexts, the problems to be addressed in these pages are those belonging to religious studies more generally. It is in religious studies scholarship and curricula that we must address the problem of understanding Islam as a religion, and beyond that, the question of what the scholar's construct, "religion," means with reference to the Islamic data.

The data fields examined in each of the essays are Islamic ones, ranging widely historically and geographically. The kinds of data are manifold, from textual, to social-historical, to ritual-symbolical. Constructive criticism of long-accepted approaches to the study of Islam and attempts to apply the methods and theories of other disciplines to Islamic religious data are presented here in the service of bringing about needed change and improvement in the study of Islam as religion. Parts One to Four form groups of essays addressed to issues in religious studies. Part Five presents two quite different responses by noted Muslim writers on Islam to the enterprise undertaken in this book. Altogether, the chapters form a conversation and discussion about Islam and the study of religion—a subject which this volume does not and can not exhaust, but to which we hope serious attention will be drawn.

Part One

Scripture and Prophet

In a style of scholarship made commonplace in nineteenth-century *Religionswissenschaft* and biblical criticism, contemporary approaches to religious studies tend to follow a common format, beginning with descriptive accounts of sacred writings and the lives and teachings of prophets, holy men, or other "founders" of a given religion. So, too, standard texts on Islam locate discussions of the Qur'ān and the Prophet Muhammad at the beginning as ingredients essential to the larger story. However useful this may be for understanding the origins and historical formation of a given tradition, the "great books" and "great leaders" approach to humanistic studies must yield to alternative ways of understanding religion. By placing the topics of scripture and prophet at the beginning of books on religions, their importance to the ongoing tradition often seems to recede as other subjects are introduced by each new chapter. Beyond the important questions of the formation of the text of any scripture and the historicity of a prophet/founder are their liturgical, ritual, and social significance as paradigmatic symbol systems in the lives of Hindus, Buddhists, Taoists, Jews, Christians, and Muslims. Philological reconstruction of the meaning, say, of Qur'ānic locutions in the time of the nascent Muslim *umma* (community) in Arabia or in the literary florescence of Middle Arabic in the eighth and ninth centuries is not sufficient evidence for understanding the cultural space occupied by the Qur'ān in a given Muslim society. Literary and historical criticism, even when extended into the history of textual exegesis, also fails to solve this central problem of religious studies.

The remedy called for is not the abandonment of historical, philological, and literary analyses of the Qur'ān or biographies of the Prophet, for the methods used in such scholarship have produced unquestionably useful results. Rather, based on the findings of textual, historical, and literary studies, religious studies must go on to ask a different set of questions about how such texts testify to the religion of Muslims. To answer the question of religion, the cultural context in which scripture and prophet are learned and internalized pedagogically, ritually, and socially must also be factored into the analysis. There is a need to discover the Islamic conceptions of "scripture" and "prophet" implicit in Muslim materials. The processes of symbolism and socialization inherent in Muslim societies as well as in the texts written within those societies are open to other interpretations than those canonized by *Religionswissenschaft* and historical studies.

Part One, then, seeks to raise a different set of questions about the traditional categories of "scripture" and "prophet." The two inquiries which follow do not attempt to lay out an entire new agenda in religious studies—it is too soon for that. Rather, limited departures are taken by each author, thereby opening a long-needed discussion in each case, yet with the recognition that other kinds of questions and approaches are possible and to be encouraged.

In Chapter 2, William A. Graham analyzes relevant passages in the Qur'ān and other sources to arrive at an Islamic sense of scripture which comes much closer to the notion of liturgical recitation than sacred writing. Although the meaning of *qur'ān* as "recitation" has long been noted in Western scholarship, Graham's point is that in religious studies we have yet to pay sufficient attention to what this implies for understanding the Qur'ān in Muslim culture. Graham makes the additional point that a better understanding of the liturgical significance of the Qur'ān may enable us to appreciate better the significance of scriptures in other religions.

In Chapter 3, Earle H. Waugh applies model theory, which he develops in the first part of his discussion, to the biography of the Prophet Muḥammad and to the ways in which prophetic biographies have been written and understood in different moments of Islamic history. It has often been noticed, for example, that Ibn Isḥāq's biography of Muhammad has served in paradigmatic ways for Islamic self-understanding throughout history. Waugh refines the discussion of models as analytical tools and then he attempts to show how Ibn Isḥāq's treatment of conflict-resolution in the life and times of Muḥammad became an authoritative model under quite different circumstances in later history, with emphasis on modern Egyptian commentators.

In sum, it is necessary but not sufficient in religious studies to familiarize ourselves with scriptures and the lives and teachings of prophets as these are presented in the classical sources. Religious world views and patterns of behavior depend in ways we have yet to understand adequately upon how religious people interpret such materials. Part One seeks to address such questions.

2

Qur'ān as Spoken Word

An Islamic Contribution to the Understanding of Scripture

WILLIAM A. GRAHAM

The appearance of a collection of essays on "Approaches to Islam in Religious Studies" underscores a widespread judgment among concerned scholars that the relationship between Islamic studies and the study of religion has been a relatively unproductive one.[1] It is not unfair to say that the broader, generic study of religious life and history has not been sufficiently informed by Islamic data, while Islamicists have correspondingly made less than satisfactory use of more general scholarly studies in religion.[2] In particular, Islamic studies have contributed little to and profited little from the phenomenological study of religion (a situation, it must be added, that they share in large part with Judaic and Christian studies[3]).

The present study is an attempt to consider a specific instance in which Islamic data and the problem of understanding those data are directly relevant to the development of a more adequate understanding of an important general concept in religion. This concept, or phenomenon, is that of *scripture*, and as obvious a topic as it might seem in the light of the uniquely scriptural character of the Islamic tradition, it has not received sufficiently serious attention even from those historians of religion with special expertise in Islamic studies. In what follows, I will consider first the idea of scripture as a generic concept in modern scholarship in religion, examining its limitations and suggesting some correctives. To substantiate these suggestions, I shall turn specifically to the Muslim notion of scripture and argue that the role of the Qur'ān in Muslim life and consciousness illumines with particular clarity an important aspect of scripture that has received little or no attention in modern scholarship, namely, its oral and aural character, its function as spoken word.

Scripture as a Generic Category

The modern scholarly use of "scripture" as a general concept has, like so many usages in the study of religion, developed out of the specific context of the Jewish and especially the Christian tradition. Only relatively recently has it become common for this concept to be generalized and applied generically to normative texts of other religious traditions.[4] The primary signification of "scripture," or of any of its European-language equivalents such as the German *Schrift*, French *écriture*, or Italian *scrittura*, was originally, and remains still specifically, the Jewish or the Christian Bible. The word derives from the Latin *scriptura*, a "writing," which in turn translates the Greek γραφή (or its plural γραφάι). The idea of divinely revealed or inspired *written* word—"the books," "what is written," i.e. "scripture"—is at least as old in the West as the post-exilic period of Jewish history and certainly attested in the second century B.C.E. in terms such as *ha-s^efārîm* ("the books"—in Greek translation τὰ βιβλία, which through Latin became "bible," "Bibel," etc.), which was used to refer to part or all of the Hebrew sacred writings.[5]

Here the related notion of a "canon" of scriptures is relevant. Although there is no specific Jewish equivalent for the Christian appropriation of κανών (lit. "rod," then "measure," "rule") to designate a formally delimited corpus of sacred and normative writings, the concept of such a corpus clearly is based upon Jewish ideas that antedate the second-century Christian concept considerably.[6] Indeed, for the first century, and most of the second, the "Bible of the Church" was "the holy books" (τὰ βιβλία τὰ ἅγια) of the Jews: the threefold collection (later known as *Tanakh*) of the Torah (= the Pentateuch), the Prophets

(*N*^e^*bī'îm*) and the other "Writings" (*k*^e^*tûbîm* = Gr. ἁγιόγραφα).[7] The subsequent Christian agreement upon a "canon" of "the New Covenant" (an "agreement" that has differed in different sectors and different periods in its specifics) completed the process whereby the idea of a canon of scripture became a shared (although differently derived and defined) concept for Christians and Jews. It is this shared concept that, many centuries later, was taken and used generically when the Judeo-Christian West began serious academic study of other religious traditions.

In this academic study (which today is no longer only "Western" but international), "scripture" has become one of those taken-for-granted categories that everyone uses with scarcely a second thought. Most students of religion would concede to scripture a prominent rank, at least in literate cultures, among important and widespread religious phenomena. "Scripture" as a generic term seems obviously applicable to texts quite different from those of Jews and Christians. No one is very exercised about the use of labels such as "Zoroastrian holy writ," "Vedic scripture," "the Tibetan canon," or "Buddhist sacred texts," or about placing them alongside "Christian scripture" or "Jewish canonical writings" as examples of the same general category of phenomena. It was upon just such texts as would fit into this kind of category that the study of religion, and especially the historical study of the major religious traditions, focused during its rapid development in the nineteenth century. Max Müller's series of text-editions, *The Sacred Books of the East*, is one kind of monument to such study; others would be the great "schools" of biblical scholarship associated with persons of the stature of Julius Wellhausen in Hebrew-Bible studies or F. C. Baur in New Testament studies.[8] The task at hand in such studies was clear: the application of historical-critical, text-critical, and linguistic analysis to the central texts of the "world religions," including those of one's own tradition.

The result of these studies, impressive and important as they continue to be, has been a continuing focus upon particular written texts that have come in various traditions to carry the sacred and normative, usually inspired, authority of scripture. The study of scripture in the major orientalist and biblical fields has, even up to the present, meant the study of documents and the historical context in which they arose. The chief concerns have been to establish an "original," uncorrupted text, to reconstruct the process of composition of the text, to analyze the text for contemporaneous historical information, and to search out key ideas of the text and trace their "sources" or antecedents. As a result, the ongoing role of a text as scripture in the subsequent life and faith of a given tradition has received relatively little scholarly attention.[9] The study of religious texts in their *function* as scriptures has been subordinated to the critical study of their earliest written forms. This is changing as more scholars are devoting themselves to the investigation of "post-classical" religion in the great world traditions, but in general "scriptural studies" devoted to tracing the historical roles of sacred texts have yet to emerge in their own right. Furthermore, the prevalent focus upon original texts and their historical contexts has meant not only that descriptive work on scripture in the later life of the various communities has suffered, but also that interest in scripture as a generic phenomenon has been small vis-à-vis the interest in particular sacred texts.[10]

The relative lack of interest in scripture as a general religious phenomenon has been especially glaring in general and comparative studies in religion. Here there has been an often noted bias in favor of "archaic" or "nonliterate" religious cultures where scripture, unlike myth, ritual, sacrifice, sacred space, or the like, is not a relevant phenomenon.[11] When treated at all in the major phenomenological works on religion, scripture has tended to be defined in accordance with textual-studies usage as "sacred writings" and correspondingly dealt with under the rubric, "holy writ," or the like. This category, in turn, has been usually paired with "holy word" in most catechisms of major religious phenomena and viewed as either an ancillary or later (and hence less "original") development of the inherently oral phenomenon of the primordial sacred word, or "word of power" (van der Leeuw.)[12] Several phenomenologists have underscored this dichotomy of word and writ by pointing out that although the written word fixes and lends permanence to the spoken word, it also threatens to kill the originally vital spirit of the oral word by incarcerating it in "the letter."[13] In this way, students of religion have reinforced the delimitation of scripture to the "black and white" text, the "canonical" collection, and the "holy writ" of theological and legal authority in a tradition.

The cumulative result of these tendencies in specialist and generalist scholarship, together with the inherent etymological connection of terms for "scripture" with writing in the West,[14] has been effectively to objectify scripture as merely a special kind of written document or book. The problem this presents is not the linkage of scripture to the written word, but the simplistic understanding of scripture as *only* the written word, only the physical text of the holy writ. Scripture has come to refer too easily to one object, albeit an important one, among the many trappings of religious life.

Underlying such an objectified usage are a constellation of attitudes peculiar to the modern Western crucible in which the history of religion has taken shape as a field of study. These attitudes center upon our understanding of language itself, which tends to be primarily script-oriented and visual as opposed to sound-oriented and oral. We are, as has been pointed out by several scholars in recent years, a typographic culture in which it is unconsciously assumed that the really fundamental form of language is the written or printed word. We have lost to a large degree the oral-aural dimensions of literate culture that characterized our own civilization well beyond the Gutenberg revolution up to perhaps the Enlightenment, and that still characterize most other literate cultures of the world today. Dominated by the silent, mass-produced, printed word, we have come to think of books as repositories of written words, data, and ideas, and hence as objects rather than living, speaking texts. Such an unconscious attitude is further reinforced by our scholarly premiums on scientific classification and "objective" analysis, both of which are peculiarly congenial to the printed page.[15] Thus it is easily understandable how we have come to assume a definition of scripture that focuses upon its normative status as a sacred and authoritative document that has been canonized or otherwise fixed and officially recognized as divinely or primordially ordained.

What is left out in this kind of objectified definition of scripture is recognition of and emphasis on the fact that "scripture" only becomes a useful and meaningful concept for the study of religion when it is understood to be a relational rather than an absolute category or phenomenon. A more adequate understanding of scripture has to include an awareness that it refers not simply to a text but always to a text in its relationship to an ongoing tradition, that is, in its relationship to persons and communities of faith for whom it is sacred and normative. So long as one uses "scripture" unreflectively to refer to *a document* rather than to *a document as it is understood by those for whom it is more than a document*, the meaning of scripture as an important phenomenon in religious life and history will be inaccessible. Similarly, the usefulness of "scripture" as a meaningful category in the analysis of religion will be minimal. Scripture, when properly seen in its relational context of meaning, refers to a living, active, immediate reality in people's lives rather than merely a completed, transmitted piece of writing.

If such a "relational" or functional definition of scripture is accepted, scriptural studies open onto various facets of religious life. Study of scriptures will involve study of the transmission and exegesis of a sacred text in contexts such as those of law, ethics, theology, mysticism, and sectarianism. It will seek to elucidate the role of the text in ritual and liturgy, and even in the broader sector of secular appropriation of and allusion to the sacred text. Especially it will include concern with the function of the text in popular piety and practice, whether these involve superstition and magic or the most elevated levels of devotional life. A canonical writing is something people read and study, a scripture something people live by and for. In dealing with scripture the historian of religion has to do with texts that "speak" to the faithful. Such texts are scriptures only insofar as the faithful *see* or, more often, *hear* in them something more than a piece of beautiful prose or poetry.[16]

Nowhere is the active function of scripture in human lives more dramatically evident than its role as spoken word. Whatever its etymology and literal signification, "scripture" is most vividly evident where it lives as an oral and aural, vocal reality. No one would want to deny that the idea of a book of holy writ, a written verbal witness of the transcendent, is central to the concept of scripture; but so also is the essentially oral nature of even the written word, especially before first paper, and then printing, made physical replication of texts easier than memorization, which is an oral-aural activity. Scripture is meant to be recited, memorized, and repeated; it is meant to be listened to, meditated upon, and internalized. It is *written word that is spoken*, because it is (ontologically as well as chronologically) spoken word before it is written.[17]

This can be demonstrated, I am persuaded, for virtually every scriptural tradition in the world today.[18] Most vividly, even radically, oral are the Vedas and later sacred texts in the Hindu tradition. Certainly traditional Jewish and Christian treatment of scripture has been far more fundamentally oral than most scholarly work on these traditions would indicate. One need only think of the primacy of the reading of the Torah in the synagogue or the massive role of *lectio divina* and *meditatio* in the Christian monastic traditions.[19] Yet because the Islamic tradition presents the case of a scripture that is at once so fundamentally oral and so firmly written a book, it offers perhaps the most vivid and convincing example of the active, oral-aural function of holy writ in the life of a religious community and culture.

Muslim Scripture as Spoken Word

In considering the role of the Qur'ān as an oral text in Islam, it is first helpful to contrast in general terms the ideas of scripture in the Jewish and Christian contexts with those in Islam. In the Muslim case, the original development of the very concept "scripture" (*kitāb*, usually translated as "book") had its own unique history. It is, however, a history that has played no evident role in determining our modern scholarly use of "scripture" in a generic sense.[20] The Islamic tradition, in contrast to that of Jews and Christians, had a generic concept of scripture from its very beginnings. The Qur'ān's own view is that there have been many scriptures, or *kutub* (plur. of *kitāb*), in the sense of sacred and authoritative, divine relations, of which the Qur'ān, or "Recitation," is the final and most complete.[21] All these scriptures have come to the various peoples of history as God's very Word, taken in each case from His heavenly Scripture (*al-Kitāb*, or *Umm al-Kitāb*, "Mother of the Book," i.e., the Book *par excellence*).[22] This fundamentally generic notion of scripture has not diminished the Muslim's consciousness of the particular ultimacy of their own scripture, but it does give to verbal revelation and scriptural texts a clear status as characteristic, recurring phenomena in the history of God's dealing with humankind.

The specific understanding of their own scripture is also different among Muslims from that among either Jews or Christians. While all three traditions have been characterized by the centrality of scripture in worship, piety, devotion, and faith, the Qur'ān stands more clearly alone as the transcendent focus of Muslim faith than does the Christian or even the Jewish Bible in its tradition of faith. It is of course true that the Torah in its most basic sense as the Law revealed at Sinai plays a role for Jews akin in significance to that of the Qur'ān for Muslims, and further that Christian, especially protestant Christian, attachment to the scriptural Word of God has been overwhelmingly important. Nevertheless, the character of the Qur'ān as the verbatim speech of God sets it apart. Whereas the divine presence is manifest for Jews in the Law and for Christians in the person of Christ, it is in the Qur'ān that Muslims directly encounter God.

Third, the concept of a canon of scriptures collected over time as a part of the ongoing record of God's dealing with His people is peculiar to Jews and Christians and distinguishes their concept of what scripture as Divine Word means from that of Muslims. For the latter, revelation was sent one final time, in the course of one prophetic career during which and immediately afterward it was collected into book form. The collected text, as God's direct Speech, has been explicitly recognized as scripture since the actual time in which it "came down." Of a process of canonization Muslims know nothing analogous to that of Jewish and Christian scripture.[23]

Finally, and most importantly for present concerns, the primary and most authoritative form of the qur'ānic text, unlike the biblical, is oral, not written. The very name of the Muslim scripture, "al-Qur'ān," underscores this. It is derived from the root *Q-R-'* with the basic meaning "to proclaim, recite, read aloud." The name "al-Qur'ān" carries the fundamental sense of "the Reciting" or "the Recitation," and it is indeed as a recited text above all that the Qur'ān has played its major role in the piety and practice of Muslims. It is this role that will occupy us here.

THE ORIGINAL MEANING OF "QUR'ĀN"

Students of Islam as well as Muslims themselves customarily think of and use the Arabic *qur'ān* primarily as a proper noun with the definite article: "al-Qur'ān," *The* Qur'ān.[24] With this they refer to the collected and written corpus of Muḥammad's revelations from God as assembled and arranged in essentially its present form by the most respected original "reciters" (*qurrā'*—also from the root *Q-R-'*) or, to give them one of their more precise names, "the transmitters of the recitation" (*ḥamalat al-qur'ān*) who were still alive in the reign of the third Caliph ʿUthmān (reg. 23/644–35/656*).[25] As a codified whole, the revelations have been known and thought of since that time both as "al-Qur'ān" and simply as "the Book" or "the Scripture" (*al-Kitāb*). This is expressed in traditional usage as "that which is between the two boards" (*mā bayn al-daffatayn*)[26] and understood in Islam theologically as "the Speech of God" (*Kalām Allāh*) preserved in the eternal Scripture of God (*al-Kitāb* or *Umm al-Kitāb*) and written down for human use in earthly exemplars (*maṣāḥif;* sing. *muṣḥaf*).

*The dual dates throughout this volume refer to the Islamic (A.H.) and Western (C.E. or A.D.) calendars, respectively.—ED.

It is obvious that "al-Qur'ān" in the later, fixed meaning of God's Word as written down in the *maṣāḥif* is necessarily a post-ʿUthmānic, or certainly a post-Muḥammadan, usage. Until the codification of what has since served as the *textus receptus*—or at least until active revelation ceased with Muḥammad's death—there could have been no use of "al-Qur'ān" to refer to the complete body of "collected revelations in written form."[27] This is not to deny that even in the Qur'ān there are hints of a developing notion of the collective Revelation in the use of the words "qur'ān" and "kitāb," but rather to emphasize the fallacy involved in "reading back" the later, concretized meaning of these terms into the qur'ānic or other traditional-text usages.

The earliest Muslim sources, in particular the Qur'ān itself, make it clear that the original understanding of the Qur'ān as scripture was focused upon the oral character of the sacred text. Fundamentally, the Qur'ān was what its name proclaimed it to be: the Recitation given by God for human beings to repeat (cf. Sūra 96:1). Such repetition served as a Reminder (*Dhikr*) and a Criterion (*Furqān*) in human worship and action; it proclaimed God's Word and kept this Word constantly before its intended hearers. In an earlier, detailed article on the earliest meaning of the word "qur'ān," I have documented this oral character of Muslim scripture in earliest Islam.[28] Some of the salient points from that study bear recapitulating here.

First is the apparent degree to which the very name "Qur'ān" (which is not attested to before the Qur'ān) was influenced by the Syriac Christian *qeryānā*. This latter term was used for the oral, liturgical "reading" from holy writ (=*lectio*, ἀνάγνωσις) and for the passage of scripture that is read aloud (=*lectio*, περιοχή, ἀνάγνωσμα, etc.).[29] Also relevant is the evident parallel in Muslim use of *qur'ān* to Rabbinic Jewish use of *q*ᵉ*rī'ā* and *miqrā'* likewise for the act of scripture-reading and the passage read aloud, respectively.[30] Miqrā' is also used as a Talmudic term for the whole Bible, one that "serves to underline both the vocal manner of study and the central role that the public reading of the Scriptures played in the liturgy of the Jews."[31] Such parallels in Christian and Jewish usage heighten the likelihood that *qur'ān* must originally have been understood by its earliest hearers to refer to *oral scripture reading* or *recitation* such as Jews and Christians practiced in the seventh-century Arabian millieu (as elsewhere), where these older scriptural traditions (along with that of the Zoroastrians, who also engaged prominently in oral recitation of scripture[32]) were very much in evidence. A "book" used in liturgy and devotions would not have been the silently read document that we today understand a "book" to be; rather, it would have been a sacred, divine word that was meant to be recited or read *viva voce* and listened to with reverence.[33]

A second argument for the originally oral-aural understanding of "qur'ān" comes from the internal evidence of the qur'ānic text itself. That the qur'ānic revelations were meant to be proclaimed aloud is evident from the recurring imperative "*Qul!*" ("Say!"), which introduces well over three hundred different passages of the Qur'ān, as well as the frequent occurrence of the verb *talā*, "to recite, follow," with similar reference to reading the text aloud. Further, in the Qur'ān, the word "qur'ān" and the other forms of its root can arguably best be understood in context if their fundamental sense of *oral, vocal* activity is retained and not anachronistically replaced with the modern idea of silent reading from a silent, written text of the *muṣḥaf*. The two most unassailable qur'ānic instances that support this argument bear repeating here:

> Observe the *ṣalāt* at the sinking of the sun until the darkening of night, and *the dawn recital* [*qur'ān al-fajr*]; truly, *the dawn recital* [*qur'ān al-fajr*] is *well-attested* [*mashhūd*]. [S. 17:78]

> Do not move your tongue with it so that you hurry too much! Ours it is to collect it and *to recite it* [*qur'ānahu*], and when We recite it, *follow the recitation* [*fa-ttabiʿ qur'ānahu*]. [S. 75:16–18]

Another body of material that argues for the retention of the essentially oral sense of "qur'ān" well after the time of Muḥammad is the Ḥadīth, or Tradition-Literature ascribed to the Prophet and codified in the second and third centuries of Islam. Among various examples cited in the aforementioned article, the following are particularly interesting.

The first is a statement ascribed to a famous poet and older companion of the Prophet, Ḥassān b. Thābit. In this, he speaks of "one who 'interrupts' the night[34] by praising [God] and reciting" (*yuqattiʿ al-layl tasbīḥan wa-qur'ānan*)[35]—a clear adverbial use of *qur'ān* to denote the *act* of reciting. Another example is the ḥadīth that reports that Muḥammad spoke highly of the person "who is constantly mindful of God in/during reciting" (*kāna rajulan kathīr adh-dhikr lillāh fī l-qur'ān*).[36] Another tradition has Muḥammad say that "in every ritual worship [*ṣalāt*] there is a recitation [or: reciting (*qur'ānun*)]."[37] A final example is a so-called "Divine Saying" in which the Prophet is quoted as saying that

> . . . the Lord says: "Whosoever is kept from petitioning Me [for help, favors] because of preoccupation with *reciting and constant men-*

tioning/remembrance of Me (*al-qur'ān wa-dhikrī*), him shall I give far better than what I give to those who ask things of me. . . ."[38]

Such usages in Qur'ān and Ḥadīth reflect the predominantly oral, recitative function of the Qur'ān in early Muslim life. They point toward the active role as spoken word that has been the distinctive mark of Muslim scripture not only in early days but throughout Islamic history. This role is evident across the entire spectrum of Muslim faith and practice, even though it has up until recently not received the scholarly attention its importance deserves. Nowhere is it more notable than in the formal cultivation of Qur'ān-recitation and its related disciplines on the one hand and, more generally, in Muslim worship and devotional life on the other.

THE FORMAL TRADITION OF RECITATION (QIRĀ'A)

Along with qur'ānic exegesis (*tafsīr*), the basic discipline of scriptural studies in Islam is qur'ānic recitation, or *qirā'a*. This word is the most common verbal-noun form derived from the verb *qarā'a* (above, p. 30), "to recite, read, proclaim." *Qirā'a, like qur'ān* but even more emphatically, retains the fundamentally oral sense of its root verb. As a technical term, it is used to refer not only to the act or practice of reciting aloud part or the whole of the Qur'ān, but also to a particular "reading" or "reciting" (i.e., pronouncing, "sounding out") of any word, phrase, or passage in the Qur'ān. This latter usage is further extended to refer to a "reading" of the entire qur'ānic text according to one of the various traditions of oral text transmission, all of which are traced back to prominent reciters (e.g. Ibn Kathīr or ʿĀṣim) or local "schools" of recitation-readings (e.g., "the people of Kūfa") in the first two centuries A.H. (seventh and eighth centuries A.D.).[39]

Qirā'a as a formal Islamic "science" (*ʿilm al-qirā'a*) encompasses both the study and transmission of the variant readings (*qirā'āt*, plur. of *qirā'a*) of the ʿUthmānic consonantal text—the written *muṣḥaf*—and also the actual art of oral recitation, or *tajwīd* ("doing well by," "rendering excellent" [the Qur'ān]), with its various traditions of vocal performance. As a joint science, the *ʿilm al-qirā'āt wa-l-tajwīd* represents the long Muslim tradition of qur'ānic textual studies. These studies rely, of course, upon knowledge of various other sciences, from grammar (*naḥw*) and philology (*lugha*) to rhetoric (*balāgha*), orthography (*rasm*), and especially exegesis (*tafsīr*). Their focus is, however, upon the exact preservation and ongoing re-creation of the living divine Word as it "came down" in oral, recited form to Muḥammad.[40]

This is not to deny the absolutely necessary role of the written text of the Qur'ān in these or other Muslim sciences, but to emphasize that the written text is always secondary. Because the written codification of the authoritative text under ʿUthmān took place before the development of an Arabic orthography that could indicate with some precision how a text actually reads, the written *muṣḥaf* could never stand alone. Its defective consonantal form allows for variant readings not only of internal vowels and inflectional endings, but even of many of the wholly unpointed consonants themselves. For these reasons, the Qur'ān had to be transmitted primarily as it had originally been given: as a recited, phonetic text. The base form of this oral text was, after ʿUthmān's time, set down in a standard but rudimentary written form and its details noted, described, and preserved by tradition (the original manuscript has not survived). As such it could serve as an *aide-memoire* but not a documentary text apart from the memorization and oral recitation of its content.[41] To read the bare text, one had to know it already by heart, or nearly so.

It seems to have been accepted from the outset that there could be various readings of the same divine text, whether because of dialectical differences among the first Arab Muslims or because even the Prophet is said to have recited the same passage in various forms at various times. The ʿUthmānic *muṣḥaf* allowed for such variety in recitation, and Muslims saw this variety as a blessing, not a curse for the community.[42] In this acceptance of divergent readings and recitative practices, they relied often for their proof-text upon the statement ascribed to Muḥammad, that "the Qur'ān was sent down according to seven *aḥruf* (lit. "letters"; usually taken as "dialects" or "modes")."[43]

As the traditional accounts of the preparation of the ʿUthmānic written codex have it, *qirā'a* and the individual *qirā'āt*, or variant readings of the qur'ānic text, were of moment from the earliest decades after Muḥammad's death because of the concern with preservation of the revelations. However, while there are also references to and some manuscripts of treatises ascribed to experts on *qirā'a* in the first two Islamic centuries,[44] it appears that the crystallization of *qirā'a* as a more formal science probably took place substantially only in the third/ninth century.[45] In any event, the culmination of this process came in the efforts of Abū Bakr Ibn Mujāhid (d. 324/936) of Baghdad[46] to systematize and give rules for proper recitation. He seems to have been the person who won recognition for seven different "readings," or traditions (*riwāyāt*) of recitation, as authentic modes of transmitting the Qur'ān. Some later scholars added three further traditions of *qirā'āt* as permissible variant systems, and still others have recognized these plus an additional four. Accordingly, seven, ten, or fourteen traditions of *qirā'āt* are sometimes cited as "authentic" in the Muslim literature, and even these traditions have branched to form subtraditions. As a result, the panoply of variant *riwāyāt* that the expert must master is quite large, even though the actual textual variations they represent are relatively minor and do not involve crucial differences in the literal meaning of the sacred text.[47]

The study of the *qirā'āt* is, as we have indicated, inextricable from the science of *tajwīd*, or actual recitative practice.[48] *Tajwīd* is the attempt to preserve the living Word of God in the full beauty and full range of meaning with which it was given to and faithfully transmitted by the Prophet. How the Qur'ān is actually rendered as recited word sets it forever apart from all other texts. The traditional authority for the special oral treatment of the sacred text is the Qur'ān itself, with its exhortation to "chant the recitation carefully and distinctly" [*wa-rattil al-qur'āna tartīlan* (S. 73:4; cf. S. 25:32)].[49] The *tartīl*, or carefully enunciated recitative chanting, of the Qur'ān has been and remains the fundamental form of the scriptural text in Islam over the centuries. *Tajwīd* has, of course, also encompassed many traditions and types of oral recitation, the most "ornamented" (*mujawwad*—from the same root as *tajwīd*) of which involve sophisticated knowledge of musical artistry as well as complete memorization, knowledgeable technique, careful comprehension, and sensitive interpretation of the whole Qur'ān.[50]

The science of *tajwīd*, buttressed by that of the *qirā'āt* and of *tafsīr*, has been the guardian and normative mediator of the qur'ānic text as living scripture in the Muslim community. Because of its predominantly oral character, *tajwīd* has received even less modern scholarly attention than the *qirā'āt*, which themselves have hardly been dealt with exhaustively.[51] It is encouraging to note, however, that in recent years several scholars, most notably Labīb al-Saʿīd,[52] Kristina Nelson,[53] and Frederick M. Denny,[54] have done much to redress this deficiency. As they demonstrate through their consideration of both the classical literature on *qirā'āt* and *tajwīd* and the living tradition of Qur'ān-recitation in its contemporary center, Cairo, it is the spoken, recited, chanted word of the Qur'ān upon which Muslim study of the qur'ānic text centers. Moreover, the science and art of the textual specialists are never isolated in the academy as, for example, modern biblical studies sometimes have been in the West. The study of *qirā'āt* and *tajwīd* opens out automatically into the public domain in Muslim society. Here it finds practical application in the highly popular artistic as well as devotional forms of oral recitation that have been one of the hallmarks of Islamic culture wherever it has spread. In turn, the formal and public recitation of the Qur'ān, whether as worship or as performance (and the two are never easily separated), is but one segment of the larger role of the Qur'ān as an oral-aural reality in Muslim life. Consideration of this larger role leads us to the heart of the functional aspect of scripture as spoken word in Islam.

THE RECITED QUR'ĀN IN EVERYDAY PIETY AND PRACTICE

The formal sciences of recitation could not have been sustained had not the practice of recitation more generally (*qirā'a*, or *tilāwa*[55]) always been central to Muslim life. Here we can only touch briefly upon this practice and related phenomena, but any discussion of the Qur'ān as scripture—especially with regard to its oral qualities—would be partial without some indication of its recitative role among Muslims of all times, places, and stations.

The Qur'ān first and foremost has been the one absolute essential of Muslim worship. This can be made vivid in various ways, but one of the most interesting is through a passage in the earliest extant work on the qur'ānic sciences, the *Kitāb al-Mabānī*,[56] which attempts to distinguish specifically qur'ānic words from the extra-qur'ānic words of God in the so-called "Divine Sayings" (above, p. 32). The *Mabānī* passage admits that the Divine Saying is a divinely revealed text, but it then proceeds to differentiate it from the Qur'ān as follows:

> It is not permissible to recite any of it [the Divine Saying] in the *ṣalāt*, for it was not sent down in the same form (*naẓm*) in which all of the Qur'ān was sent down—which [Qur'ān] we have been commanded to recite (*umirnā bi-tilāwatihi*), which is written in [our] copies (*al-maṣāḥif*), and the transmission of which has come to us generally attested in every generation.[57]

The functional orientation of this distinction between qur'ānic and other divine words is striking. Here it is the Qur'ān's form as a text intended for recitation in *ṣalāt*, the daily ritual of worship, that distinguishes it. Later theological distinctions of "inimitability" (*iʿjāz*) or the like notwithstanding, it is above all the function of the Qur'ān as spoken word in worship that sets it apart.

Indeed, the reciting of the Qur'ān is what has been called "the very heart of the prayer-rite,"[58] and no *ṣalāt* is valid without recitation of at least the Fātiḥa, or "Opening" (S. 1). It is expected that one or more shorter sūras (chapters) or verses will also be recited.[59] It is quite common to precede or follow the *ṣalāt*-rite proper with substantial recitation from the Qur'ān,[60] and Qur'ān-recitation in general is a highly preferred form of religious devotion at any time. The fact that its language is the sacred Word of God in "an Arabic recitation" (*qur'ānan ʿarabīyan*[61]) has deterred Muslims from translating it and, conversely, has spurred even Muslims who know no Arabic to memorize shorter or longer passages in order to be able to worship in *ṣalāt* and apart from *ṣalāt* by reciting the Qur'ān. Among many possible examples illustrative of this is an interesting account by a French traveller to Singapore over a century ago. He tells of walking one day in the Malay quarter of the city and hearing children's voices apparently chanting a lesson from a nearby house. Going in, he found an old Malay with a white beard sitting on the floor together with over a dozen children and leading them in recitation—he from a book, they from pieces of paper. Questioned by the visitor as to what was being recited, the old man replied that it was the Qur'ān, in Arabic, which he admitted he did not understand, but which he could sound aloud from the written page. Asked further why they would be learning words they could not understand, the teacher replied that in reading them aloud, the children learn them by heart.

> The sons of the Prophet ought to have this Word in their memory so that they can repeat it often. These words are endowed with a special virtue. . . . In translating [them] we might alter the meaning, and that would be a sacrilege.[62]

While the matter of the special virtue conveyed by the very sound of the qur'ānic Word is interesting in itself,[63] most vivid in the preceding story is the express feeling that Muslims need to be able, as early in life as possible, to recite from the Qur'ān in its original form with some ease. Memorizing from the Qur'ān has always been basic to elementary education in every corner of the Muslim world. Ibn Khaldūn remarked long ago that "teaching the Qur'ān to children is one of the signs of the religion (*shaʿāʾir al-dīn*) that Muslims (*ahl al-milla*) profess and practice in all their cities."[64] One of the most cherished honorifics a Muslim can earn is that of *ḥāfiẓ*, one who "has by heart" the entire scripture. Traditionally such complete mastery of the entire text has been requisite for any accomplished religious scholar (*ʿālim;* plur. *ʿulamāʾ*) in any of the religious sciences. One does not have to read long in Muslim texts nor listen often to any *ʿālim* speak to discover how the ring of the qur'ānic text cadences the thinking, writing, and speaking of those who live with and by the Qur'ān.

Anyone who has spent any length of time in a Muslim society will have remarked also the degree to which the lilting refrain of qur'ānic recitation occupies a prominent place in the public sphere. The ḥadīth that says, "The most excellent form of worship and devotion (*ʿibāda*) among my people is reciting the Qur'ān,"[65] has been taken to heart in Muslim practice. In that most social and communal of all Muslim religious events, the month of fasting in Ramaḍān, the nights are filled with the sound of Qur'ān-recitation in the mosques. Indeed, the basic recitative division of the Qur'ān into thirty parts is held to be for the purpose of reciting one part (*juzʾ*) in each night of Ramaḍān.[66] In practice, the whole is often recited in one night by the most zealous individuals or groups who repair to the mosques for this purpose.[67]

Another popular form of public *tilāwa* is the group chanting associated both with the formal *dhikr* sessions of the ṣūfī brotherhoods and with the popular *dhikr* sessions at certain mosques, especially tomb-mosques. *Dhikr*, the "remembrance" of God in litanies of devotion, involves the chanting of formulae and texts steeped in the language of the Qur'ān, and qur'ānic recitation itself commonly begins such sessions.[68] I have witnessed one popular *dhikr* held each Friday after the evening prayer at the tomb of "Sīdī Maḥyiddīn," Muḥyi'l-Dīn Ibn al-ʿArabī (d. 638/1240) in Damascus. In this gathering, the men who crowd into the tomb chamber to sit on the floor all join in a sing-song recitation in popular *dhikr* style which focuses at least in the first hour or so on favorite sūras of the Qur'ān.

In contrast to such group chanting is the session in which listeners and reciters come together to hear the Qur'ān recited by a series of individual practitioners of *tajwīd*. Cairo is particularly well known for its varied forms of this kind of session, which is known as a *maqraʾ*. Most of these are associated with mosques and take place regularly one or more times a week. The most prestigious are those at places like the Imām Shāfiʿī mosque and the Azhar University mosque, but there are many smaller, more private, or local mosque-settings for the *maqra'*.[69] Still another kind is the *nadwa*, or listening session held often in private homes and attended by cognoscenti of the art.[70] In this latter type of session the musical aspects of recitation often receive greater attention, although it is never easy to distinguish the artistic from the religious elements of Qur'ān recitation and listening. Thanks to the works of Nelson and Denny, we have interesting documentation of some of the inner dynamics of varied *maqra*'s in Cairo today. These studies point up the degree to which *tilāwa* is at once a demanding art form, popular entertainment, and sometimes even performing contest, as well as always an act of devotion and piety and a formal part of the transmission of the Qur'ān in its most perfect possible form.[71]

Yet the active role of the Qur'ān as spoken word among Muslims is still more pervasive than even the preceding examples from ritual, devotional, and public life can adequately convey. From birth to death, virtually every action a Muslim makes, not to mention every solemn or festive event in his or her life, is potentially accompanied by spoken words of the Qur'ān, whether these be entire recited passages or simply discrete qur'ānic words or phrases that have passed into everyday usage. Such a qur'ānic word may be the simple *basmala*, "In the name of God, the Merciful, the Compassionate" (*bism allāh al-raḥmān al-raḥīm*) that precedes countless daily acts such as drinking or eating, just as it precedes all but one sūra of the Qur'ān. Or it may be the ubiquitous *mā shā' llāh* ("whatever God wills!") of S. 18:39 and *al-ḥamdu lillāh* ("Praise be to God!") of S. 1, both of which punctuate Muslim speech even outside of the Arabic-speaking world.[72]

As an example of longer qur'ānic passages heard in daily life, one thinks immediately of the Fātiḥa, Sūra 1, which every Muslim knows by heart and which is recited not only in every *ṣalāt* but on virtually every formal occasion, be it the signing of a wedding contract or prayer at a tomb.[73] There is also the powerful Sūra of Unity, or Pure Devotion, 112, which enters into most prayers and forms the basis of countless litanies of praise; or the final two sūras, 113 and 114, that fend off evil (al-Muʿawwidhatān) and hence figure prominently as talismanic recitations; or the prayer for forgiveness in the final verses of Sūra 2, "The Cow" (al-Baqara), which are known as "the seals of the Baqara" and often are recited before going to sleep; or the powerful and moving strains of Sūra 36, Yā Sīn, which one recites at every burial and also on the "Night of Quittance" (*Laylat al-Barā'a*), a kind of Muslim All-Soul's Night when life and death in the coming year and the deeds of the past year are popularly held to hang in the balance.[74] These are but a few one could mention, as anyone well knows who is aware of how popular the "Throne Verse" of S. 2:255 and the Sūra "Light" (24) also are.

What Ghazālī said of the Qur'ān long ago still holds today: "Much repetition cannot make it seem old and worn to those who recite it."[75] The powerful presence of the rhythmic cadence of qur'ānic *tilāwa* is everywhere evident in traditional and much of modern Muslim society: ". . . the book lives on among its people, stuff of their daily lives, taking for them the place of a sacrament. For them these are not mere letters or mere words. They are the twigs of the burning bush, aflame with God."[76]

None of the preceding is meant to belittle the importance of the written form of the Qur'ān or any other of the great scriptural texts of human history. The Qur'ān in particular has been written and is visible in magnificent fashion: its tradition of manuscript illumination and calligraphic artistry is one of the wonders of the Islamic cultural heritage. The written qur'ānic word embellishes virtually every Muslim religious building as the prime form of decorative art. Nor is the reverence and honor shown the written Qur'ān-text in Muslim piety any less striking and impressive. All such facts simply underscore what has been argued here: that the scriptural word, even where its written form is most prominent, is always demonstrably a spoken word, a recited word, a word that makes itself felt in personal and communal life in large part through its living quality as sacred sound. Our easy dichotomizing of oral word and written word will no longer do as a way of talking about religious texts, let alone about stages of religious development. Orality characterizes the "scriptural" as well as the "pre-scriptural" forms of religious life. If that clearest, even most extreme instance of what Siegfried Morenz has called "book-religion,"[77] namely the Muslim treatment of the Qur'ān, presents us with a scripture that is oral as well as written, we would do well to ponder the implications of this for our general understanding of scripture as well as our specific interpretation of it in particular traditions.

3

The Popular Muḥammad

Models in the Interpretation of an Islamic Paradigm

EARLE H. WAUGH

The phenomenological approach to the history of religions has forced the discipline to look to "lived" experiences as the foundational area for investigation, both to escape the charge of esoterism and to be true to its scientific calling. A child of the Enlightenment, history of religions has also searched for rational principles underlying the manifold variety of this experience. But emphasis on investigating what people do and how they act rather than what they say they believe has brought the discipline into sharpened conflict with many religious people; some confessing believers argue that even the tools of analysis are flawed and must ultimately be subjected to the revealed will of God, regardless of whether or not the results make sense. One practical outcome of the standoff between believers and scholars from outside the tradition has been a professional reluctance to find ways of applying history of religions methodologies to Islamic materials, with both the study of religion and of Islam the poorer for it. In this chapter, I shall make a modest attempt to suggest that there are ways around the impasse, illustrated by a study of the Prophet's life.

Model Theory and the Study of Religions

Scholars and believers alike have long held that understanding the "Prophet" in Islam could not be limited to a historical recounting of his days on earth. Indeed, we get little beyond the stories of his birth before it becomes obvious that another, more powerful dimension has had an impact on the very telling of that history. The details become too rich and multihued, defying any simple evaluative procedure. Thus, sacred biographies provide data that cannot be confined to a historical record. A similar problem exists in the analysis of types of religious leadership. Joachim Wach, following Max Weber, argued that there were identifiable types of religious authority and that the scientist of religion would do well to investigate the organization and constitution of the group around each type.[1] Among the types are figures who may be considered "classic" examples. Several scholars, including Joseph Kitagawa, have found the classic types as a convenient and illuminating focus around which to build studies of religious leadership.[2] The category of prophet, however, is fraught with problems, since, by nature, the charismatic vision is mediated through the individuality and personhood of the prophet himself. Beyond the common dramatic tenor in which prophets achieve their ends, and the charisma that is said to be expressed in them, commonalities are hard to find. The claim of pious Muslims that Muḥammad is unique has more truth than our penchant for categories would seem to allow.[3]

These observations suggest that any study of "Muḥammad in Islam" that concerns itself only with the Prophet's life and career, but which hopes to deliver some final assessment, is doomed before it begins. The reason is not the defectiveness of the methods, but the assumption that a historical biography can hope to exhaust what the Prophet both was and now appears to be. A much fairer starting point is to acknowledge that Muḥammad cannot be located on any single plane, whether it be social, political, psychological, or religious. In history of religions terms, he is a paradigmatic figure, as these passages so vividly depict:

> The apostle of God grew up, God protecting him and keeping him from the vileness of heathenism because he wished to honour him with apostleship, until he grew up to be the finest of his people in manliness, the best in character, most noble in lineage, the best neighbour, the most kind, truthful, reliable, the furthest removed from filthiness and corrupt morals, through loftiness and nobility, so

> that he was known among his people as "The trustworthy" because of the good qualities which God had implanted in him.[4]
>
> We used to prepare his evening meal and send it to him. When he returned what was left, Umm Ayyub and I used to touch the spot where his hand had rested and eat from that in the hope of gaining a blessing.[5]

If we accept the paradigmatic nature of the Prophet, how can we best uncover the various strands that make up that totality? Despite the fact that Muslims have made copious studies of the many details of his life, purported and actual, they are reluctant to cut perceptions of the Prophet free from a solidly historical interpretation. Such reactions are significant; we know that ways of perceiving truth are directly influenced by the deeper expectations and commitments of the human spirit. For example, the quest for the historical Jesus would not have been so intense had Albert Schweitzer and his followers not believed in the discoverability of pure historical fact apart from the system of convictions of the Christian church. So too, Muslim assertions about Muḥammad's life must be placed in the larger parameters of the ongoing religious experience of the *umma* (community of believers), which gives context and meaning to all assertions, whether historical or otherwise.

Another dimension of history of religions methodology has been to examine religious data for its scaffolding, that is, to search out the structures that give coherence and continuity to the material, thereby determining some of the inner dynamics of the religious life. Historians of religions from Max Müller to Mircea Eliade have practised this art. Yet, despite the fact that much of this analysis is based upon the desire to discover the religious impulses implicit in the data, the patterns thus discerned appear to say more about the abstracting abilities of the scholar than of the tradition they are examining. Thus, historians of religions are often criticized for having provided little more than "sermons." Part of the problem admittedly has to do with the supposed neutrality of "patterns" discerned in religious data. Here I am referring to the works of Eliade (such as *Patterns in Comparative Religion*) where the patterns appear to be religiously powerful yet can be used as an interpretive tool in many contexts by the researcher. It is probably impossible for a Western scholar to evaluate the sacred tree among primitive peoples without anticipating in some way what he knows of Christian symbols. Such expectational assumptions can distort interpretation, especially when these assumptions become the basis for the analysis of an entire tradition.[6] With regard to Muslim material, there is the added problem of the hiatus between Islam's concern for law and the dominant categories of the history of religions.[7]

The nature of the material itself should tip us off about the inherent structures of that material; but because the shape given to the structures is not monovalent, the focus must be on models rather than patterns as the locus of the investigation. This acknowledges that the analytic task itself requires a sort of idealized withdrawing of a recurring form from its matrix in the material, and hence consciously admits that what we look for never has the same objectivity as a scientific fact. This point would be contradicted by scholars such as Robert Baird (who speaks of categories) and most likely even by Eliade (patterns). Nevertheless, the attempt to find meaning already orders the way "facts" are linked together, and the notion of model better fits the manner in which we use our analytic skills to make sense out of the manifold data.

The concept of model has a considerable history. First used by mathematicians Eugeneo Beltromi and Felix Cline[8] to aid in explanation of non-Euclidean geometry, it was adapted by logico-mathematicians such as Gottlob Frege and Bertrand Russell; from there, model was utilized in linguistics, first by Charles F. Hockett in 1954. Hockett argued that "by a model of grammatical description is meant a frame of reference within which an analyst approaches the grammatical phase of a language and states the results of his investigation. In one sense there are as many models as there are different descriptions . . . but in another, and very important sense, most grammatical descriptions seem to cluster about a relatively small number of distinct models; it is with these archetypal frames of reference that we are concerned here."[9] Since then, models have received multidisciplinary applications and consequently have taken on a number of different meanings. Yuen Ren Chao identifies thirty different meanings drawn from general model theory, a number of which depend upon their own disciplinary situation for definition.[10]

In his famous book, *Models and Metaphors*, Max Black analyzed various senses of the term "model," including the construction of miniatures, the making of scale models, analog models, mathematical models, and finally theoretical models.[11] Perhaps his most controversial discussion centered on his adaptation of Stephen Pepper's *root metaphor* which Pepper called an implicit or submerged model operating on a writer's thought.[12] Black preferred to call these metaphors "conceptual archetypes": "By an *archetype* I mean a systematic repertoire of ideas by means of which a given thinker describes by analogical *extension*, some domain to which those ideas do not immediately and literally apply."[13] He notes the case of four mathematicians who found that they were unable to solve the problem of dissecting any rectangle into a set of unequal squares. They were manifestly unsuccessful until they began applying different theories, and suddenly landed on the theory of electrical networks. The authors reported that "the discovery of this electrical analogy was important to us because it linked our problem with an established theory. We could now borrow from the theory of electrical networks and obtain formulas for the currents—and the sizes of the corresponding component squares." Black adds, "This fascinating episode strikingly illustrates the usefulness of theoretical models."[14]

Drawing on Black's work, the most famous religionist to use model theory was Ian Ramsey of Oxford University. Beginning in the early sixties, Ramsey argued in a number of books and lectures[15] that "it is by the use of models that each discipline provides its understanding of the mystery which confronts them all, and indeed its own contribution to the fellowship of faith and learning which should characterize a university."[16] He went on to say that his "main point has been that whether the models are scientific or social, they are born on insight, which in this case reveals for each of us his own subjectivity."[17] Ramsey called this a disclosure model.[18] He went beyond Black by arguing that models do not just *represent* ideas of reality but have cognitive content: "But where I believe I would not so much collide with [Max Black] as go beyond the position he takes up, is in the cognitive significance which I give to insight and imagination; it is in my emphasis on the objective reference of all disclosures."[19] Models, then, are not just imaginary perceptions brought to bear upon unsuspecting data, but insights into the true nature of things which, though they may appear to contradict what is normally held to be true, say something meaningful about the reality from which they arise.

Similarly, models from various disciplines could say something important about reality, but could not provide an ultimate model. Even theology was limited in what it could say. The best it could do was to step back and point to a "further dimension" or "witness to the depth which each alone misses and conceals."[20] Ramsey affirms, however, that even theology would have to learn to live with diversity, and he accepts the position that the price for model theory in theology is the possibility of many ways of understanding Christ and the church.[21] Picking up on Ramsey's theme, others have tried to develop the notion of model by conceiving its function in different ways. Ewert Cousins, for example, wants to extend model theory into the area of religious experience.[22] He, therefore, sees model theory working at two levels. "One level would deal with religious experience in search of what we call 'experiential models.'" By this he means the structures or forms of religious experience, the term "experiential" implying the subjective element and the term "model" implying the variety among religious experiences. The second level of the method concerns the expression of religious experiences in words, concepts, and symbols, that is, biblical imagery, Christian creeds, and theological systems. Such expressions are identified as "expressive models" taking all those forms that religious man utilized in explicating his personal religious experience. It is the work of scholars to probe the experiential model, isolate and explore it, and then "chart the co-relations between the experience and its expressive model."[23]

Cousins adds new dimensions to this model theory by arguing that both expressive models and experiential models can change.

> The change from the Ptolemaic to Copernican universe affected man's self image and challenged some of his cherished religious ideas. From the time of the renaissance to the 19th century debate raged over the status of the cosmology of Genesis in relation to that of sciences. With the aid of biblical scholarship, theologians began to see cosmological models as expressive models in which man formulated his religious experience. Thus the theologians would accept an evolution in cosmological models which did not undermine the significance of the Genesis narrative. For they could see in the Genesis cosmology the expressive model of a religious experience that transcends the primitive cosmology.[24]

As an example of a new experiential level, Cousins points to Teilhard de Chardin as one who expresses a new cosmic sense in religious faith. Cousins holds that this cosmic sense indicates the way in which humankind is now experiencing a new earth and a new universe. He puts great stock in the human experience of space as a way of developing a new religious sense.[25] Cosmic Christology for him is a profound theological expression of this new experiential model. By proposing the use of models in this way, Cousins hopes to free theology from the restrictiveness of its past since he sees the current crisis of theology as partially answered by the limiting visions out of which it operates.

Let us return to the earlier differentiation between structure and model. Some clarification can be added which will help our analysis. Structure has to do with a religion's composition; it is first and foremost the scaffolding upon which the tradition stands. In Cousins's language, it is the experiential model. Islam has quite clearly gone through several experiences that have altered the way Muslims have perceived their faith: the codification and universalizing of the Shariʿa, the rejection of the Greek mindset expressed by the Muʿtazila, the expansion of the Shiʿa tradition, and the interaction with the West in modern times, to mention only some of the more significant. Thus these experiential models have changed during the development of Islam. This is not to say that all aspects of the tradition have changed, but that new or different elements result in shifts within the system that have had repercussions for the religious mood of the believers. At the very least, the paradigms, those crucial elements of a belief system, are altered in content or in relation to one another within the system. What remains central, however, is that the whole tradition retains its distinctively Muslim character. Any interpreter must, in the final analysis, return to that touchstone if what he says is to be valid.

When it comes to uncovering the modes of expression within the tradition, however, the researcher may utilize any number of models, from whatever sources, in plumbing the expressive models. All that is necessary is that, in Ramsey's terms, they "disclose" the reality they address. Some models fit better than others, yet it is possible that all applicable models can disclose. For example, the confrontation model may be more helpful in delineating a religious truth than irenic attempts at either peace or brotherhood. In the final analysis, the validation of model theory comes from a sense of consonance with other data within the cultural or scientific community, and not from the religious community itself. Hence model evaluations may at times contradict the more general and normative structures of a religion, if for no other reason than that the community does not perceive itself in that way at the moment. Still, the fact that such an analysis can be made demonstrates that the religion has a richness and variety that can be so interpreted. It is one way, most religionists would agree, that a tradition grows in self-understanding.

By virtue of this "disclosing" nature of models, we can also affirm their functional dimension. They are explicative. A good illustration comes from my father, who, in answer to my childhood query as to why the stars shine at night, pointed out that there were holes in the floor of heaven. Eminently satisfying at the age of four, it was later replaced by talk of corpuscular or wave theories of light and light miles. Models are not representational then, in the sense of replicating reality in a more recognizable form, but are pedagogical and psychological in intent. They relate the world around us to the psychological and intellectual needs of our time. This also suggests that they are disposable, for they may work at explaining something to us up to a point where we recognize their limits, and then we move to an entirely different system of expression. Hence the Qur'ān may be a central paradigm in the Muslim community, but determining how and why and in what sense it is may require us to work with several models as we try to explicate those realities.

It should be clear that use of the term "model" here is not in a singular "Eliadian" sense of having mythic, theophantic qualities. This sense has difficulties when applied to Muslim material, principally because Muslim religious sentiment has little official place for myth. Its conscious religious life has been largely lived in moral behaviour, Qur'ānic exegesis, and historiography to such a degree and in such a manner that myth and myth-making are relegated to the *jāhiliyya* or to local and thus inferior custom. Myth does exist in Islam—at popular levels in the Eliadian sense, and in officialdom in a more refined sense—but the problems of applying the term may well be insurmountable. Under these circumstances it seems much better to acknowledge the *potential* of an image, concept, or notion to elicit an appreciative response among Muslims. Those that do elicit such responses can be held to be powerful, since they come out of the lived experience of the believer. If images and concepts have this characteristic, they hold promise for deepening our understanding of the Muslim religious life.

The Islamic paradigm of the Prophet is the focus for our application of this theory. What follows must necessarily be suggestive but in the first section we will consider a model that comes to the fore in the identity of the Prophet in Ibn Isḥāq's biography of the Prophet (*sīra*). In the second, we will briefly examine some treatments, especially among modern writers. In the third, we will consider models of

Muḥammad under the impact of new and radical ideologies. Our concluding section will attempt to explore how models assist this kind of examination.

Ibn Isḥāq's Muḥammad: Conflict Resolution in the Early Umma

It is well known that the famous *sīra* of the Prophet by Ibn Isḥāq stands as a plateau among the early writings and oral narratives accorded to the Prophet-literature that can be designated as *maghāzī-sīra*.[26] This kind of writing is, in fact, the oldest Muslim historical material in Arabic to come down to us.[27] Since the Sira has been treated as "history," it has been subjected to numerous studies by Muslims and Western students alike, and inevitably finds its way into any attempt to describe the first century and a half of Islamic history. Wansbrough, in his recent study, *The Sectarian Milieu*, holds that this literature contains "the earliest formulations of Muslim identity" and that the conceptual motivation was polemical.[28] Positing the model of polemic, as reflected in earlier scholars' works (Bauer and Wellhausen),[29] he sees early Islamic identity as the story of competing confessional groups, each holding itself to be orthodox, working within a political structure which was benign enough to ride above the internal tensions until a consensual compromise could meld with the state.[30] Wansbrough's view is that process rather than structure is the investigative strategy: "The process in question may be envisaged as twofold; (1) linguistic transfer/adaptation of *topos*/theologoumenon/symbol to produce an instrument of communication and dispute (lingua franca); (2) distribution of these elements as confessional insignia (sectarian syndrome)."[31]

This is, of course, a very suggestive hypothesis, did it not appear to presume a *Sitz im Leben* dominated by Judeo-Christian ideology. One wonders whether the pagan environment of Arabia has sufficient place in this analysis. But Wansbrough's study fruitfully points out that we are dealing with a genre of literature that operates within the demands of a scholarly elite whose perceptions are tied to the requirements of their circles, and thus must be evaluated with those literary-religious demands in mind. In short, the *mythos* Ibn Isḥāq creates reflects his interaction within a larger community.

One is not far into Ibn Isḥāq's work until he or she realizes that this is something tantamount to an early Muslim Homeric *Odyssey.* The activities and characteristics of the hero are of epic proportions, implying and shaping the destiny of a people. The normative tone pervades, urging the reader to make a judgment. The question remains: to whom was the book directed? Some hints can be seen from one of the prime tensions underlying the book: the conflict between the north and south within the Hijaz. For Ibn Isḥāq this conflict resolves into multihued tensions between the ancient and distinguished Himyarite kingdom of the southern area and the *nouveau riche* Quraysh of Mecca. The former is defined by a dialogue set around the vision of the old Yamanite king Rābiʿa b. Naṣr. The experience had terrified him, but he asked the soothsayers to interpret it without divulging its details. The result was:

> His kingdom shall be ended by an apostle who will bring truth and justice among men of religion and virtue. Dominion will rest among his people until the Day of Separation, the day on which those near God will be rewarded, on which demands from heaven will be made which the quick and the dead will hear, men will be gathered at the appointed place, the God-fearing to receive salvation and blessing. By the Lord of heaven and earth, and what lies between them high or low I have told you but the truth in which no doubt . . . lies.[32]

The eschatological event that is crucial is, of course, the coming of Muḥammad and "his people," an occurrence that sets the stage for a new reign that will only be broken by an apocalyptic judgment day that will decide the fate of all humankind. It follows that the true descendants of the Himyarite kingdom are the people of the Prophet, a claim that neatly circumvents the Quraysh, since the intervening hegemony had been that of Persia and Abyssinia.[33] Moreover, Ibn Isḥāq deliberately has the Prophet setting the Quraysh straight as to how they managed to continue in power: "When God sent Muḥammad he specially recounted to the Quraysh his goodness and favour in turning back the Abyssinians in order to preserve their state and permanence."[34] He suggests that their rulership was based upon their continuing the ancient religious traditions: "They are the people of God: God fought for them and thwarted the attack of their enemies."[35]

Thus the primary sin of the Quraysh was that they did not accept the eschaton when it occurred; the reason given for their blindness was that they forsook the true religion for the worship of stone.

> They say that the beginning of stone worship among the sons of Ishmael was when Mecca became too small for them and they wanted more room in the country. Everyone who left the town took with him a stone from the sacred area to do honour to it. Wherever they settled they set up and walked round it as they went round the Kaʿba. This led them to worship what stones they pleased and those which made an impression on them. Thus as generations passed they forgot their primitive faith and adopted another religion for that of Abraham and Ishmael.[36]

So deluded were the Quraysh that their response to the monotheism of the Prophet was to cry out: "Would he make the gods into one God? That is indeed a strange proceeding!" Thus the forgetfulness of the truth by the Quraysh becomes the focus for the message of the Prophet, and the burden of his people. The conflict between the north and the south was expressed in religious terms as a battle of the old religionists of Himyarite background who remained true to the eschaton and recognized it, and those who forgot it and went their own way. During the life of the Prophet it was translated into the anatagonism between the *anṣār* [Helpers] of Medina, who recognized the Prophet long before the Meccans, and those of the Quraysh who had converted only at the last minute.

The conflict was resolved by the Prophet in a meeting specially called to deal with disaffection among the Ansar when the Prophet gave gifts to the Quraysh and the Bedouin but nothing to them. The confrontation is all the more remarkable because the Prophet says, in effect, you have me, while all they have is goods and flocks:

> Are you disturbed in mind because of the good things of this life by which I win over a people that they may become Muslims while I entrust you to your Islam? Are you not satisfied that men should take away flocks and herds while you take back with you the apostle of God? By Him in whose hand is the soul of Muḥammad, but for the migration I should be one of the Anṣār myself. If all men went one way and the Anṣār another I should take the way of the Anṣār.[37]

The result was many tears from the Ansar along with, "We are satisfied with the Apostle of God as our lot and portion."

The significance of this passage cannot be what seems like an easy way out for the Prophet. Conflicts with such long-standing resentments cannot be overcome in one meeting, whether the leader offers himself in lieu of inequity or not. The important point is that this conflict was resolved in the meaning and value of the Prophet himself.

In effect, the presence of Muḥammad and kinship with him in a larger cause was worth more to them than all the gifts he had given. The conflict was resolved at a deeper and more meaningful level—in the personhood of the Prophet. We are left to conclude that the endowment of honour and respect to the Prophet had right from the beginning involved a complex network of political and personal meanings, which could only be resolved by the growth of piety around the Prophet. As a result, the Prophet-image took on meaning divorced from any individual situation or value and became a symbol into which the community could invest its higher meanings and commitments.

It is, perhaps, not too much to suggest that Ibn Isḥāq was signaling a move by some of the Muslim literati into a magnification of the Prophet and his house that was characteristic of the Shiʿa, not because of loyalty to ʿAli or his cause, but because loyalty to the Prophet was the only avenue that sidestepped the knotty political and religious problems they saw around them, yet still connected them with the great sense of pride they had in Arabia's Himyarite past. The Prophet's life became the one acceptable medium that could free them from the present moment and yet could answer their needs for a symbol of continuity among the changes that rapid expansion now brought. In doing so, they opened the Sira to new forms and interpretations.

Muḥammad Among Modern Writers: Struggle for Universality

When we turn to modern textual data—Middle Eastern and primarily Egyptian—the one thing that strikes us on the surface is the predominance of overwhelmingly traditionalist viewpoints.[38] Even such a vigorous and bright intelligence as Ṭāhā Ḥusayn could write in *Fī l-shiʿr al-jāhilī:* "Yes, when we engage in the study of Arabic *adab* [literature] and its history, we must forget our national consciousness and everything that it represents, our religion and all that is related to it; we should not be concerned with whether the questions will contradict either nationality or religion; we should be constrained by nothing but the methods of true scientific investigation."[39] Yet, when he writes a three-volume work, *ʿAlā hāmish al-sīra,*[40] he does little more than write a popular account of the Prophet's life; indeed, he says in the introduction, "Man has other capabilities that want to be satisfied no less . . . than reason. Perhaps the stories do not satisfy logic and are not appropriate for the methods of scientific thought; yet the feelings are satisfied nevertheless. Their reading is a help in passing the time and in the bearing of the cares of existence."[41]

This is not the place to trace the sad saga that attended the publication of Ṭāhā Ḥusayn's *Fī l-shiʿr al-jāhilī*. Suffice it to say that the political suppressions and active religious machinations of the conservative religious element in Egyptian society weighed heavily upon him, though this explanation is hardly intellectually satisfying. Nevertheless, it does indicate that for emotional and religious reasons Ṭāhā Ḥusayn could not bring to bear the kind of scientific tools he had available; some of these reasons had to do with the nature and role of the Prophet's life in a traditional society. That he could use his scientific approach to the other contexts, but not here, indicates how symbolically powerful the Prophet's life had become. So closely was it tied to conservative orthodoxy that Muslim identity could not allow modern criticism to have free reign.

This is reflected, too, in ways in which religious styles can be used to interpret his life. In a book by the Egyptian al-Azhar University scholar, Muḥammad Muḥyī al-Dīn, published by the Higher Council of Islamic Affairs, entitled *Sayyidūna al-Muḥammad: Nabī al-raḥma wa rasūl al-hudā* [Our Lord Muḥammad: The Prophet of Mercy and the Apostle of Guidance], one would expect a much more mystical interpretation of the Prophet, especially after this introduction:

> To you, my beloved apostle of God. A word of fidelity, love: in dedication to a noble and prophetic life history, through which all the world is perfumed with a pleasant aroma throughout all ages. I lived through that experience with all my inner being and was transformed, carried back through the era of immaculate prophecy. I saw your faithful companions around you listening with their humbled hearts and purified souls, and my eyes were filled to overflowing on seeing you; and my heart won your approval and satisfaction. . . .

Yet when one turns to Muḥyī l-Din's treatment of the *isrāʾ* and *miʿrāj* (concerning Muḥammad's miraculous night journey to Jerusalem and ascent into Heaven) he simply expresses wonder at God's divine power, sketches the controversy over whether Muḥammad went in spirit or in a body, and closes with the admonition that it behooves all Muslims to believe in it since Muḥammad was truthful. The only really stimulating detail in Muḥyī l-Dīn's account is that Imām Jaʿfar al-Ṣādiq interpreted the star in the Qur'ānic verse, "by the name of the star when it falls," as Muḥammad's return from his journey.[42]

Comparisons and adaptations which make the Prophet appear equal or superior to other great leaders, on the other hand, are acceptable. Thus in ʿAbbās Maḥmūd al-ʿAqqād's work on "Muḥammad's Genius"[43] one finds a series of arguments, utilizing strategies of such military commanders as Napoleon and Hitler to prove Muḥammad's military superiority. For example, Napoleon used to think that the ratio of moral power to numerical value was three to one; ʿAqqād holds that Muḥammad had achieved this long before Napoleon had. Similarly Muḥammad's use of surveillance and information gathering was almost proverbial, far sooner than Napoleon's famed developments in the area.[44] ʿAqqād's comparisons with Hitler focus on Hitler's use of exploratory missions, the purpose of which was to parachute behind lines, disrupt communications, and instill fear within the populace. Muḥammad used the exploratory mission not to demoralize the people but to obtain information: "This military method adopted by Hitler had its own admirers and detractors. Those who admired it would say it was beneficial . . . those to whom it appeared negatively divine that this method was based on compulsion." Muḥammad's use of the exploratory mission was thus superior to Hitler's because it was based upon ideological persuasion rather than demoralization. It was based on the Muslim principle that there is no compulsion in Islam.[45] ʿAqqād's appeal to these figures was surely not made from great respect for their moral stature in history; the goal was to situate the Prophet in the highest counsels of military ability. The appeal to Hitler and Bonaparte is made, too, because they are recognized by both Europeans and Egyptians as exemplary tacticians. By demonstrating Muḥammad's superiority to these, ʿAqqād raises him above the locale of Arabic history to world history.

With these perspectives in mind, when we come back to Ṭāhā Ḥusayn's *Sīra*, the same intent to raise Muḥammad to international status can be noted. Rather than military prowess, Ṭāhā Ḥusayn stresses the universality of human reason. The eloquence of the Qur'ān is not just a miracle, it is a miracle of reason; he makes a character say:

> In all that I have seen and known concerning prophets, I have seen nothing stronger than that related to Muḥammad, God bless him and guard him. He was a man of whom opponents and enemies demanded miracles, but who dissociated himself from their idea and proclaimed to them that he was human like them, and that he was

> not sent to dazzle *minds* with great occurrences, but was sent to recite to people a Qur'ān which speaks to their *minds* and fills them with guidance, and speaks to their heart and makes them feel compassion and generosity.[46]

Ṭāhā Ḥusayn saw Egyptians, and indeed all modern Muslims, as the amalgamation of Greek and Arabic cultures—rationality and scientific principles on the one hand and the will and sensitivity of feeling on the other. The Prophet was the reflection of that view: his *Sīra* is a continuous integration of those two tendencies. It is hard to escape the view that Ṭāhā Ḥusayn's overriding image of Muḥammad comprises everything in both Western and Eastern cultures, as he saw them.

This, then, is the linkage with the Muḥammad of Ibn Isḥāq: what may be applied to the Prophet are those perceptions within the *Sitz im Leben* of the conservative Ulama of the hour. Only those models which are consonant with the traditional Muḥammadan biography, but which make the Prophet more universal, can be accepted. Stress is placed upon an idealized Prophet, not upon the limitations of a common man.

The Contemporary Muḥammad: Catalyst of Radical Ideology

Where most writers heretofore incorporated their orientation into the interpretive structures of the *sīra*, some have seen the power of the Prophet to be transparent—the Prophet radically altered the culture and society in which he lived. As a symbol, Muḥammad expresses the dynamics of a true Muslim believer. The expression of such revolutionary ideology is, perhaps, put no more succinctly than by Aḥmad Ṭālib, a leader in the Algerian revolution of the 1960s. Yet in justifying his activism, Ṭālib reinterprets early Islam. His first plea is to return to Muslim origins to make a "pilgrimage to our sources," so that believers could see if Islam (that is, essentially, the Qur'ān as it was revealed and then applied) has attained a solution to the problem and, in the event of a positive response, to make clear the originality of that solution.

> The Prophet himself did not opt to live far away from the camp of men. He did not say to youth: "Sell what you have and follow me." On the contrary, he worked and toiled among things just as they are. He did not achieve the glory of the just, except by way of the risk of his life. He only made triumphal entry into Mecca after confronting

> every danger and being subjected to every taunt of sarcasm. At Medina, he was not content merely to be the preacher of the new faith: he became also the leader of the new city, where he organized the religious, social and economic life. We see him sharing personally in the construction of the Mosque and the dwellings of the emigrants. Later, carrying arms, he put himself at the head of his troops. Charged to deliver a message he opted for action, because he was convinced that a message can only pass from the realm of life by taking the hard road of involvement.
>
> Thus, Islam commends action—we plainly see—just as, no less explicitly, it condemns craven aloofness from it.[47]

Summing up his argument for social activities, Ṭālib writes:

> Having responded . . . to the effect that Islam is a philosophy of engagement and roundly condemns all forms of desertion from duty, it remains to show how this philosophy is distinguished from those doctrines of action which abound in our day. It seems to me that the answer to that can be found in this verse: "Say: 'Act, and God and the Prophet and the believers will see your doing." (S. 9:105). In other words, the Muslim must be a man of action ["Act"] but his doings must be ruled by a moral factor ("God sees what you do") and should conform to the perfection of a model ("and his Prophet") and also have the good of the community as their goal ("and the believers").[48]

In an entirely different vein, Khālid M. Khālid, another graduate of al-Azhar, demonstrates yet another orientation. In a work whose title means in English "Thus Spake the Apostle," (reminiscent of Nietzsche?) he takes up science and culture and Muḥammad's perceptions relative to them. When Muḥammad speaks about learning he does not mean the mere gleaning and storing of details but the active integration of *fiqh* [discerning the Law] into one's life. He argues that fiqh has an encyclopedic sense, such that the insights one forms during one's wide range of knowledge and experience will continuously build his cultured character. *ʿAmal al-fiqh* [Practical application of fiqh] can be interpreted "as an instructor who conveys this knowledge to the recipient, and the recipient will receive this information, digest it and through his better understanding, better evaluation and the spark of his intellect and the genius of his feeling be more knowledgeable than this teacher."[49] Consequently Muḥammad as the expression of the *ʿilm* [science, knowledge] that is working towards a higher culture is alive today, in the way individuals are developing. There is, then, a continuous metamorphosis of the individual under the power of the *ʿilm* of the Prophet.

The proof of these views rests upon the extraordinary emphasis the Prophet gave to learning, attested in the Hadith: "a single scholar (*ʿālim*) is much harder on the devil than one thousand worshippers (*ʿibād*)." Khālid interprets this to mean that "the devil would find his way quite easily to any worshipper that is not enlightened by the light of learning itself, whereas all [of] Satan's attempts would fail to encircle a worshipper that is enlightened by learning, its guidance and its light."[50] Hence, in a manner that perhaps Nietzsche would have appreciated, at least in part, Khālid argues that the true objective of knowledge is personal development: "The objective of learning is the creation of a human individual who is constantly in the process of perfecting his or her processes of thinking and feeling, along with the development of consciousness and will."[51] The validation for this is the Prophet: "The Apostle of God used to ask us to stand so that our shoulders touched, and often he indicated by his own hand how to straighten our lines for prayer; moreover he used to say 'Let those who are knowledgeable in mind and heart be next to me in line, and those who are less than they in that respect follow them, and so on.'"[52]

Such strikingly different interpretations as those we have just considered suggest that the religious and cultural situation of contemporary Muslims has called for a radically modified role for the Prophet. As a paradigmatic figure, he is no longer just a theological expression; he is recognized explicitly as a galvanizing and religiously powerful impulse within the Muslim community. Not content with a perception of the Prophet that limits him to the founding of the umma or to the historical locale of traditional Muslim thought he is seen as a present-day catalyst for social and religious achievement, with an existential meaning for a Muslim world facing the problems of change and uncertainty.

Model Theory and the Prophet

To what extent has our use of model helped us "disclose" meanings in *sīra* materials? In the first place, we have argued for a direct relationship between the *Sitz im Leben* of each creative expression of *sīra* so that, in Cousins's words, we can discover the "experiential" setting out of which the expression is made. In the second place, we have taken the Prophet-image itself to be inexhaustible, that is, to carry with it meanings which may be developed and even explored beyond that found in its original setting.[53] Third, because the model itself has no particular religious entailments, it allows us to explore language that has itself become weighted with its own tradition. Fourth, we have found patterns within the religious lives of Muslims that open up dimensions for further study, namely, what relationship is there between the conflict resolution of Ibn Isḥāq and the social catalyst of Aḥmad Ṭālib? How do they portend crucial religious structures in the umma? What role has veneration for the Prophet played in allowing Muslim religious thought to remain in touch with the experience of the believers? Immediately we can see a number of further linkages. Consequently, testimonial literature, like this gem from Ibn Isḥāq can serve as a basis for the historian of religions in his analysis of Islamic piety.

> Those gone by never lost one like Muḥammad
> And one like him will not be mourned till Resurrection Day
> More gentle and faithful to obligation after obligation;
> More prone to give without thought of any return;
> More lavish with wealth newly gained and inherited
> When a generous man would grudge giving
> what had long been his.
> More noble in reputation when claims are examined;
> More noble in princely Meccan ancestry;
> More inaccessible in height and eminence
> Founded on enduring supports,
> Firmer in root and branch and wood
> Which rain nourished making it full of life.
> A glorious Lord brought him up as a boy
> And he became perfect in most virtuous deeds.
> To his knowledge the Muslims resorted;
> No knowledge was withheld and no opinion was gainsaid.
> I say, and none can find fault with me
> But one lost to all sense,
> I shall never cease to praise him.[54]

Part Two

Ritual and Community

Whether in ancient civilizations myth provided the basis for ritual or vice versa was a question that animated *Religionswissenschaft* in the late nineteenth and early twentieth centuries. If ritual was to be understood, then, in relation to myth, evidence could be drawn from the textual accounts of Creation and the cosmic cycle of the New Year, which were plentiful enough in Ancient Near Eastern textual and archaeological materials. The myth/ritual categories shed new light on the cultural history of ancient Israel and the formative histories of Judaism and Christianity. Semitic and classical philology and *Religionswissenschaft* seemed impotent to move beyond the period from Antiquity to Late Roman times, however, to analyze ritual in the youngest cognate Semitic religion, Islam.

The reason seems plain enough in retrospect. Neither Islamic sources nor Islamicists say much about myth. The Qur'ān is not structured around the great cosmic cycles of Creation and the eschaton; the Prophet Muḥammad's persona has not been seen to be framed by miracles and *Heilsgeschichte* but rather by the political history of the Hijaz in seventh-century Arabia; and the First of Muharram—the Islamic New Year and a minor occasion by comparison to Hajj and Ramadan closing feast days—refers not to cosmic renewal but to Muḥammad's politically necessitated emigration to Yathrib. Thus, without the presence of myth by which to understand ritual, historians of religion have seemed to lack the necessary grounds for a comparative study of ritual that would include the Islamic materials. The declaration that Islam is absent of any significant mythology has cast a vast scholastic penumbra over the data the myth/ritual approach has relied upon. Such light as we have had until recently came from such sources as the historian Snouck-Hurgronje, the anthropologist Westermarck, and the adventurer Burton, who undertook the task of providing Europeans with descriptions of Islamic rituals, primarily the pilgrimage to Mecca and local rites of passage.

Leaving aside the question of the extent to which *mythos* does or does not play a role in Muslim world views, the evidence of ritual behavior in Islamic society is rich and diverse. The more recent ethnographies of Clifford Geertz and Victor Turner, based on what many call "symbolist" cultural anthropology, have influenced a renaissance of ritual studies that take some account of Islam. The work of Lévi-Strauss has stimulated limited exploration of structuralist analysis by some observers of Islamic culture. The interpretation of ritual behavior, like the study of religious texts, is seen to be susceptible to semiotic theory—a hermeneutics that regards religious expression in word *and* deed as *meaningful* within a cultural system of signs and symbols. Whether or not one accepts the particular views of culture retailed by Geertz, Turner, or Lévi-Strauss, their attention to the significance of religious behavior has provided religious studies scholarship with more powerful prescriptions with which to correct myopic oversight of the study of ritual in Islam.

The scope of the newer ritual studies as they apply to Islam can enrich our understanding of traditional topics in Islamic studies. The

Shiʿi *taʿzīya*, Sufi *ṭarīqas*, visitation to saints' tombs for *baraka*, and the performance of Qur'ān recitation—to name just a few—are symbolic activities of deep significance in Islam. The question for religious studies is not whether ritual exists much in Islam but how to approach the study of the many kinds of ritual activity in Islam. In a word, the newer trend in ritual studies is not to identify and isolate ritual data for analysis but rather to locate such data within the broader cultural matrices in which they occur and presumably find their meanings.

Part Two recommends a reorientation of our thinking about ritual as structured, meaningful behavior in Islamic culture. In Chapter 4, Frederick M. Denny starts out by examining why Islamicists have all but ignored the highly performative aspects of the religious duties of Islam. His treatment of the problem offers a number of possibilities for future research and ways of approaching the variegated forms and expressions of symbolic activity in Islamic society. Denny suggests several ways which scholars studying other traditions have distinguished among different types of rituals, and he recommends where similar steps might be taken with the Islamic materials.

In Chapter 5, William R. Roff singles out a particular ritual assemblage in Islam, the annual pilgrimage to Mecca, which he examines in light of Turner's revision of van Gennep's theory of "liminality." With greater use of the Islamic materials than Turner made in his well-known studies, especially the usually overlooked Hajj manuals written for pilgrims, Roff brings greater insight into the applicability of Turner's thesis and its limits. As Roff points out, Turner, like most Islamicists, had dwelled on the activities and symbolic meanings at Mecca and its environs, the sacred spacial and temporal center of Hajj activities. An equally important set of questions surround the rites of separation and reincorporation of the Hajji from and back into his particular societal environment and the socio-psychological dimensions of status enhancement this entails.

4

Islamic Ritual

Perspectives and Theories

FREDERICK M. DENNY

If the study of Islam as a whole has been relatively neglected in the history of religions, the systematic study of ritual within traditional Islamic studies has been recessive, too. Why this is so can only be speculated upon, for Islam itself places great emphasis on ritual activities. Thus, Wilfred Cantwell Smith, for example, has counseled translating the word *sunnī* not as "orthodox," but "orthoprax."[1] And Bousquet has written that if *ʿibādāt* ("religious observances") is translated as "cult"

> we are committing something of a theoretical error (Tor Andrae), for it has quite correctly been said that, strictly speaking, Islam knows no more of a cult, properly speaking, than (Snouck Hurgronje) it does of law; nor, we should add, of ethics. *Fiḳh* is, in fact, a deontology (the statements of the whole corpus of duties, of acts whether obligatory, forbidden or recommended, etc.) which is imposed upon man.[2]

Bousquet overstates the issue but he has a valid point in suggesting that to *know* the truth—which is a possible translation of *fiqh*—requires *doing* it as well. This is what Smith may have in mind with his translation "orthoprax." It is not a question of knowing versus doing, or of doctrine versus ritual; rather, it is a question of emphasis between the two poles of a single symbol and action system. Islamic ritual is an expression of Islamic doctrine, but this is not to say that the latter is either logically or chronologically prior to the former. The two are mutually confirmatory moments in a unified process of religious discovery and discipline. *Tawḥīd* is not merely a matter of theological propositions, but also a living realization: the "making one" of God by total submission and service. At the center is the experience of God, which is then articulated and maintained by religion. Theological issues have been of great importance in the history of Islam, but legal and ritual concerns have been even more so. *Kalām*, "dogmatic theology," has never been recognized by "orthoprax" Sunnis, at least, as an autonomous science apart from *fiqh*, "jurisprudence."

The *fiqh* books always begin with ritual duties by considering the four "Pillars" (*arkān*): canonical prayers (*ṣalāt*), alms (*zakāt*), fasting (*ṣawm*), and pilgrimage to Mecca (*ḥajj*). The first Pillar, *shahāda* (confession of God's unity and Muḥammad's apostleship), is usually not discussed, but taken for granted. The actual enumeration and explication of the requirements for Salat are always preceded by a detailed discussion of purification, *ṭahāra*, the indispensable condition for all acts of worship. Ritual ablutions are themselves complex processes, requiring detailed elucidation. Muḥammad is reported to have said, "Purification is half of faith." Also, he is credited with saying, "The key to Paradise is worship (Salat); the key to worship is purification."[3]

Ritual Studies and Islamic Studies

What is the key to understanding Islamic ritual from outside the tradition? Is it simply to accept what the official sources say about it? If so, one will have a fairly easy time of it, and the occasional confusion of differing details among the Muslim schools of jurisprudence (*madhāhib*) will offer no more difficulty than they do to Muslims. But then, what are to be accepted as *official* practices? If one reads in the Hadith one finds all sorts of practices that are recommended or at least not condemned. But if one reads Ibn Taymiyya or Wahhabi literature, for example, the field of acceptable ritual behavior shrinks drastically as the range of corrupt and detested practices expands. Yet these practices are often embraced by masses of Muslims who regard them as part of the true religion.[4]

Let us consider a practical case. Occasionally in my lectures on Islamic practices a Muslim or two in the class will challenge me on this very point saying, "That is not true Islam. Why are you telling the class these things?" Then I will ask if the practice, say, of seeking intercession from a saint by visiting his tomb is, in fact, practiced by some Muslims. The answer, if the student is knowledgeable about actual behavior, will be in the affirmative but with a qualification and very often a condemnation of the practice as well. Students are often puzzled and frustrated, however, because of the conflict between normative and descriptive approaches to the analysis of behavior. Clifford Geertz's title *Islam Observed* is a shrewd acknowledgment of this conflict, and his comparison and contrast of religion in Morocco and Indonesia is an instructive essay in definition and description.[5] One has only to delve into a study like Nadel's *Nupe Religion* to read of practices associated with Islam that would make the most liberal Muslim (or scholarly observer, for that matter) uneasy.[6] Of course, Nadel was not concerned with how far practice agreed with doctrine; he was not studying that abstraction we call "official Islam," but rather Nupe society and values, including religion.

One approach is, then, to concentrate on "deontology," that is, on the consideration of the Shariʿa as the Muslim science of duty (*deon*), of which scholars like Bousquet, Snouck Hurgronje, and Andrae have reminded us, and which is considered by Muslims to be above criticism. Our discussions in this case would have as their object the idealized form of ritual behavior as found in the original sources. Also, we would not deliberately provoke objections from guardians of normative Islam who understandably consider excursions into folklore and pagan survivals at the least as the misapplied association of customs (a sort of anthropologist's *shirk*) or at worst as an attempt to undermine and discredit what Muslims hold to be sacred. What is needed is much more sensitive and informed attention to Islamic sources and discussions on ritual. From the orientalist's viewpoint, the materials have been sifted with primary attention to their historical provenance; such scholarship has its place, but so far it has been practiced with little regard for synchronic structures of meaning. What I propose instead is to follow the sedulous discipline that the *fuqahāʾ* (Muslim doctors of law) and Islamists alike must share if they would analyze and interpret normative ritual requirements in a manner that brings out the meaning within its proper Islamic contexts. For example, a preoccupation with Jewish parallels to the Salat in a study that seeks to understand Muslim worship may hinder and even prevent an understanding of the primary subject, which has a life of its own. That is, one must first of all seek to understand and appreciate the peculiar quality of conviction that renders Salat meaningful to Muslims.

Faith is, as the old German maxim goes, both *eine Gabe und eine Aufgabe*, "a gift and a task." Does this imply that outsiders who study Islam should somehow submit to the revelation for methodological reasons? Can we as scholars claim objectivity and free inquiry while at the same time we maintain convictions and participation in the religious object of our research? In short, what is the relation between understanding a faith and having a faith? The student of tribal religion often takes for granted that he or she will at some point be ritually incorporated into the life of the group. "Paris is well worth a mass," whether in avoiding a fatal challenge, as Henry of Navarre did, or publishing praiseworthy monographs, as Burton and Snouck did.[7] The problem of the difference in perspectives between observer and actors is as old as social science and has not yet been entirely eliminated even by sophisticated field techniques centering on the "participant-observer."[8]

Ritual is for the participant a reenactment of a profound truth. As Geertz has put it, it is realizing that religion is at the same time a model *of* and a model *for* the world.[9] Does one need to be a Muslim in order to capture the essence of Islamic ritual? It depends on what "capturing the essence" means. It may mean conversion. Santayana has expressed this memorably:

> Any attempt to speak without speaking any particular language is not more hopeless than the attempt to have a religion that shall be no religion in particular. . . . Thus every living and healthy religion has a marked idiosyncrasy; its power consists in its special and surprising message and in the bias which that revelation gives to life. The vistas it opens and the mysteries it propounds are another world to live in; and another world to live in—whether we expect ever to pass wholly over into it or not—is what we mean by having a religion.[10]

But having a religion is not what we mean by *understanding* a religion, and understanding is not the same as believing. Embracing a religion, finding "another world to live in" is not itself a scholarly enterprise. Neither is the discipline of religious studies a world to live in; rather it is a highly diverse product of a much wider world that most of its professors share, having as one of its biases a seemingly insatiable curiosity—which borders at times on the meddlesome—about other peoples and world views.[11]

Capturing the essence does not require anything so drastic as conversion, but it does demand sympathy and respect as well as openness to the sources, human and textual, that are centrally meaningful to the adherents. In any case, one cannot convert to Islam for purposes of scholarly convenience or authenticity. What is more, the Muslim colleague who would undertake history of religions scholarship is under the very same constraints as the non-Muslim as far as making sense of the tradition to the scholarly world at large. As Fazlur Rahman points out in Chapter 12 of this volume, being a Muslim does not by itself guarantee that one's explication and interpretation of Islam will be either clear or balanced. Seeing oneself, one's own tradition from the "inside" is at least as difficult as attempting to understand from the outside, particularly if wider communication of the findings is envisaged. The sympathetic scholarly study of a religious tradition to which one does not personally adhere is neither an exercise in piety nor a pretense at being an insider.[12] It is rather the limited project of attempting to know whatever can be communicated and to share it with any other humans who have the interest and intellectual discipline to absorb it. The basic premise is that humankind is one, and what we call Buddhist, Islamic, Christian, or Aztec theodicies, for example, are ways in which fellow human beings have discerned, codified, and communicated facts and feelings, practices and beliefs. History of religions is not theology, nor is it a "new humanism." It is much more modest. It is simply one of a number of related disciplines both in the humanities and the social sciences by which we attempt to explain and interpret ourselves to ourselves. Personal articulations about God have nothing to do with the discipline in any normative sense. To insist that they do is to change the subject, which is humankind. But this does not make history of religions a thoroughgoing humanism, either, especially in an ideological sense, however useful its findings may be for that purpose.[13]

The study of Islamic ritual is not a mysterious business, although the paucity of published materials on the subject in relation to its obvious central importance may seem paradoxical.[14] Nothing could be easier for the outsider than the observation of Muslims at prayer or engaged in a variety of other ritual activities, both official and popular. The fault for neglected study of Islamic ritual lies with the scholars, not with the Muslims. That a now generally acknowledged oversight has been allowed to persist is a testimony to the failures of scholarship and not to any opaqueness or intractability of the subject matter. But herein lies a problem. One needs to examine both texts and contexts, and the divergences between the two will require scholars to make certain decisions about interpretation. The historian of religions strikes out on his own at this point in striving to make sense of issues that may well be neatly accounted for within Islam.[15]

Snouck Hurgronje's precise and penetrating historical study of the Hajj was published several years before his actual sojourn in Mecca during the spring and summer of 1885, and is thus an example of the type of painstaking orientalist scholarship that has traditionally been based on texts and carried out in an academic setting. All that one needed to know about the Hajj from the formal standpoint was plentifully available in written sources. And in classical Islam, *fiqh*, once established as positive law, needed no *riḥla*, "trip to the field," but only *kitāba*, "writing" things up from available texts." Yet it was Snouck's *riḥla* that made it possible for him to provide a perceptive contextual examination of Mecca and its peoples, a sort of early "Islam Observed."[16] Materials on so central an Islamic ritual as the Hajj cannot be limited to manuals on *manāsik al-Ḥajj*, those distillations from *fiqh* works that guide pilgrims through the entire process in an orderly, if abstractly perfect, textbook fashion. Each Hajj is the same, the official sources suggest, and the attention of the faithful toward achieving perfect performance of the rites is a testimony to abidingness.

It is also possible to acknowledge, however, the pristine perfection of the ritual duties performed by Muslims as spelled out in the Qur'ān and Sunna, even when they do not regularly fulfill them, or when they irregularly observe them. What does the scholar do when confronted with a duty unperformed by persons claiming to be devout; or with additional practices unprescribed in the Shariʿa but diligently observed in local practice? It does not increase our understanding to scold the former and correct the latter—that is the Mulla's task; in either event a statement is being made about Islam as a perceivable reality. Islamic sources do not provide much in the way of analytic models to deal with such a problem, although all of the elements are readily available. And it should be added immediately that it is not Islam's task to generate conceptual frameworks for scholarly analysis beyond the obligations of *daʿwa*, in the sense of "mission."

Elements of Ritual in Islam

The most basic term for Islamic ritual is *ʿibāda*, "worship, service," of inferiors toward their superior, their Lord. All of the official duties of Islam are subsumed under *ʿibāda:* the five Pillars constitute the main categories of Islamic ritual and lesser events are arranged under them in orderly fashion. For example, the *ʿĪd* of Sacrifice is inextricably rooted in the Hajj. The festival of fast-breaking (*ʿĪd al-fiṭr*) serves to punctuate the ending of the Ramadan fast. The special Salats of earthquake or eclipse are variations on the standard form, as is the Salat at the graveside. All is orderly and minutely regulated. Four of the five Pillars have a strong communal reference and, in fact, are fashioned to express and channel the driving force of the first, the Shahada, which itself implicitly contains the fuller features of Muslim faith (*īmān*), to which belong statements about belief in God, angels, prophets and their books, the Last Day, and divine decree. Two of the Pillars also have a strong spatial reference, for both Salat and Hajj are focused on the Kaʿba in Mecca. Three—Salat, Sawm, and Hajj—also have strong time references. So we have in these several ritual clusters a full range of dealings in sacred space and time. Nor are all things of equal status. Some matter, for example, is impure by nature and not by circumstance (pig, carrion, and dog), whereas some is impure only because of contact with impurity, which can be avoided or removed. Thus in Islam there is what in ritual studies is referred to as the aspect of "separation," or a system of separations, based not merely on time and space but also on purity and pollution.

When legal terms are considered, we see not a sharp distinction between the sacred and the profane, but a kind of shading off from the one toward the other, as in the sequence *jā'ir* and *mubāḥ* (neutral) toward *farḍ* and *wājib* (performance rewarded, omission punished), and from *sunna* and *nafl* (performance rewarded, but omission not punished) all the way to *makrūh* (disapproved but not punished) and finally *ḥarām* (absolutely prohibited, with punishment). A sharper distinction is seen when the division is limited to *ḥarām* and *ḥalāl*, "forbidden" and "permitted." Note that these terms do not mean, at least etymologically, "impure" and "pure"; they are legal concepts and reflect the primary notion of obedience to God's command. *Ḥarām* also means "sacred," but not in the English sense, which is restricted to the notion of "holy." Rather in the French sense of Durkheim's "things set apart and forbidden." There is ambiguity in the term, for it can be interpreted as "forbidden: unclean" and also "forbidden: ultraclean." The related "*ḥaram*" is limited to positive sacrality and would thus be equivalent to the English "sacred." One might be inclined to substitute taboo for *ḥarām*, but the latter term is native to Islam and has its own constellation of related meanings, however much it may be found to overlap with taboo. In such cases as this the historian of religions has the opportunity and duty to qualify the application of concepts (taboo) in cross-cultural studies to the actual meanings of similar notions (*ḥarām*) within a particular tradition. Thus we may learn about "taboo" through the study of "*ḥarām*," and not simply vice versa.

Pollution avoidance has considerable ritual meaning for Muslims and is one of the most prominent indicators of the general bipolarity of things in Islam. The Qur'ān has numerous pairings of opposites, as indeed the Arabic language in general frequently displays. The people of the "left" are contrasted with the people of the "right." The *dār al-islām* (Abode of Islam) is set over against the *dār al-ḥarb* (Abode of Conflict). Each of these orientations has a direct connection with purity (right) and pollution (left). So benefit and blessing proceed from the right whereas baleful effects are to be expected from the left. One enters a mosque with the right foot first; one leaves leading with the left. The opposite is the case when entering and leaving a privy. The left hand is used for humble tasks, whereas the right is reserved for eating and touching others. The Kaʿba itself had been oriented from most ancient times according to a right-left sense, and this has been maintained in Islam though not without some alteration and confusion.[17]

Pollution avoidance also pertains to food. Mary Douglas's absorbing and convincing analysis of Jewish dietary regulations argues that the intricate conditions pertaining to lawful and unlawful foods reflect the uncompromising monotheism of the people who codified them in Leviticus.[18] This is useful for an approach to Islamic regulations, which are similar in certain instances to the Jewish ones. The will to *tawḥīd* is fundamental, *mutatis mutandis*, in both traditions. The means by which Islam arrived at its positions on food, however, must be quite different, anchored in part on the authority of Arabian traditions as well as in the Qur'ānic affirmation of God's law as given to Moses. Douglas's intricate and ingenious discussion of classifications, eschewing what she calls "medical materialism," could serve as an extended footnote to any *faqīh*'s [Muslim lawyer's] ventilation of the issue, right up to its climax. "The dietary laws," Douglas observes, "would have been like signs which at every turn inspired meditation on the oneness, purity and completeness of God. By rules of avoidance holiness was given a physical expression in every encounter with the animal kingdom and at every meal."[19]

Earlier I introduced but did not explore issues of space and time in Islamic ritual. This pair of classifications has been exploited extensively by historians of religion, but rarely does one encounter a treatment of them with reference to Islam, except, of course, in unelaborated remarks on the Kaʿba as "navel,"[20] for example, or *Laylat al-Qadr* as the sacred time of the descent of the Qur'ān, observed around the final days of Ramadan each lunar year. Now, to say that Islam has much to offer comparativists on the subject of sacred time and space does not in itself advance our understanding very much, nor is it necessary to spawn a school of studies which in some circles would render Islam more appealing to scholars who adore those categories and invoke them on all occasions. What is needed is attention to the spatial-temporal dimensions and orientations of Islam for purposes of better understanding Islamic symbolism as it is understood from within. Space and time are universal categories, and the ways in which religious persons discern and relate to them are often widely shared. Yet, once the relatively low-level, albeit necessary, rehearsal of mythic and ethnographic parallels has been accomplished, we still have to focus on the particular *Islamic* awareness and applications. Beyond that it is likely that such research will be of wider application in comparative religious studies in general.

Toward an Analysis of Ritual in Islam

With the appearance of Islam in world history, the old Arabian way of life, *al-jāhiliyya*, the "Time of Barbarism," had been superseded. A new era and a new dispensation had begun, and zero point was the dramatic emigration of Muḥammad and his Companions from Mecca to Medina. The new calendar was arranged, without intercalation, to be independent not only of the old Arabian lunar year but especially of all solar reckoning which was traditionally linked to the structures of agricultural society and religion.[21]

Both God and his believers transcend the regularity and the vicissitudes of the seasons which in turn are controlled ritually; a peculiar order is imposed upon them. The Islamic ritual year comprehends and dominates the mundane year, resolutely denying any intrinsic value to seedtime and harvest, to breeding and lambing, to cool summer retreats to Ṭā'if or London, and to other meaningful and satisfying seasonal activities, while at the same time blessing them all with its lordly progress in a regular round of visits. The word *ʿīd* contains the notion of "return" as well as festival, but the point of return is on a calendar that slides slowly behind the "seasons." God is jealous, holy, and will not permit any association of natural time or season with himself. Put another way, one should not see time as having independent value apart from God, for it is mere duration. The pagan Arabs of the Jahiliyya lamented that "Nothing but Time destroys us" (Qur'ān 45:24). An astonishing "Divine Saying" (*ḥadīth qudsī*) exclaims: "The son of Adam should not say, 'Curse Time!' For I am Time! I send the day and the night, and if I wished, I would take them away."[22] There is considerable mention of time in the Qur'ān particularly in passages warning of the Last Day, and Hereafter, and so forth.

The Islamic calendar and indeed the Islamic day are pregnant with ritual meaning, and beyond the canonical observances are many others of local or folk origin such as saints' festivals.[23] The five daily prayers provide a vigorous testimony to the dominance of ritual concerns in people's lives by calling them from mundane occupations to remembrance of their ultimate orientation. Each performance of the Salat is an exercise in liminality marked off by the ablution and "intention" (*niyya*) at the beginning and the "peace" (*taslīm*) at the end. The Hajj is, of course, a mighty expression of liminality and communitas in Victor Turner's sense,[24] with its potent combination of space and time focused on the center of the world, Mecca, a true *axis mundi*. But in the Salat itself there is also a strong spatial orientation toward the *qibla*, the direction of the Kaʿba in Mecca, when the whole Umma at worship effects an implosion of spiritual energy and celebrates its unity of people and purpose. Wherever the Muslim prays, he is during those moments spiritually at the center. I once discussed this with Javanese Muslims and was told that although Indonesia is a great distance from Mecca the Kaʿba itself is in their hearts and that there is a sense of closeness not only to Mecca during prayer, but also to all other Muslims wherever they may be on the face of the earth. This is typical of Islamic religious sentiment. The development of astronomical and mathematical studies in Islamic civilization was in no small measure related to the enduring ritual requirement of being in a proper *qibla* orientation wherever prayers were offered up.[25]

Sacred space in Islam is markedly different from sacred space in other traditions, particularly the older religions of agricultural orientation in the Ancient Near East. Theodor Gaster described in *Thespis* a phenomenon which he named the "topocosm," a complex interrelationship of the individual, society, time, and location centered in the seasonal round with a comprehensive cosmology.[26] The major components of the seasonal pattern are rituals that are divided into two categories, rites of *kenosis*, "emptying," and rites of *plerosis*, "filling."

> The former portray and symbolize the eclipse of life and vitality at the end of each lease [i.e., on the land and its reproductive powers], and are exemplified by lenten periods, fasts, austerities, and other expressions of mortification or suspended animation. The latter, on the other hand, portray and symbolize the revitalization which ensues at the beginning of the new lease, and are exemplified by rites of mass mating, ceremonial purgations of evil and noxiousness (both physical and 'moral'), and magical procedures designed to promote fertility, relume the sun, and so forth.[27]

Gaster's useful model is only partially applicable to orthodox Islam. The topocosm idea itself does not apply, but kenotic and plerotic rites are present. The first category includes the Tenth of Muharram, especially as observed by Shiʿites with self-flagellation, the *taʿziya* ("passion play"), and so forth. The Ramadan fast belongs in this category, as do individual voluntary fasts, although one must very carefully consider the elements of the former and not make facile comparisons with other rituals of self-denial, for example the Christian Lent, which is an entirely different kind of observance. To some extent the state of *ḥarām* on the Hajj is kenotic, but that complex ritual process also features the plerotic rite of blood sacrifice (which is kenotic only from the victim's vantage point). The sharing of the food and general rejoicing, not only on the Field of Sacrifice at Mina, but also and especially throughout the Islamic world during the Festival of the Sacrifice again illustrate the communal aspects of Islam and its universality.

The rites of *kenosis* and *plerosis* are not topocosmic as far as the Pillars are concerned, but in popular Islam the story is different, for there are definite throwbacks to an earlier, agrarian-based world view. One example is the great *moulid* (*mawlid*, "birthday") of Sīdī Aḥmad al-

Badawī which is held each autumn in Tanta in the Egyptian Delta.[28] This celebration is essentially Egyptian, it is observed according to the solar calendar, and it cuts across sectarian and even traditional religious lines. The Moulid festival has a strong fertility dimension, to the point that older descriptions of activities were laconic in the extreme.[29] I refer here not to the mosque-centered activities, but to some of the local folk practices that go on far into the night. To a marked degree the Tanta Moulid is also an important agricultural trade fair. Another example is the Nupe of West Africa who, although partially Islamized, adhere to a seasonal calendar and combine both pagan and Islamic rites, the latter being essentially public and with an emphasis on joyful celebration, what Gaster calls *plerosis*.[30]

The widespread saint cults of Islam satisfy the desires of people for holy places nearby. In Egypt, indeed, it is generally thought essential that each village should have a proper mausoleum shrine (*qubba*) housing a local saint's remains. This edifice and its attendant ritual observances reflect Islamic principles, to be sure; but they also play a significant role in maintaining the community's self-respect and sense of propriety. Despite the virulent attacks by Ibn Taymiyya,[31] the Wahhabis, and other reformers against local saint veneration, the longing for local shrines to visit and from which to receive blessings appears to be ineradicable. And these establishments, which are often *ṭarīqa*-oriented, maintain among their adherents and even wider circles a strong sense of identification with a pristine past faithfully remembered in *silsila* (spiritual lineage) and *mawlid* (*moulid*, meaning birthday festival). Until the eighteenth century, the Hijaz and Najd had many saints' shrines and mosque-tombs, and the pattern of the sacred enclave (*ḥarām* and *ḥawta*) extended back well into Jahiliyya times. According to R. B. Serjeant,[32] the sacred enclave, centering in a saint's tomb, is still a very prominent part of Yemenite Islam and folk religion. In East Java the mosque-tomb complex of Sunan Giri (near Surabaya) reflects the Hindu-Buddhist past with characteristic Majapahit touches in the architecture, extending even to the placement of carved *nāga*s protecting the tomb itself. Significantly, the saint's remains are aligned with the *qibla* of the adjoining mosque, so that the worshippers face Sunan Giri as they bow toward Mecca.

Central to any discussion of ritual in comparative religion are rites of passage, particularly the model of Arnold van Gennep[33] with its phases of separation, transition, and incorporation in a new status. W. Montgomery Watt has written that there is no *rite de passage* into the Umma, and he is right.[34] There is simply a confession of faith and the assumption of the duties as set forth in the Pillars. For an adult male convert there is also circumcision, but it is not absolutely required. Islam does know ritualized changes of status, however, and they are worth examining in detail by scholars. Most rites of passage are "critical" rather than "calendrical," in Titiev's sense.[35] That is, they are geared to the needs of individuals and usually do not explicitly represent the bonds of society as a whole, although they may do so implicitly. Important critical rites of passage among Islamic peoples, though not all are universally observed, include birth, *ʿaqīqa* (haircutting sacrifice), circumcision, marriage, mastery of certain phases of the methods (*ṭarīqa*) of Sufi practice and receiving the Sufi cloak (*khirqa*), recitation of the Qur'ān, and death rites. Other critical rites, though not "of passage," attend eclipses, battles, earthquakes, and other ominous or auspicious natural occurrences. Often boys' puberty rites are calendrical as well as critical and serve to symbolize renewed strength and the future leadership of the larger group. The often-elaborate ceremonies surrounding circumcision, for example in Egypt, are true rites of passage whose liminal stage may include even the donning of articles of female clothing before the dramatic status change which takes place with the cutting of the foreskin.[36] Calendrical rites are always communal and Islamic calendrical rites—the major ones of the religious system—are especially potent partly because of the highly imperialistic lunar calendar which dominates and slowly makes its way around the seasons as a sort of guardian of time.

A seldom investigated but nonetheless fruitful topic for the study of Islamic ritual behavior is Qur'ān recitation, where there is an immediate and strong relationship between text and context. That is, it is not simply a question of the correct practice of recitation based on the knowledge of "readings" (*qirā'āt*), and the rules of pronunciation, stops, and starts (*waqf wal-ibtidā'*), and so forth. The condition of the reciter, the place of performing the recitation, and the attitude of the listeners are also of critical importance. Generally, group or individual recitation aims at a *khatma*, a "completion" of the entire text within a set period, which may be a day, three days, a week, a month, or other time frame, pacing the progress by means of the liturgical divisions of the text. It is customary when the *khatma* is achieved to proceed immediately to the opening sura, al-Fātiḥa, and read it together with the first five verses of the second sura, al-Baqara. This symbolizes the eternity of the Qur'ān as a perfect cycle that keeps pace with the calendar and indeed adds to the sanctification of Islamic time. Reciting the Qur'ān is akin to a sacramental act in that divine power and presence are brought near.

There is even a kind of "divine Magic" to the Qur'ān, as Seyyed Hossein Nasr has admitted. "The formulae of the Quran, because they come from God, have a power which is not identical with what we learn from them rationally by simply reading and reciting them. They are rather like a talisman which protects and guides man. That is why even the physical presence of the Qur'ān carries a great grace or *barakah* with it."[37] The Qur'ān constantly informs the daily lives of the Muslims by means of the many socially exchanged phrases of greeting, gratitude, praise, and amazement that have been mined from it. These phrases figure prominently in the rituals of social relations and serve as a code of communication, blending the personal with the communal in acceptable ways. A medieval Muslim study that provides rich materials for analysing the ritual uses of the Qur'ān is Al-Nawawī's *Al-tibyān fī ādāb ḥamalat al-qur'ān* [an exposition of the proper procedures for those who bear the Qur'ān].[38] The sources the author used were traditional, but the arrangement and discussion of them were original and of great interest for ritual studies in that they provided an authentic Islamic approach to the ordering of religious behavior.

Matters for Further Discussion

This paper has merely touched on a few of the more prominent areas of ritual interest in Islam. Nothing has been said, for example, of *zakāt*, "mandatory alms," which is included among the major duties of Muslims. Perhaps it is to stretch the concept of ritual too far to include almsgiving. But then Zakat has its strict rules and applications, is included among the *ʿibādāt* ("acts of worship"), and is frequently mentioned in the Qur'ān right after Salat (e.g., S. 2:43, 83; 5:12; 9:5). With reference to the Islamic calendar, certain kinds of property are taxed at the end of the year, and *zakāt al-fiṭr* comes at the close of Ramadan. Zakat is something more than the practice of civic virtue, or even charity, for it has a transcendental basis and embraces the entire Muslim community. And, with respect to pollution issues, Zakat is reckoned to make pure that property remaining to the giver; indeed purity is tied up with the very meaning of the root "*zakā*" in the first place.

Here it appears that we have a uniquely Islamic form of economic ritual practice, one that is integral with other practices—Salat, Sawn, the Hajj—and intersects key planes of ritual experiences such as sacred time, pollution avoidance, and community enhancement.

A more fundamental topic from the methodological standpoint is that of ritual terminology. There needs to be a thorough survey and analysis of the terms, concepts, and idioms of ritual found in the Islamic languages, preeminently in Arabic, and a relating of them to more or less universally used scholarly terms. Such a task is beyond the scope of this paper but suggestions of the lines it might take have been made above. The standard *fiqh* books provide the bulk of source material for such a study. And here it is clear that anyone who attempts to unpack Islamic ritual terminology will first have to master a wide range of legal issues. This is beyond the range of most scholars of comparative religion, a fact which should make outsiders pause and reflect when they are criticized by Muslim experts for oversimplifying or just plain bungling issues because of inadequate training in the sources, however intelligent and up-to-date they are about method and theory in the academic disciplines.

This paper was begun with the intention of saying more about "official" versus "popular" Islam. Although there are important dimensions to this distinction, it is in some respects a red herring. It is better to view ritual ideas and practices among Muslims as elements of a total symbol and action system than as a set of mutual antagonisms. This is not to ignore the existing tensions and contradictions, nor to shrink from making definitive statements about what constitutes normative practice.[39] The study of ritual is the study of actual behavior as much as it is the mastery of ideal forms. Islam defines itself not only by its norms, but also by its acts—that is, Muslims define Islam in its various forms without even being conscious of doing so. It is the task of scholars, if not of believers, to make intellectual sense of those forms and those acts. Some of my alert Muslim students will probably continue to object, "But, Dr. Denny, that's not true Islam!," and I will try to be Socratic and encourage them to explore descriptive along with normative kinds of data, even though I am sympathetic to the point they are wont to make.

5

Pilgrimage and the History of Religions

Theoretical Approaches to the Hajj

WILLIAM R. ROFF

In an article first published twenty years ago, Wilfred Cantwell Smith remarked, "Anything that I say about Islam as a living faith is valid only in so far as Muslims can say 'amen' to it."[1] Leaving aside contingent questions about how many—or how few—Muslims may in such circumstances constitute a court, this states very plainly a pressing concern for all historians of religion. There is little point in devising analytical categories—sociological, psychological, materialist, or other—which purport to explain religious phenomena or invest them with meaning for others, if such categories command no acceptance from adherents of the religion concerned. Yet a great many religious phenomena, in their social behavioral aspects especially, seem to require of the historian tools of analysis that go beyond those available from within religious systems themselves. What one must in consequence do, I assume, is find some way of drawing inferences from the observed practice and expressed ideas of religious actors that at once fulfill the need of the historian for structured understanding of social process and meet with acceptance from believers. Cantwell Smith again put the matter succinctly: ". . . where the encounter is between the academic tradition of the West and a particular religion, the statement that is evolved must satisfy each of two traditions independently and transcend them both by satisfying both simultaneously."[2]

Jacques Waardenburg has noted the emergence of what one might call the new epistemology of modern Islamic studies, describing in detail some of the questions currently asked of Islamic religious data, under the influence especially of the social sciences. It is to one of these questions that I should like to draw attention, namely, "What general political or social role or function do different Islamic ideas and practices perform . . . apart from the specifically Islamic religious meaning they are meant to have for believers?"[3] This is truly a hard question, for in the spirit of Cantwell Smith one does not, of course, wish actually to strip idea and practice of the specifically religious meaning they are meant to have, but rather to make (secular) analytical discoveries about how religious meaning and intention, as understood and enacted by believers, inform the specifically social functioning of the ideas and practices under consideration.

The institution I want to consider in this respect is that of the Hajj, the pilgrimage to Mecca—or more accurately (for "pilgrimage" may in some respects mislead) the ritual assemblages that are performed there at the annually appointed time, as they have been since the year A.H. 10 (A.D. 632) or somewhat earlier. My starting point is that although many millions of Muslims have made their way to Mecca and performed the Hajj since the first/seventh century, and that on the basis of this and other evidence they may be seen as attaching considerable religious significance to it, no adequate methodology has been devised for analysis of its import and meaning for historical Islam. However little studied in this respect, the Hajj has nonetheless been and continues to be the subject of frequent generalized comment and assertion in historical contexts, most of which, however (from Western or non-Muslim scholars in particular), precisely does strip the phenomenon of much of its religious meaning, choosing instead to emphasize mainly its more readily accessible epiphenomena of ideological dissemination and status enhancement. It is hardly necessary to turn to that most political of Islamists (and prolific writer on the Hajj) Christiaan Snouck-Hurgronje to recognize this. At the most general level, A. J. Wensinck, in his long article on the "Ḥadjdj" in the second edition of the *Encyclopaedia of Islam*, addresses himself only in his final two or three lines to the matter of its "spiritual influence," concluding abruptly, "This is known only to God." When Bernard Lewis adds, in the same context, that the Hajj was beyond doubt "the most important agency of voluntary, personal mobility before the age of great European discoveries [and] must have had profound effects on all the communities from which the pilgrims came, through which they travelled, and to which they returned," he is stating something that is certainly true but which does not necessarily touch upon its specifically religious meaning.

When the Hajj was first proclaimed as one of the principal duties towards God of believers able at least once in their adult lives to make their way to Mecca (Qur'ān, S. 3:91), and for some little time thereafter, all Muslims lived within the confines of the Arabian peninsula, the majority in the Hijaz itself. By the eighth century, Muslims were more numerous outside the peninsula than within it, and many lived as far away as Spain in the west or Sind in the east. A few centuries later, substantial Muslim populations existed throughout much of the world, from the further extremities of sub-Saharan Africa to China. Despite this vast expansion of Muslim peoples, and the resulting difficulties and distances entailed by the journey to Mecca, the model for the Hajj remained (as it now remains) the one established in the lifetime of the Prophet and testified to either by Qur'ānic injunction (which is relatively sparse) or, principally, by the hadiths concerning the "farewell" Hajj of the Prophet himself, made in 10/632. It is this assemblage of rites, as set out in the texts and as performed by historical Muslims, that constitutes the reality of the Hajj and that must in consequence form the central subject of analysis.

The remainder of this paper will try to survey some possibilities in this respect, particularly those raised by consideration of ritual passage in general.

Although, as observed, the nature of the journey to the Holy Places does not play any significant role in the exemplary Hajj, it is nevertheless obvious that even residents of Mecca must "leave home" to begin their Hajj, so that in an important sense their case is no different from that of the Indonesian who must travel round half the world. For both, territorial as well as symbolic passage is involved, and it was in territorial passage that Arnold van Gennep saw a framework for discussion of the ritual assemblages he called *rites de passage*.[4] Departure from the profane, crossing the threshold of the sacred, and incorporation—the classic stages set forth, maplike, each accompanied by its appropriate rites—are reducible in kind to three: pre-liminal, liminal, and post-liminal, or those of separation, transition, and aggregation. It is manifest that pilgrimage within many religious traditions may be seen as conforming to this pattern, not least the Hajj, where the sacred territory is explicitly the center of the world, with at its own center the *bayt Allāh* or House of God. This intense sacredness of place is restated five times a day in *ṣalāt* (canonical prayer) by all Muslims. Performance there of the Hajj is obligatory, contingent only upon capacity to get there. The holy places can, of course, be visited by Muslims at any time of the year and the *ʿumra* or lesser rites performed. The Hajj, however, may be undertaken only during the appointed days of *Dhū l-ḥijja*, the last month of the lunar year, and accordingly takes place at a sacred time as well as within a sacred place.

With this as a starting point, let us examine, at least briefly, the structure of the Hajj, as it may be represented in *rites de passage* terms. For Muslims who come from a distance and at considerable trouble and expense, the two months preceding Dhu l-hijja, from the end of the fasting month of Ramadan onwards, often have a preparatory character and are known as *mawsim ḥajj*. During this period, funds with which to make the journey are finally assembled, arrangements are made for dependents left behind, and the details of travel are completed. It is important that the money used to make the Hajj be "good" money; funds acquired by dishonest or doubtful means, or without due consideration for others, render acceptance of the Hajj by God impossible or unlikely. Borrowing to make the Hajj is in many societies not unknown but is frowned upon; indeed, among the preparations enjoined upon intending pilgrims are the extinction of personal debts and obligations before departure.

In this respect, as in certain others, leave-taking tends to have a testamentary or even funerary character.[5] Though this may in the past have derived in part from the dangers and uncertainties of the journey, its symbolical relevance is equally clear. The pilgrim is severing himself from his past life, and must embark on the journey away from it in a spirit of purity. He is enjoined, accordingly, to repent of all sin and make what amends are possible, to ask pardon of friends and relatives, and in general to set his affairs in order. An additional association with death is afforded by the practice adopted by many pilgrims of carrying with them cotton cloth to be soaked in the holy water of Zamzam, later to form their burial shroud.[6] Actual departure is accompanied by much ambiguity of feeling, with mingled sentiments of great cheerfulness and joy on behalf of those making the hallowed journey, grief and tears as for those lost to life.[7]

The precise day and time for the pilgrim's departure from his house and hearth is often, as in Malaysia and Indonesia, determined by some form of (extra-Islamic) divination, to seek the most propitious time for setting forth. This established, a communal meal is held in the pilgrim's house, attended by kin, neighbors, and close friends, symbolizing "the mystical and social unity of those participating in it,"[8] and in this manner restating the social matrix from which the pilgrim is about to separate himself. Prayers are said on this occasion for the journey, and blessings sought from the intending pilgrim, no blessing being more highly regarded than that conferred by one about to perform the Hajj, and enter God's sanctuary, save for the one he confers upon his return.[9]

Describing the foregoing in general terms, and citing al-Ghazālī and others, Gaudefroy-Demombynes draws attention explicitly to their *rites de passage* nature, and notes that around the departure of pilgrims has been established an assemblage of rites which together form "une première étape entre la vie laique et une existence qui va être de plus en plus voisine du sanctuaire."[10] Having settled his affairs and taken leave of his family, the pilgrim sets out "comme s'il sortait ce monde." At the moment of leaving, or just before, the pilgrim performs a ritual prayer of two *rakʿa*s, and follows this with the recitation of special suras of the Qur'ān, of which the most usual is the utterance of Noah upon completion of the Ark (S. 11:41): "In the name of God be its course and its mooring," thereby emphasizing the apocalyptic nature of the undertaking.[11]

For many pilgrims, especially from Asia but often also the Maghrib (North Africa), the journey was, in fact, by sea. But whether by sea or land, pilgrims have through the ages moved for the most part collectively, in pilgrim ships or land caravans. Though preceded by penitence, the journey itself is not regarded as penitential by nature, even when its rigors must have made it appear so. Pilgrims have chosen at times to make hard the way in penance, or to enhance the merit of accomplishment, but as with Ibrahim Adham, who walked from Turkestan to Mecca halting at every step to perform a prayer of two *rakʿa*s, this was regarded as superfluous and not productive of the desired effect,[12] and the Prophet is said to have disapproved of self-mortification while on the Hajj.[13] The collectivity of the journey has for most Muslim pilgrims been its main feature, and must for many have been the first true departure not merely from an ideally repented past but from the familiar social structures and roles of everyday life.

Victor Turner, who has done so much in recent years to transform processual analysis, has discussed at length the nature and character of this essentially "preliminal" stage of the pilgrimage process. The individual's movement away from his structural involvements at home represents "at once a negation of many, though not all, of the features of preliminal social structure and an affirmation of another order of things and relations. Social structure is not eliminated, rather it is radically simplified; generic rather than particularistic relationships are stressed."[14] Turner speaks also of the ambiguity of the journey, in which as the route becomes increasingly sacralized at one level it becomes increasingly secular at another.[15] This was perhaps more obviously true of the pilgrimage by land—as witness the incremental ostentations of the official caravans from Morocco or early royal pilgrimages from the western Sudan, with their kettledrums and sideshows, their slave girls and itinerant traders.[16] Yet a young Sumatran pilgrim in the 1920s could write of the way in which the long sea voyage out of sight of land, of fixed markers, while affording the opportunity to dwell upon oneself and the purpose of one's life, to take part in congregational prayer, to sit reading the Qur'ān to oneself in a soft voice, offered unfamiliar opportunities, too. The ship was crowded with pilgrims from all over the Indonesian archipelago, and several marriages occurred between young men and women from widely scattered places and differing social groups, "very easily, without many of the conditions and requirements that apply on land."[17] A recently published guide to conversational Arabic for Malays about to make the Hajj has on the cover a young man reading the same book in a deckchair by the ship's rail while a modestly dressed but attractive young woman stands nearby gazing at the horizon; its title is *Teman Haj* (Hajj Companion).

If socio-structural identities, barriers, and norms begin to dissolve or become elided by the collective journey in favor of a greater emphasis on brotherhood, and on the commonality of the experience and intent and a more open field of choice in relationships, this process reaches its further symbolic stage as Mecca itself is finally approached. Entry into the sacred space that surrounds Mecca must be preceded, at the appointed markers (*mīqāt*s) by a sequence of purificatory rites that mark the last stage of leave-taking from the habitual and the profane, and complete severance from this-worldly connections and statuses, from the past (as one enters the "sacred time" of the Hajj to reenact in minute detail the rituals performed by the Prophet and the first Muslims), and from all sin. Divesting himself of his ordinary wear, the pilgrim rids himself of body hair and trims his beard and nails (which may not be cut again until desacralization), makes a full ritual ablution (*ghusl*), and after uttering a solemn statement of intention concerning the rites he intends to perform in Mecca, clothes himself afresh in the *iḥrām*, the two seamless white cloths that must be worn during the Hajj that follows. Women, though not required to wear *iḥrām* of the same constituents, don a not dissimilar plain (usually white) shift that must conceal the female form while leaving face and hands uncovered. In this state, without rank, gender, or other ascribed social status beyond that of those who are *Muslim* (in submission to God), the *muḥrimūm* (those in the state of *iḥrām*) are forbidden all sexual intercourse and all acts of violence, killing, or uprooting. Leave-taking and separation are complete, and the pilgrim is free to move upon the precincts of the Holy City, navel of the world, as a guest of God, calling aloud the pilgrims' invocation known as the *talbīya:* "What is Thy command? I am here, O God! What is Thy command? I am here!"

This total, symbolic separation from the social and temporal bonds of the known mark what Van Gennep, and following him Turner, see as the beginning of the liminal or transitional stage of the ritual process, from which eventually the devotee emerges in some respect changed, indeed "as though newly born from his mother's womb."[18] The Hajj proper, which extends over some days, is marked by a series of central, essential, collective rituals that have been frequently described—the *ṭawāf* or "circumambulation" of the Kaʿba on arrival in Mecca, that *saʿy* or "traverse" between Safa and Marwa, the *wuqūf* or "standing" at ʿArafat, the sacrifice at Mina, and the stoning of the pillars. It is this period as a whole, then (if most acutely at its most congregational moments) that is characterized by liminality with respect to habitual social structure, and accordingly by what Turner would call social anti-structure, or in its experiential dimension "communitas," "a spontaneously or normatively generated relationship between levelled and equal, total and individuated human beings, stripped of structural attributes."[19]

This experience of communitas clearly lies at the heart of the Hajj, and its ritual and symbolic content merit the closest analysis in *rites de passage* terms. I cannot embark on this here, though I should like to draw attention to Partin's unpublished and seemingly little known study of the Hajj, which among other things sees in this connection the *ṭawāf* of the Kaʿba and the kissing or touch of the black stone as paramountly rites of incorporation.[20] More generally, descriptive accounts of the Hajj by participants make clear the emotional power of absorption in a common act of worship in undifferentiated association with fellow Muslims from all parts of the earth, of all colors and all conditions. The Mecca approached by the pilgrim, calling aloud the *talbīya*, is itself seen as spatially liminal and removed from time; "it is not a place; it is the Beginning, the Present and Forever."[21] In the richly symbolic acts that follow, amidst a host of religious artifacts hitherto known only in an almost mythic way—from the *ṭawāf* in the steps of the Prophet himself to the prayers enacted with the multitude at noon[22] in the valley of ʿArafat (the place of knowing) pleading God's forgiveness and the acceptance of one's Hajj—the pilgrim seeks to find in transcendence of the mundane and the temporal some alteration in his inner state, from sin to grace, an enhancement of being that will return him changed.

One of the best known of American Muslims, Malcolm X, wrote in the moving account of his Hajj that he sent to the newly formed Harlem Mosque, that

> there were tens of thousands of pilgrims, from all over the world. They were of all colors, from blue-eyed blonds to black-skinned Africans. But we were all participating in the same ritual, displaying a spirit of unity and brotherhood that my experience in America had led me to believe never could exist between the white and the non-white. . . . on this pilgrimage, what I have seen and experienced, has forced me to *re-arrange* much of my thought-patterns previously held, and to *toss aside* some of my previously held conclusions.[23]

Many pilgrims do indeed return from the Hajj changed, in a number of obvious and outer, symbolic ways—wearing, perhaps, Arab dress, in distinction to that in which they arrived; often having taken new names, in token of their rebirth; and with a new status designated by the title "*ḥajji*." It may reasonably be assumed that the pilgrim returns changed also in his perception of Islam and the Muslim community, its imperatives and strengths. He belongs in consequence both to this larger community and to his own national and local, rural or urban, one, and by virtue of having reenacted the origins of the faith at its font he is uniquely capable of linking the two and revitalizing in his person that to which he returns. How the Hajji's new persona and new status are employed by himself or recognized and accepted by others has clearly differed at different times and in different places, in relation to the society and the social structures to which he belongs and within which he is reintegrated. To say this is to do no more than acknowledge that historical content must be given to what is otherwise an analytical paradigm. But that the paradigm may be useful seems clear—most particularly insofar as it offers some promise of assisting in the elucidation and understanding of the social role and functioning of the specifically religious meaning of the Hajj, historically and comparatively.

All the evidence, from early Hadiths to modern accounts, suggests that the Hajj does, at least ideally (the *ḥajj mabrūr*), involve transition. From what to what? Van Gennep saw *rites de passage* as effecting the transition of an individual "from one defined position to another," instancing birth, social puberty, marriage, fatherhood, advancement to a higher class, occupational specialization, and death.[24] Turner, employing a much wider conception of status and role, and of ritual process, saw the transition as being from one "state" to another, "state" denoting "a more inclusive concept than status or office and [referring] to any type of stable or recurrent condition that is culturally recognized."[25] Lack of clarity or definition concerning these constructs of "position" and "state" has troubled others,[26] and troubles me. It is apparent that there is one sense in which Van Gennep's model of ritual passage would do little more than elaborate upon the Hajj as a source of (and mechanism for) status enhancement—which as we saw at the outset can at best offer only a partial and external view of the phenomenon, and one which avoids consideration of its specifically religious meaning. Turner's ritual passage, though much richer and more resonant in religious terms, has as its end point (even in his more recent and extended study of Marian pilgrimage)[27] a "state" that goes largely unexamined and assumed. His concern is much more with the "liminal" stage of pilgrimage process than with the "post-liminal." If we are to follow Van Gennep and Turner in developing analytical categories that will serve to illuminate our understanding of the Hajj, this must give us some concern. But the attempt is surely worth the effort. As Abū Yazīd of Bistām was quoted by al-Hujwīrī as saying, "On my first pilgrimage I saw only the temple; the second time, I saw both the temple and the Lord of the temple; and the third time I saw the Lord alone."[28]

Part Three

Religion and Society

The impact of religion on society and of socio-economic factors on religion have occupied historians and social scientists since the pioneering works of Max Weber and Karl Marx. The study of religion and society has captured the public interest perhaps more than any other aspect of religious studies. Is there a "civil religion" in the United States which shapes public policy and discourse? Did the United States err in Iran by failing to appreciate the role of the Shiʿi Ulama? Why have scholars generally failed to predict or meaningfully assess the excrescence of religious fundamentalism in both industrial and nonindustrial societies during the past decade? These are hard questions that government and business are wont to have answered without much help from the academy.

Truisms about Islam and society are always stated but seldom examined adequately in most of the textbooks around which scholars attempt to build religious studies curricula. For example, it is commonplace to observe that the separation between *dīn* and *dawla* (religion and politics) is unknown in Islam; yet whether order in Muslim polities is a result of the Shariʿa inducing Muslim involvement in political-economic governance or, to the contrary, social order results from the restrictive focus of the Shariʿa on religious duties and local social responsibility—leaving the affairs of state to those in power—is a legitimate question to be asked. Every beginning student knows Islam is a "religion of the Book." Thus it is often assumed that the written scripture and the literary tradition of law and commentary it has generated frame the cultural context in which all Muslims learn and live out their religion. How this actually works among the large numbers of devout Muslims among the peasantry and urban poor who are functionally illiterate is a question seldom raised. One of the most pernicious truisms is the old cliché that Islam is a "religion of the sword." The concomitant assumption is that the vast populations of the Middle East, Africa, the Indian Subcontinent, and Southeast Asia converted successively (and rapidly) to Islam through physical coercion, ignoring conceptual and other cultural factors. The obvious and necessary distinction to be made between the static categories of normative (theological) and actual (sociological) religion entails the less frequently noticed principle that the tension between religious ideals and social realities constitutes the dynamic human context in which religion is acted out.

Heraclitus's question of whether the stream that continuously rushes past is the *same* stream each moment reasserts itself in the study of religion and society. The richly ambiguous term "tradition"—a conservative concept by definition—creates a semantic field of fixed terms for describing and analyzing religious data despite obvious historical, geographical, and ethno-linguistic differences. Clifford Geertz demonstrated the problem by comparing Islam in Indonesia and Morocco with a much greater preponderance of evidence of difference and change than Heraclitus had standing beside a stream. Nonetheless, we *are* able to communicate effectively about the natural and social world around us using terms like "stream," "religion," and "tradition." We tackle the differentia that make similar things also seem different by making such distinctions as—in the case of Islam—between great tradition/little tradition, normative and popular religion, and so on. Are such academic devices useful to the study of religion and society?

In Part Three, several of these issues in the study of religion and society are taken up by two scholars who survey some of the literature and offer approaches of their own to particular problems. In Chapter 6, Marilyn R. Waldman shows how the recent work of anthropologist Jack Goody (and others) on the social transmission of culture by literary means in contrast to oral (or both) is a useful way to frame different kinds of questions about Islam. What is the effect of literacy on a culture previously based on oral transmission? The usual emphasis upon classical Islam—the growth of a literary tradition, institutions of learning, and so on—has induced scholars to all but disregard the oral component of Muslim culture, most noticeably in the case of the Qur'ān itself. As Waldman suggests, the shift from "non-listed" (oral) to "listed" (literary) modes of transmission helps account for several developments in the formation of the Islamic tradition as well as certain differentiations within Islamic society today.

In Chapter 7, Richard M. Eaton tackles a quite different problem, that of conversion. The usual Western image of religious conversion is that of a dramatic altar call. In the history of Islam, however, whole tribes and regions became Muslim over periods of time, some brief and others more extensive. Pointing to the apparent anomaly of large numbers of illiterate *jatis* in India turning to a "Book" religion, Islam, Eaton argues that Sufi shrines played important social and symbolic roles in the conversion process. He examines the dimension of conversion involving the shift or integration of cosmologies of different cultural systems to accommodate the changing social, economic, political, and geographical conditions of a people.

6

Primitive Mind / Modern Mind

New Approaches to an Old Problem Applied to Islam

MARILYN R. WALDMAN

The history of religions can be taught in two ways—theologically or humanistically—that is, in terms of the action of absolute higher reality in the world, or in terms of human beings' responses to the perceived presence of that "higher reality." Furthermore, it can be taught in terms of "religions" plural, stressing the separateness of various traditions; or in terms of "religion" singular, stressing religiosity itself as a shared dimension of human experience. Though a humanistic approach can be expressed in terms of religions plural or religion singular, it tends to be reinforced by the latter, and to promote it as well.

To many committed adherents of given religions, the humanistic approach has understandably seemed appropriate to all traditions but their own, for which only the theological approach yields an adequate explanation. When the humanistic approach is extended to their own traditions, they often feel a sense of insult and denigration. In the case of modern Euro-American studies of Islam, the obvious presence of a tradition of sometimes malicious misconceptions exacerbates an already problematic situation. Quite naturally Euro-American scholars can appear to devout Muslims to be persisting in their willful misunderstanding and belittling of Islam in the safer guise of an academically pure, universal analytic.

Eventually, the old argument about the unbridgeable gap between the outside observer and the inside participant is engaged, as in the essays by Abdul-Rauf and Rahman.[1] Since what follows is a secular, humanistic, largely anthropological approach to the history of Islam by an outside observer who cares deeply to see Islam presented sympathetically to a Euro-American audience, some explanation of my stance on these methodological issues is in order.

First, I assume that any human being's understanding of a religious tradition, hers or someone else's, is *limited.* I further assume qualitative differences among the understandings of all insiders and outsiders, and the possibility that on some levels the outsider's understanding or response can be superior. For example, one can imagine a pietistic Catholic whose response to the mass, attended hundreds or thousands of times, is so routinized that a sensitive and susceptible outsider responds to its power in a more immediate and spiritual way. Or one can posit an orthodox Jew, brought up in a very legalistic household, who can empathize more with *sharīʿa*-minded Islam than a secularized youthful Muslim can. No one has a monopoly on understanding, and no one has an understanding that cannot be deepened or broadened, even by an outsider, even if the outsider only remarks on something that seems unremarkable to an insider.

The uniqueness of a tradition truly shows up only when religion singular is the subject, that is, only when a given tradition can be set in the context of all human religiosity. The humanistic approach does not deny the theological; it brackets it so as to make compassionate mutual understanding possible. It argues that there is something on some level that we all have to learn from one another, even if some of us must add the theological approach to be satisfied fully.

Curiously, the humanistic approach may be consistent with the theological on a structural level while at the same time it is opposed on an ideological one. An example of this paradox is A.F.C. Wallace's classic article, "Revitalization Movements," in which he analyzes the conditions associated with the appearance of prophetic figures. Other than the fact, an important one to be sure, that Wallace locates the causes of prophetic movements in the "natural" dynamics of society qua organism, his analysis is consistent with traditional accounts, for example, Muslim accounts of Jahiliyya ["Time of Ignorance" in Arabia prior to

Islam], which also stress the appearance of deviant behavior, (e.g., female infanticide, which the Qur'ān itself denounces), and argue that messengers are always sent to communities that have been made ready in all respects.[2]

This apparent paradox leads me to argue that, in fact, the anthropological approach can help non-Muslims understand certain aspects of what Muslims tend to claim—that religion must be embedded and integrated in the total life of the community, and that secularization by modern technology does not necessarily constitute an advance. The special value of the anthropology of religion for the study of Islam is that it begins with the assumption that religion cannot be separated from other dimensions of culture. Ironically, when made by most anthropologists, that assumption leads to a secularization of religion; for a devout Muslim, it could be used to spiritualize secular life. Even with different values attached to it, the assumption that religion cannot be separated from other dimensions of culture might provide a bridge.

What I want to discuss in this essay follows directly from these remarks. For I am exploring here the nature of the relationship between any technique for the collection, management, and release of information, and the mode of thought that the use of the technique seems to imply, especially as that relationship applies to the history of religion. And I am asking of that relationship the classic chicken-and-egg question, "Which came first?" Two homely examples will help me begin.

Some years ago in India, when the teaching of the rhythm method of birth control seemed to offer a solution to the problem of the birth-rate, an apocryphal story arose about the technique that field workers used to teach it to illiterate women. The women were given an abacus-like set of beads, blue on either end and red in the middle, and told that when a blue bead was pushed over, they were safe, and vice versa for the red. The beads were used, but the pregnancy rate among users failed to decrease: the women were using the beads, but according to a mode of thought with which they were more comfortable. When sexual relations were desired, a blue bead was pushed into place; when not, a red.

In the summer of 1979, an older man, an engineer from British Columbia, riding on a train into the Norwegian fjord country, ignored the scenic beauty to complain about the problems of metric conversion for manufacturers of machine parts. At the end of his complaint, he rather peevishly attacked metric thermometers, saying, "And besides, I'll never feel warm at 20°!"

In the real world, we observe all the time such adoptions and uses of new techniques of information storage and management by an individual or group whose existing mode of thought is tied to and reflects older techniques. Perhaps in time the Indian women could have come to understand their bodies' fertility cycles in the terms implied by the bead contraption. Perhaps in time the British Columbian will actually come to think in terms of the scale of measurement he now uses out of convenience and necessity, rather artificially. But in both cases, one point is clear: the use of a technique may produce rather than be produced by a new mode of thought. And the emergence of a technique and its adoption is part of a very complex process that cuts across cultural lines, vertically and horizontally.

These are the main points, the broad implications, of Jack Goody's *The Domestication of the Savage Mind*[3] and of a series of other works that lead up to it. Once Goody's ideas are taken into account, many controversies in the study of Islam may turn out to be artificial.

A certain amount of background is in order. Goody's findings were made in reaction to a variety of what can be called "-chotomous" thinking about the history of culture that have permeated the study of religion: dichotomous explanations of the history of thought that rely on pairs like "primitive/modern," "big tradition/little tradition," "high culture/low culture," "elite culture/folk culture"; and trichotomies such as "primitive/archaic/modern," or "primitive/traditional/modern." Of course, "-chotomous" thinking is particularly problematic in fields like Islamic studies, where both or all parts of any "-chotomy" seem to be present in varying proportions simultaneously in most specific cultural settings.

Early Reactions to "-Chotomous" Thinking

A growing rejection of "-chotomous" thinking exists in the study of the history of culture, and particularly of any notion of "progress" from one mode of thought to another. In 1974, Stanley Diamond published a book of essays under the title, *In Search of the Primitive: Critique of Civilization*,[4] in which he argued against applying ethnocentric Western notions of progress to non-Western societies. He also tended to romanticize the primitive, decrying the contemporary disjunction between the affective and cognitive modes and criticizing modern Western civilization itself.[5] As Eric Wolf put it in his foreword, "For Diamond, then, the primitive is both a historical phase in man's career, and an existential aspect of his being."[6]

It was in these ways that Diamond contributed to new forms of thinking about the primitive/modern dichotomy. Even when his Marxist rhetoric is discounted (e.g., "The telephone is not an abstractly or inherently 'rational' instrument, but an integrated aspect of the repressive culture of monopoly capitalism."), he does demonstrate that measures used for the specialness of "modern" culture do not, in fact, show any real progress from primitive to modern, and that elements considered modern can be found in the primitive and vice versa.[7]

Robin Horton has made a contribution similar to Diamond's. In an article on the scientific revolution, he argues that the popular anthropological assumption of a dichotomy between primitive and modern derives from a misreading of Durkheim. Horton shows that Durkheim was actually trying to demonstrate a continuity between premodern religious thought and modern scientific thought, or rather to show the former to be protoscientific.[8] Although Horton has been accused of comparing the wrong aspect of primitive thought with modern scientific thought, his notion of a primitive-modern continuum has begun to gain currency.[9]

Clifford Geertz has carried on these revisions by designing a conceptual framework that can be applied to the dynamics of any cultural situation and that does not imply any evolutionary hierarchical arrangement of different modes of thought.[10] The framework involves a definition of religion that focuses on "(1) a system of symbols which acts to (2) establish powerful, pervasive, and long-lasting moods and motivations in men by (3) formulating conceptions of a general order of existence and (4) clothing these conceptions with such an aura of factuality that (5) the moods and motivations seem uniquely realistic."[11] These religious symbol-sets provide not only a "model for" the world, that is, a guide to living *in* it, but also a "model of" the world, an explanation of an order that appears to be rooted in the structure of the universe.

Thus, for Geertz, religion both expresses and shapes the world in which humans live, in a fundamental and ultimate way. Using such a definition of religion as this, the observer can approach any given situation in its own terms. Changes in religious modes of thought would be explained by all the broader cultural and material changes that can affect the social construction of symbol systems. And these changes, in turn, can be affected by a society's working out the meaning and implications of its symbols. Religious symbols represent the ultimate but acquire their meaning in the context of human consciousness. The difference, say, between what we call primitive and modern thought would then be a variation in the construction of symbol systems, not an improvement in it.

Let us take as an example the continuing appearance of new visual representations of the symbol of the crucifix, as in the iconography of Father Goode's black Catholic church in Brooklyn:

> Inside Our Lady of Charity Roman Catholic Church in the Bedford-Stuyvesant section of Brooklyn, visitors are struck first by the naked body of a black Jesus over the altar, suspended against a mural of the continent of Africa, done in bright orange, red, greens, and blues, with slave ships anchored off the western shore. To the right of the altar is another bright mural featuring many black faces and the legend, 'The black family celebrates survival.'[12]

From this example it is perhaps more obvious how a given symbol can come to represent, for a given community, a "better" guide to living in the world and explanation of how it is the way it is, but better only in the sense of more appropriate.

Marshall Hodgson, in his exploration of what he calls the "technicalization" of Western European culture in the eighteenth century, takes a different approach to the problem of continuity and discontinuity. His argument is that the cognitive features we take to be innately modern or Western might be products rather than causes of changes in techniques of production and information gathering.[13] In class at the University of Chicago, Hodgson used to like to tell the story of an early English bureaucrat, who, desirous of trying to rationalize Britain's export trade, sent a request to a northern harbor-master for monthly figures on coal export. The harbor-master duly totaled the year's exports and divided by twelve, sending back a single average figure, which, of course, did not reflect the fluctuations that interested the more "modern" bureaucrat. Eventually, though, if regular use of the "proper" new techniques of data-gathering gained enough currency, they might suggest not only new questions about the economy to the bureaucrat but also even a new way of thinking about it to the harbor-master. In a similar way, the use of punch cards to keep tabs on Ellis Island immigrants in the nineteenth century suggested new questions about social statistics that could be answered with them.[14]

Edward Hall, in a book published after Hodgson's, concentrated on the impact of such techniques, or tools, on cognitive development, by utilizing the concepts of extension and extension transference. By extension he means any use of the environment as a tool for extending a mental process, e.g., the use of a stick rather than the hand for flattening and rolling dough.[15] He goes on to explain what tends to happen to extension as these systems elaborate themselves further and further.

> It is . . . paradoxical that extensional systems—so flexible at first—frequently become quite rigid and difficult to change. Confusion between the extension and the processes that have been extended can explain some but not all of this rigidity. . . .
>
> Extension transference (ET) is the term I have given to this common intellectual maneuver in which the extension is confused with or takes the place of the process extended. . . .
>
> Extensions often permit men to solve problems in satisfactory ways, to evolve and adapt at great speed without changing the basic structure of his body. However, the extension does something else; it permits man to examine and perfect what is inside the head. Once something is externalized, it is possible to look at it, study it, change it, perfect it, and at the same time learn important things about oneself.[16]

Hall finds Extension Transference [ET] to have several inherent problems, problems that have implications for the study of religion as well. First, if the ET process goes into second and third generations, the first-generation extension "is overshadowed and frequently viewed as though it had no structure." Second, Hall sees ET as a source of alienation from self and heritage.[17] In this connection, one might think of the early Arab philologists who would corner Bedouin coming into Basra with the caravans in order to find out what certain words meant in pre-Islamic Arabic poetry or even in the Qur'ān. One might also recall the critiques by the Muwahhidun or of an Ibn Taymiyya of using "extensions" of revelation—*ḥadīth* and *furūʿ* ["branches" i.e., applied law]—as a substitute for the process of revelation itself as depicted in the Qur'ān. She might also observe that the written Qur'ān is an extension of the oral one, and that Muslims' insistence on remaining as close to the process of revelation itself by maintaining the oral Qur'ān as the real one has represented a kind of awareness of the dangers of Extension Transference. In Hall's terms, what is interesting about the Qur'ān is that ET did not take place—that the extension, the written Qur'ān, did not become confused with the process of revelation, which is kept alive by the persisting orality of the true Qur'ān. Application of these ideas produces an interesting reading of the Sura of the Clot—a dynamic and productive tension between spontaneity and permanence—between *Q-R-'* and *Q-L-M*. *Q-L-M* when read as pen implies alphabetic writing and hence a book; but if it is taken to signify not a pen per se but a writing implement that engraves in stone, then the permanent Word is always vitalized by its performance, that is recitation (*Q-R-'*). This way of looking at Islamic revelation may also point out a major distinction between Islam and Judaism and Christianity. In certain forms of both of the latter, the pious focused so much on extensions, e.g., exegetical activity, that they lost sight of the process of revelation, which neglect eventually led to reactions aimed at recapturing it. Not so for Islam.

Goody's Analysis of the List as a Form of Composition

In his emphasis on the power that extensions can come to have, especially through the process of Extension Transference, Hall comes very close to the perspective of the most recent work I will discuss—Jack Goody's *Domestication of the Savage Mind*. Refining his previous work on literacy and culture, Goody, however, goes even further than Hall by arguing that many observable changes in modes of thought were actually produced by what appear to be extensions of them. In particular, he focuses on techniques of writing and recording and on the control and manipulation of those techniques by specialized and restricted groups. To oversimplify his argument, one can say that the emergence and development of writing has been associated with new forms of recording and storing information, in particular, the list, in the broadest sense possible, that is, a fixed, ordered, graphic presentation. Many changes that we think occur in the realm of cognitive capability or orientation have been preceded by changes in the nature of communicative acts and, in particular, by changes in techniques of collecting, recording, storing, and releasing information. I shall quote Goody's account of this process at length:

> . . . writing, and more especially alphabetic literacy, made it possible to scrutinize discourses in a different kind of way by giving oral communications semi-permanent form; this scrutiny favoured the increase in scope of critical activity, and hence of rationality, scepticism, and logic to resurrect memories of those questionable dichotomies. It increased the potentialities of criticism because writing laid out discourse before one's eyes in a different kind of way; at the same time increased the potentiality for cumulative knowledge. . . . No longer did the problem of memory storage dominate man's intellectual life; the human mind was freed to study static 'text' (rather than be limited by participation in the dynamic 'utterance'), a process that enabled man to stand back from his creation and examine it in a more abstract, generalized, and 'rational' way. . . .
>
> I want to suggest that the presence of writing, leading amongst other things to these developments in the activity of list making, alters not only the world out there but the psyche in here; at least a recognition of its role should modify our understanding of the processes involved. . . . I would argue that the graphic representation of speech (or of non-verbal behavior, though this is of more limited significance) is a tool, an amplifier, a facilitating device, of extreme importance. It encourages reflection upon and the organization of information, apart from its mnemotechnic functions. It not only permits the reclassification of information by those who can write, and legitimises such reformulations for those who can read, but it also changes the nature of the representations of the world (cognitive processes) for those who cannot do so, whether they are the non-reading element of societies with writing (a very large category over the five thousand years of written experience) or the population (usually children) that have not yet reached the point in time when they can read, either because they do not yet have the ability or because they do not yet have the opportunity.[18]

It should be noted that Goody is not arguing that listing behavior does not exist at all in nonliterate societies but that it takes on special forms and rigidity in cultures with alphabetic literacy. In this connection, it was interesting to observe at the conference at which these papers were delivered what changes occurred when written versions were presented orally. The features of fixed written order most salient for Goody (e.g., the possibility of the eye's being referred forward and backward, or moving voluntarily to achieve a kind of contemplative reflective mode) were suppressed in favor of immediacy and spontaneity. Footnotes that could be brought forward and integrated or used as glosses were; sections with recalcitrant footnotes were omitted.

The problem with using Goody to talk about Islamic civilization, especially its religion, is that he addresses only very late in his book the situation more common there—neither a totally literate nor totally nonliterate society—but one "where language takes both written and oral forms (for all or for a proportion of people)."[19] For as Goody points out only ten pages from the end of his book, in such a society we must be interested in the interplay between the two. For example, Earle Waugh points out how complex can be the role of the Muhammad paradigm in a literate contemporary society; our studies of only partially literate societies in nineteenth-century West Africa show how much more complex the role can be there, and how even new written biographies can emerge from the interplay.[20]

Furthermore, in early Islamic society, we have a case of ever-expanding literacy and of contacts among literate persons originally educated in different traditions. In fact, Goody's ideas might help explain conflicts between those who favored oral and those who pushed for written transmission, but unfortunately, complexities of this sort are beyond the scope of Goody's book. Similarly, he fails to make enough subtle distinctions among types of literacy for us to know immediately where Islamic culture would fit. That is, Goody *breaks down* "-chotomous" thinking but does not substitute a useable continuum.

Despite these problems, Goody's general findings can be useful in the study of the history of Islam. If we look at the emergence of Arab-Islamic culture and its gradual adoption of literacy at the high-culture level, we can observe the importance of listing activity of all sorts. But before an attempt can be made to apply some of these ideas to Islam, a summary of the hypothesis to be tested is in order: 1) any view of the varieties of modes of thought in or over time that is hierarchical or evolutionary obscures the complexities of any given system, especially in regard to relationships among different modes in the same culture; 2) changes in modes of thought are preceded by changes in techniques of storing information that arise from other causes; 3) the focus on the emergence of new techniques and their utilization by various segments of a society helps explain situations that are problematic when looked at in terms of cognitive change of other sorts.

Applying Goody's Analysis to the History of Islam

Let me start with one simple example, the relationship between the emergence of lists of the attributes of God and the development of the Muslim conception of God. One possibility, the obvious one, would be to say that as the Muslim scholars' view of God expanded and became more complex, detailed lists of attributes appeared that expressed that view. From Goody's point of view, the situation would be quite the opposite: As the Qur'ān itself became "listed," that is, arranged in fixed order according to some criteria of listing, further listing of the contents or part of the contents of the Qur'ān according to other principles of listing followed naturally. These lists, in this case, of attributes, came to be used widely for all sorts of cultural reasons as yet unspecified. As they spread, they affected the development of the Muslim conceptualization of, ability to, conceptualize God, and presumably the list of questions which structured early Islamic theology as well. It is interesting to note, however, that early *kalām* discussions of the matter of attributes did not, in fact, proceed from the standard lists then circulating but from more selective ones.

A similar problem has been raised by Marshall Hodgson in his classic article on the Shiʿa.[21] Hodgson's revisionism in that article involves his perception of an eighth-century reading back of the *naṣṣ* imamate [leadership by "designation" of one's predecessor] into a much more fluid pre-eighth-century environment. But even Hodgson assumed that the appearance of lists of the Imams' genealogies signaled the appearance of a new way of looking back at Shiʿi history. But Goody would probably urge us to look at the role of the linear genealogies themselves in forming the notion of the *naṣṣ* imamate. That is, was the ability to list and ponder the significance of the lists a requirement of the formation of that sense of genealogy?[22] And further, what was the role of literacy and its extensions in the development of Shiʿi ideology? Does the *naṣṣ* imamate develop, for example, among more literate groups?

When we turn to the "listing," that is the editing, of the Qur'ān, Goody's ideas continue to be suggestive, especially when we combine them with the results of William Graham's recent study of *ḥadīth qudsī*.[23] If we assume, as Goody might, that the "listing" or arrangement of the Qur'ān into a book *did not* involve a corresponding editorial decision that it was the exclusive locus of Divine Word, we could then go on to reason that the ultimate separation of Divine Word and Prophetic Word, which Graham details, was encouraged by the very presence of the "listed" version of the former, as well as later, the "listed" version of the latter. We might even want to explore whether the conceptualization of Qur'ān as "book" was made possible by the very *ability* to canonize the order of its contents.

In this connection, it is interesting to note the survival of ways of handling the Qur'ān that preserve its prelisted characteristics. Although there are traditions of reading the Qur'ān straight through in the order of the standard version, a liturgical cyclical, ordered recitation did not become part of the *ṣalāt* (as it did of Jewish ritual). Where it does exist, as Frederick Denny points out, the overstitching of end and beginning seems to emphasize its nonlinearity.[24]

In fact, the very principles of ordering chosen by the Qur'ān's editors militated against linearity of handling. Obviously, the pondering or repeated recitation of small portions of the Qur'ān, without regard to their place in the whole, always remained a pious act. And yet the grouping and ordering of Qur'ānic verses have not been without impact, especially for the structure of *tafsīr*. But the combination of what I would call "listed" and "nonlisted" qualities also explains the selective perceptions that nonliterate Muslims can have of the scope and contents of the Qur'ān.[25] The question then remains: what role did the ordering of the Qur'ān have in the development of Muslim notions of it as a Book competitive with other Books? And to what extent did opposition to its being edited come not from the desire to preserve variants but either from resistance to the techniques of the literate, or to the authority that its canonization would give them, or from disagreements over which written techniques were to be employed?[26]

We come next to ask what the relationship was between the development of the *Saḥīḥ* [authoritative] collections of Hadith and the Sunni conception of Sunna. Again, we might tend to assume that the fixing of the Hadith into the "canonical" corpura was the product of clear-cut cognitive decisions on the nature of the Sunna. But following the approach I have been developing, we might wonder about the degree to which the decision to incorporate the Hadith made it possible for a fixed concept of the Sunna to develop. Much of the controversy which engaged Schacht and Abbott, among others, failed to take into full account the nature of literacy and its role in various types of recording of early Hadith.[27]

Finally, using Goody's approach, we could look at the question of religious behavior at different cultural levels. When we compare the form of the Pilgrimage (*ḥajj*) to Mecca with Visitation (*ziyāra*) to certain local saints' tombs, the obvious differences in the form of behavior seem to imply different cognitive levels.[28] The Meccan Ḥajj, with its fixed linear sequence of events, is eminently orderly with a fixed significance assigned to each event. The action during many Ziyaras has no fixed sequence and the significance of each act varies from time to time and from actor to actor; the Shiʿi Ziyara, however, appears to be more fixed in sequence and meaning.[29] Goody would argue that the ability of the literate to list a sequence, in this case a temporally ordered chain of events and acts, and then to ponder and refine it, produces in an almost circular way the cognitive capacity to carry out its demands. It would be useful to relate the more or less sequential nature of pilgrimage rituals to differing conditions of literacy.

This contrast between different types of pilgrimage would lead us also to question the significance of the Meccan Ḥajj for different types of people who participate in it. In a lecture at The Ohio State University some years ago, Mujahid al-Sawwaf commented that North African female pilgrims respond to their arrival at Jidda not with the appropriate prayer of arrival (a literate form, after all) but rather with joyous ululation.[30] He further reported that members of sub-Saharan *ṭarīqas* [Sufi organizations] hold *dhikr* ceremonies during the afternoon of "Standing on ʿArafa," when other behavior would be more appropriate according to the accepted "list" of Hajj steps. In each case the written sequence of events and its significance are being subverted by a non-literate understanding of the type of event the Hajj represented and the degree of flexibility its form can endure.

Drawing out the implications of Goody's ideas has enabled us to raise many new and stimulating questions about several central phenomena in Islamic religious history: lists of the attributes of God, the Shiʿi *naṣṣ* imamate, the canonization of the Qur'ān and Hadith, and the organization of the Hajj and other visitations to holy places. The new questions have arisen because our hypothesis focused our attention on changes in techniques in collecting, managing, and releasing information and on the variable understanding of those techniques naturally present in any society that contains vastly differing levels of literacy. Without such an approach, certain types of anomalies must constantly be explained—for example, why groups that have apparently developed a new mode of thought continue to behave as if they had not.

With such an approach, what seems anomalous becomes predictable and in fact central to any understanding of the process of change itself.

If through further, more detailed, research we do determine that modes of thought change as a result of changes in techniques for the management of information, then the focus of the historian of religion will gradually shift to those moments when such new techniques come into use. If Goody is right, the historian of religion will also find a way to link changes in modes of religious thought to other cognitive changes, all of which would be affected by changing profiles of literacy over time and space.[31] Finally, we will have to deal with the question of how our own analytic lists and categories distort the reality of religious communities whose literacy was or is of a different sort from ours.

As has been shown here, the humanistic approach to the *history* of a tradition, in the sense that it is also phenomenological, raises another problem: a tradition cannot be *defined* through its historical and cultural manifestations. Any normative definition of its ideals and central impulses will constantly be called into question by the sometimes widely differing versions that appear in various times, places, individuals, and groups. Any adherent to Islam who defines it in terms of a received idea beyond time and place will be discomfited by the seriousness with which historical phenomena as they present themselves are treated in an approach like this. And such an individual may again feel that any focus on the behavior of believers rather than on the "real" received system of belief has a malevolent intent.

These days one of the most vexing problems in the study of Islam, for Muslims and non-Muslims alike, is precisely this relationship between what Fazlur Rahman calls normative Islam and forms of Islam that "deviate" from it.[32] Rahman blurs the distinctions between what many modern scholars call great and little traditions by arguing (1) that the great tradition is not so monolithic as tends to be assumed and (2) that the little traditions share a normative core—Qur'ān and Sunna—with the great ones. Maintaining a minimal core may, in fact, prove necessary to Muslim/non-Muslim communication so long as beyond that a nonhierarchical, nonevolutionary approach to the various historical manifestations is employed.

My own justification for seeking to make the faith of others accessible through a humanistic approach derives from my ultimate commitment to correcting the ethonocentrisms that have produced our misconceptions in the past. It is echoed in Arnold Toynbee's plea for a rejection of parochialism in favor of world history:

> In order to save mankind we have to learn to live together in concord in spite of traditional differences of religion, civilization, nationality, class, and race. In order to live together in concord successfully, we have to know each other's past, since human life, like the rest of the phenomenal universe, can be observed by human minds only as it presents itself to them on the move through time. . . . For our now urgent common purpose of self-preservation, it will not be enough to explore our common underlying human nature. The psychologist's work needs to be supplemented by the archaeologist's, the historian's, the anthropologist's, and the sociologist's. We must learn to recognize, and as far as possible, to understand, the different cultural configurations in which our common human nature has expressed itself in the different religions, civilizations, and nationalities into which human culture has come to be articulated in the course of its history. 'All of human history is relevant to present and future human needs.' 'The knowledge of the history of mankind should be one of mankind's common possessions. . . .' We shall, however, have to do more than just understand each other's cultural heritages, and more even than appreciate them. We shall have to value them and love them as being parts of mankind's common treasure and therefore being ours too, as truly as the heirlooms that we ourselves shall be contributing to the common stock.[33]

If the humanistic approach as I have described it is a vehicle for secular moderns to come to an understanding, so be it; otherwise they may have no point of entry at all. The quality of commitment *will* inevitably be missing from analyses by the noncommitted. But their empathy with that commitment must still be nurtured by developing enough knowledge and respect to see how it could be a focus of faith for others.

7

Approaches to the Study of Conversion to Islam in India

RICHARD M. EATON

The expansion of Islam east of the Middle East has been, apart from a few notable exceptions, a relatively understudied subject. This is especially remarkable when one recalls that, by far, the world's greatest number of Muslims reside east of Karachi. The reasons for this neglect of scholarship, however, are not far to find. First is the identification of the Arab Middle East with the historical heartland of Islam, which makes it the natural object of study of classicists whose scholastic concerns often focus on the formation of cultural traditions. Second, despite its universalist claims and its undeniable status as a world religion, Islam is related to Arab ethnicity, language, and culture in complex ways that have always somehow made the study of Arab Islam a more legitimate or proper field on the Islamist's agenda than "Eastern" or sub-Saharan Islam. And third, for at least a century, severe methodological problems have prevented scholars from explaining the formation, through conversion, of the majority of the world's Muslim population living beyond the Middle East. There have appeared few convincing answers to such basic questions as: What is conversion per se? Can conversion to Islam be fit within a larger conceptual category, or must it be considered unique? By what indices can it be measured? What forces favor or hinder its progress?

Nonetheless, scholars of various persuasions have recently taken a lively interest in the study of Muslim conversion movements. It is the aim of this paper to explore some of the approaches to this topic as it concerns one important area of the Islamic world—South Asia—with a view to isolating some of the problems encountered in previous studies and to suggesting a more comprehensive hypothesis explaining the phenomenon.

Theories of Conversion to Islam in India

Most explanations of conversions to Islam in India can be reduced to three basic, and in my view inadequate, theories. The oldest of these is the "religion of the sword" theory. As a theme in the Western historiography of Islam it has a long and weary history that dates from the time of the Crusades; and for Indian Islam, too, it has always had its advocates. Yet as Peter Hardy has recently observed, those who argue that Indian Muslims were forcibly converted generally failed to define either "force" or "conversion,"[1] leaving us to presume that a society can and will change its religious identity simply because it has a sword at its neck. Precisely how this mechanism worked either in theoretical or practical terms, however, is seldom spelled out. Moreover, proponents of this theory seem to have confused conversion to Islam with the extension of Turko-Iranian rule in North India between 1200 and 1765, a confusion probably originating in a too literal translation of primary Persian accounts narrating the "Islamic" conquest of India.[2]

But the most serious problem with this theory is its incongruence with the geography of Muslim conversions in South Asia. A glance at the geographical distribution of Muslims in the subcontinent (see map on p. 108) reveals an *inverse* relationship between the degree of Muslim political penetration and the degree of conversion to Islam. If conversion to Islam had ever been a function of military or political force (however these might have been expressed) one would expect that those areas of heaviest conversion would correspond to those areas of South Asia exposed most intensely and over the longest period to rule by Muslim dynasties. Yet the opposite is the case: those regions of the most dramatic conversion of the population, such as Eastern Bengal or Western Punjab, lay on the fringes of Indo-Muslim rule, whereas the

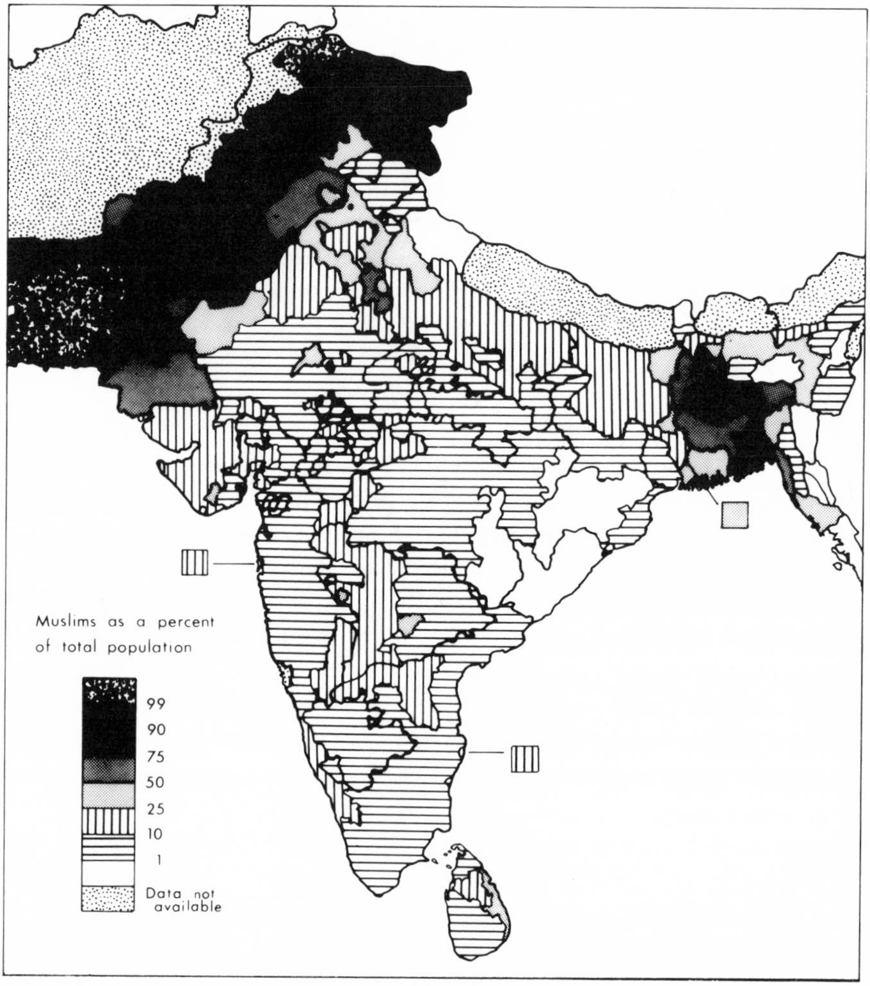

Geographical distribution of South Asian Muslim population. [Adapted from J. Schwartzberg, ed. A Historical Atlas of South Asia *(Chicago and London: University of Chicago Press, 1978), p. 94].*

heartland of that rule, the upper Gangetic Plain, saw a much lower incidence of conversion.[3]

A second theory commonly advanced to explain the conversions of Indians to Islam is the "political patronage" theory, or the view that Indians of the medieval period converted in order to receive some nonreligious favors from the ruling class—relief from taxes, promotion in the bureaucracy, and so forth. In the early fourteenth century, for example, Ibn Battuta reported that Indians presented themselves as new converts to the Khalaji sultans who in turn rewarded them with robes of honor according to their rank.[4] But individual conversion for political gain frequently lacked conviction, as witnessed by the more spectacular cases of apostasy: Khusrau Khan, a fourteenth-century usurper of the Delhi Sultanate; or Harihari and Bukka, the cofounders of the Vijayanagar Empire. Then, too, nineteenth-century census reports speak of land-holding families of medieval Upper India declaring themselves Muslims either to escape imprisonment for nonpayment of revenue, or to preserve ancestral lands in the family name.[5] More important examples of the "political patronage" phenomenon were the cases of groups coming into the employment of Muslim rulers and in this way gradually acculturating themselves to Indian Islam. The Kayasthas and Khatris of the Gangetic Plain, the Parasnis of Maharashtra, and the Amils of Sind all cultivated Muslim culture by virtue of their filling the government's great need for clerks and administrative servants at all levels, which Aziz Ahmad compared with the later "westernization" process.[6] Finally, the acculturation of captured soldiers or slaves, severed as these men were from their families, formed another dimension of this process.

Adequate though the patronage thesis may be in accounting for the relatively light incidence of Islamization in the political heartland, it cannot explain the massive conversions to Islam that took place along the political fringe—especially in the Punjab and Bengal. For political patronage, like the influence of the sword, decreases rather than increases as one moves away from the Delhi heartland toward the periphery.

What is needed is some theory that would explain the phenomenon of mass conversion to Islam on India's periphery and not just in the heartland, and among India's millions of peasant cultivators and not just among urban elites. To this end a third theory is frequently invoked, one which has for long been the most popular explanation of the phenomenon—the "religion of social liberation" theory. Elaborated by British ethnographers, Pakistani nationals, and Indian Muslims among many others, the substance of the theory is that the Hindu caste system is a rigidly discriminatory form of social organization and that the lowest and most degraded castes, recognizing in Islam an ideology of social equality, converted to it en masse in order to escape Brahmanical oppression.

This theory, too, has serious problems. The first is that it commits the fallacy of reading the values of the present into the peoples or events of the past. Are we to assume that before their contact with Muslims the untouchables of India possessed, as though they were familiar with the writings of Rousseau or Jefferson, some innate notion of the fundamental equality of all men denied them by an oppressive Brahmanical tyranny? To the contrary, it seems that Hindu society of medieval India was more influenced by what Louis Dumont calls the principle of *homo hierarchicus*, or of institutionalized inequality, than by the principle of *homo equalis*.[7] Beyond that, a careful reading of Persian primary sources suggests that in their presentation of Islam to Indians, Muslim intellectuals did not stress the Islamic ideal of social equality as opposed to Hindu caste, but rather Islamic monotheism as opposed to Hindu polytheism.[8] Moreover, even if it were true that Islam had been presented as an ideology of social equality, there is abundant evidence that former Hindu communities failed upon conversion to improve their status in the social hierarchy and that, to the contrary, they simply carried over into Muslim society the same practice of birth-ascribed rank that they had had in Hindu society.[9]

But the most damaging problem with the "liberation theory," as with the two others discussed above, appears when we return to the map (p. 108) and observe the geographical distribution of the South Asian Muslim population. Before the dislocations consequent upon the Partition of 1947, the areas with the highest percentage of Muslims were Eastern Bengal, Western Punjab, Northwest Frontier, and Baluchistan. Now from both historical evidence and anthropological studies we know that the bulk of the population in Baluchistan and the Northwest Frontier were not converted communities at all, but descendents of the immigrants from the Iranian Plateau. This leaves East Bengal and West Punjab as the two areas of the subcontinent possessing the highest incidence of Muslim conversion among the local population. What is striking about those areas, however, is that they lay not only far from the center of Muslim political power, as noted, but that their indigenous populations had not, at the time of their contact with Islam, been integrated into the Hindu social system. In Bengal, Muslim converts were drawn mainly from Rajbansi, Pod, Chandal, Koch, or other indigenous groups which had had but the lightest contact with the Hindu religious or caste structure, and in the Punjab the same was true for the various Jat clans that came to form the bulk of the Muslim community. Since the greatest incidence of Muslim conversions occurred among groups that were not fully

Hindu in the first place, for the vast majority of South Asian Muslims the question of "liberation" from the "oppressive" Hindu social order was simply not an issue.

Toward a New Theory of Conversion: Accretion and Reform

Much more in keeping with the geography and chronology of Muslim conversions in India would be, I would suggest, an understanding of mass conversion as a process whereby preliterate peoples on the ecological and political frontier of an expanding agrarian society became absorbed into the religious ideology of that society. Proceeding from the theoretical work of Nehemia Levtzion, and before him of A. D. Nock,[10] I would further divide this process into two subprocesses, that of accretion and that of reform. Whereas the simplest model of a conversion movement would be one beginning with accretion and ending with reform, we should not see this process as any necessary or irreversible march from the first to the second. A closer examination of individual cases of Muslim conversion movements in India reveals more complex patterns—some, for example, oscillating back and forth between accretion and reform, others stuck on accretion indefinitely, remaining unaffected even by the powerful reform currents of the nineteenth century.

What precisely characterizes these processes? In a cognitive sense, the accretion aspect of conversion sees a people either adding new deities or superhuman agencies to their existing cosmological stock, or identifying new deities or agencies with existing entities in their cosmology. Accordingly, the supernatural agencies Allah, khizr [the Qur'āanic *Khidr*], or the swarms of *jinns*, for example, may either be grafted onto an already dense cosmological universe, or identified, by name, with existing agencies. But in either case the original cosmology is essentially retained. In the reform dimension of the process, on the other hand, Islamic supernatural agencies are not only distinguished from the preexisting cosmological structure, but the latter is firmly repudiated. This is accompanied with greater attention given to the all-encompassing power of one Islamic agency in particular, the Supreme god Allah, who assumes the function and powers of all other agencies in the former pantheon. In a history of religions framework, this corresponds to what Max Weber has called the process of religious rationalization, that is, the absorption of many lesser beings by one universal, supreme god.[11]

In terms of social organization, the accretion aspect of conversion entails no Muslim communal exclusiveness or even distinctiveness. Persons will identify themselves as Muslim inasmuch as they worship Allah, for example, or refrain from eating pork—two attributes which in this aspect of the conversion process might be loosely understood as the defining features of Islam. But this by no means prevents them from participating in village propitiation of a local goddess to ward off smallpox or in joining village devotions to an *avatar* of Krishna. Social integration is sustained by other than ritual means, too. A recent study of the Meo community of Rajasthan, a community which for many centuries has adhered somewhat loosely to Islam without responding to reformist pressures, shows that while their practices relating to personal life cycles are Islamic (e.g., practicing circumcision, burying their dead), their institutions respecting relations with their Hindu neighbors are non-Islamic (e.g., marriages are clan exogamous and not cross-cousin; inheritance follows local, not Muslim practice).[12] In strictly social terms, in other words, they are still a relatively indistinct community.

In the reform dimension of the conversion process, however, the community perceives itself as socially distinct and consciously acts upon that perception. Accordingly, the group not only resists participation in non-Muslim rituals, but will, for example, adopt Islamic inheritance customs for daughters as well as for sons, a practice which decisively separates the Muslim community from its neighbors. Or, even more decisively, it might adopt cross-cousin marriage patterns, regarded by many Hindus as simply incestuous. Such practices become more prevalent to the same extent that the Muslim community becomes conscious of its adherence to a single model for social and ritual action, a model whose source of authority stands wholly outside of one's ancestral locality.

Finally, one can distinguish between accretion and reform in terms of the overall socio-political environment in which each process takes place. For mass conversions, anyway, the earlier phase of the process generally accompanied integration into the outer fringes of one of the expanding Indo-Muslim states which, from the twelfth century on, pushed ever outward from the Delhi Doab heartland in the north-central region of the subcontinent. What is critical here (and I will return to this theme of political/ecological integration at the end of this paper) is that this integration always took place in a *regional* context (a region in India) whether one speaks of the expansion of Tughluq power into fourteenth-century Punjab, of the Bahmani Kingdom into fifteenth-century Deccan, or of the Mughal Empire into sixteenth-century Bengal. In these circumstances whatever Muslim elements were added onto the existing stock of beliefs and practices, they were not perceived as representing a "world" religion, but only the particular beliefs and practices associated with a local saint, a local *qāḍī* (Muslim judge) or the spiritual power of a local shrine. On the other hand, the context of reform was always a worldwide one, inspired by a vision of Islam as a world religion—or rather, *the* world religion, with Mecca as its geo-spiritual hub. Reform movements, or the reform aspect of the conversion process, are typically initiated by someone freshly returned from the purifying experience of a pilgrimage to Mecca, an experience which, among other things, heightens one's awareness of the universal truth of Islam as opposed to the local and very particularized idioms in which it may be expressed.

Yet the questions remain: how can we measure the growth of a conversion movement, and what are the agents stimulating or shaping it? If we understand religion as "an institution consisting of culturally patterned interaction with culturally postulated superhuman beings,"[13] it can be argued that three sets of symbols, or names, mark such interaction as distinctively Muslim as opposed, for example, to Hindu or Christian. One set of symbols refers to man's identity in relation to the superhuman beings, for example, names of persons such as ʿAbd al-Rahman "slave of God."[14] A second set of symbols refers to the identity of superhuman beings in relation to man, that is, man's names for the gods, such as "Allah" instead of "Iswara." A third set of symbols refers to the identity of the sacred place in which the interaction takes place, as in mosques instead of, say, Vaisnavite temples or shrines devoted to the mother goddess.

Although these three sets of symbols will not tell us why a conversion movement took place, they can be used as indices by which we can plot the geographical and chronological expansion of Islam in India, or elsewhere for that matter. For example, the naming pattern of a single Punjabi Jat group, the Sials, suggests that from the thirteenth to the early nineteenth century the Muslim self-identity of this group proceeded at a very slow rate indeed.[15] In the early fifteenth century, 10 percent of recorded Sial males had Muslim names; for the mid-seventeenth century, 56 percent; for the mid-eighteenth century, 75 percent, and for the early nineteenth century, 100 percent. This is, I think, a most revealing index of the gradual process of group identity formation.

Just as socio-religious identity is reflected in changes of personal names, it is also reflected in changes in the names of those superhuman agencies with whom people interact. It is this index, moreover, that most dramatically distinguishes the accretion aspect from the reform aspect of the conversion process. Turning from the medieval Punjab to medieval Bengal, consider the names that local Muslim poets used to denote the one, supreme god of the Qur'ān. The sixteenth-century poet, Haji Muhammad, referred to him as Allah, Khuda ("God" in Persian), and Gosain ("master of the herds"), adding that he assumes limitless forms. The late sixteenth-century poet Sayyid Sultan referred to him as Iśvara, (Supreme god, "lord"), adding that he resided in every entity. Shaykh Mansur (fl. 1703) named him Khuda and Prabhu ("master"), Niranjan (Supreme God, lit. "without emotion"). The eighteenth-century poet Ali Riza referred to him as Iśvara, Allah Yagat Iśvar ("lord of the world"), Niranjan, and Kartar ("creator").[16] In a land where the cult of the mother goddess had great popularity, the sixteenth-century Bengali poet Sayyid Murtaza addressed Fatima as "the mother of the world" (*jagat-janani*).[17] Similarly, Sayyid Sultan identified the Prophet as a manifestation (*avatar*) of God.[18] What these poets were doing, of course, was laying the intellectual foundations for their readers' adhesion to Islam; that is, by matching up the cognitive categories drawn from Islam with those drawn from local traditions, they were making possible the process of identification, which is one of the hallmarks of the accretion aspect of conversion.

A third index of growing Islamization consists in changes in the identity of the sacred place in which religious interaction takes place. Table 1 is an abbreviated list showing the chronology of mosque construction in Bengal between 1200 and 1800. It is true that the construction of mosques, especially small, private mosques, may reflect only a patron's desire to perform a meritorious act and may not necessarily indicate the expression of popular piety. On the other hand, the appearance of congregational (*jāmiʿ*) mosques, intended as they are to accommodate the religious needs of entire populations of towns or villages, does give some idea of the chronology, and also the geography, of the growth of the Muslim community. The table, for example, certainly suggests that although Muslim *rule* in Bengal dates from the

Table 1
Mosque Construction in Bengal, 1200–1800

YEARS	ORDINARY MOSQUES	*JĀMIᶜ* MOSQUES	TOTAL MOSQUES
1200–1250	1	0	1
1250–1300	2	0	2
1300–1350	1	0	1
1350–1400	1	1	2
1400–1450	4	0	4
1450–1500	46	7	53
1500–1550	21	18	39
1550–1600	11	1	12
1600–1650	3	0	3
1650–1700	4	0	4
1700–1750	4	0	4
1750–1800	2	0	2

Source: From Shamsud-din Ahmed, ed. and trans., *Inscriptions of Bengal* (Rajshahi: Varendra Research Museum, 1960) vol. 4, pp. 317–338.

thirteenth century, Muslim *society* cannot be said to have emerged there until two centuries later.

If the above data provide some of the indices of conversion, what are its agents? Some writers have focused on the Muslim merchant who, interested in economic profit, thrived best under conditions of internal stability. While evangelism was not his aim, the social contacts resulting from the expansion of commerce and the condition of mutual trust in which commerce thrives, created favorable conditions for social accommodation and, to some extent, acculturation. Generally speaking, this process was, then, more typical along India's coasts—from Gujarat down to Malabar and Coromandel, and up to Bengal—than it was in the Muslim states of the interior.

Along the Konkan and Malabar coasts, accordingly, we find the earliest Muslim mercantile communities, which have thrived over a thousand years. In the early tenth century the Arab traveler Masᶜudi noted that an Arab trading community along the Konkan coast, which had been granted autonomy and protection by the local rajah, had intermarried considerably with the local population.[19] The children of such marriages, brought up formally with the father's religion, yet carrying over many cultural traits of the non-Muslim mother, contributed to an expanding community which was richly described by Ibn Battuta in the early fourteenth century.[20] But by virtue of this community's close commercial contacts with Arabia, reflected in religious terms by its adherence to the Shafiʿi legal tradition, the foreign aspect of the community was always present and made social integration with the Hindu community difficult.[21] In the last analysis, then, while it is true that Muslim merchants founded important mercantile enclaves and by intermarriage expanded the Muslim population, they do not appear to have been important in provoking religious change among the local population.

A far more influential agent in the conversion process was the village Qadi or judge, one of the key figures that accompanied the establishment of Muslim regimes as local powers. Although a thorough study of the role of the medieval Indian Ulama (*ʿulamā'*), and especially the Qadi, has yet to be written, preliminary evidence points to the central and continuing role that local judges played in establishing a measure of uniformity among the various rural folk who, for various reasons, adhered informally to Islam. Qadis were appointed by central and provincial authorities to apply Islamic law in all towns or villages having a Muslim population. And while Qadis theoretically applied Muslim religious law (*sharīʿa*) only to those criminal and civil cases involving Muslims, they also settled cases involving Muslims and non-Muslims, thereby drawing the latter into the legal and social orbit of Islam. In this way all manner of disparate groups would have had some of their most important affairs decided by men who, in theory at least, represented a single religious and legal tradition. With reference to the late nineteenth century, district gazetteers repeatedly reported that while particular Muslim "castes" were lax, avoided beef, kept Hindu festivals, or worshipped Hindu deities, they at the very least respected the Qadi and used him to officiate at their marriages and funerals.[22] Qadis thus stood not only as representatives of the court among peasants, but also as models of their religion before the semi-Muslim folk of the countryside.

What is more, the Qadis represented above all the *literate* aspect of Islam, as living reminders that Islam in the last analysis is a religion of the Book. Recent anthropological research has drawn attention to the great importance of the literacy of an incoming religion as a variable that explains the appeal of that religion to preliterate societies.[23] The point is that the Qur'ān, as the unchanging Word of God, possessed immense power, and consequently appeal, among preliterate peoples whose previous cults had not been stabilized by the influence of literacy. Thus, in the history of Islam in India, one important reason that Islam sank such deep roots in areas such as East Bengal or West Punjab was that the native populations of those regions were far less integrated into the literate tradition of the Brahmans than were the peoples of upper India. Although upper India had been for centuries the center of Muslim administration, the incidence of conversion to Islam there was as a consequence relatively low.

The agent of conversion that has, however, received the most attention is the Sufi. There is an enormous literature on this theme, commencing with Thomas Arnold's fervent portrayal of Sufis as Islamic "missionaries" among non-Muslims.[24] A close reading of the primary sources, however, would not support this portrayal. In their own writings and in the contemporary biographical accounts of them, Sufis do not appear to have been concerned with conversion. In fact, the sort of self-conscious, highly organized effort along the lines of a Christian missionary society, implicit in Arnold's writing, is at variance with the social roles actually played by medieval Indian Sufis.[25]

If a living Sufi had only minimal influence in the religious life of non-Muslim Indians, a deceased Sufi, especially one blessed with sainthood by the local population, could literally work miracles. This was because the charisma or *baraka* of a spiritually saturated Sufi saint became, with time, transferred to his tomb. And since brick and mortar shrines have much greater longevity than flesh and bone Sufis, self-sustaining centers of religious power were able in this way to grow and span many centuries. Moreover, a saint's *baraka* also adheres to those of his family descendants who inherit spiritual authority associated with the shrine, which also extends the longevity of *baraka*. For example, both the grandson and the shrine of Baba Farid in Pakpattan, Punjab, became so thoroughly identified with Baba Farid the saint, who died in 1265, that when Ibn Battuta visited Pakpattan in 1334 he actually wrote of meeting Baba Farid himself. In fact, the living person whom the famous world traveler met was the grandson who had inherited the spiritual and temporal leadership of the shrine complex.[26] An even more dramatic example of a saint's *baraka* growing after his death is seen in the faith common people had in the Chishti Sufi, Sayyid Muhammad Husayni Gisudaraz Bandanawaz, who died in 1422. Writing in 1609, the historian Firishta could observe that "the people of the Deccan have such respect for the saint that a Deccany, on being asked whom he considered the greatest personage, the Prophet Mahomed or the Syud [Sayyid Muhammad], replied, with some surprise at the question, that although the Prophet was undoubtedly a great man, yet Syud Mahomed Geesoo-duraz was a far superior order of being."[27]

It was faith like this that explains the tremendous growth of hundreds of shrines all over the Subcontinent, each providing a localized focus of votive worship. These shrines differed a good deal from each other, some specializing in terms of the community to whom they administered, and others in terms of the ailment or complaint the devotees would bring to them.[28] But they all shared in common a mediating capacity between the devotee and Allah, thereby not only softening the theological chasm between man and God, but also presenting God in a locally accessible idiom.

If it is true that the Qadi and the saint's tomb were the most important agents in the Islamization process, we are still confronted with the vexing problem of the geography of conversion. I have argued that the theories of the "religion of the sword," "political patronage," and "religion of social liberation" all fail to account for the exceptionally high incidence of conversion on the political peripheries of medieval India and the relatively low incidence of the heartland. Yet if the agents I have identified as most crucial to the conversion process—the Qadi and the Sufi shrine—were scattered throughout the Subcontinent, how can their agency help explain the geography of the issue? As noted, one variable in explaining this is the degree of integration of a region into a literate tradition—in this case Brahmanical Hinduism—prior to its contact with Islam. Also important are those elements of the social and ecological situation within a region that enabled Qadis or Sufis to have greater effect in patterning religious change on the frontiers than in the heartland. As a rule, India's most extensive conversion occurred not in the great agricultural plains but in the pastoral plains or forested regions—areas, in other words, where religious patterns had not yet been stabilized by literacy as represented and sustained by Brahmans. For it was not Hindus who most readily converted to Islam, but nonagrarian forest or pastoral peoples whose contact with Brahmanism and caste stratification had been either casual or nonexistent. The process of the absorption of these peoples into Islam was, in fact, similar to the integration of aboriginal peoples into the Hindu caste and ritual structure that had taken place earlier in Indian history. As D. D. Kosambi wrote with reference to that earlier movement, "The major historical change in ancient India was not between dynasties but in the advance of agrarian village settlements over tribal lands, metamorphosing tribesmen into peasant cultivators, or guild craftsmen."[29]

It is of the utmost significance, then, that those areas of the most massive conversion to Islam, such as East Bengal or West Punjab, were fringe areas both from the point of view of the socio-ecological frontier of Hindu agrarian society, and also from the point of view of the political frontier of the Muslim state. The consistent aim of the latter—and here reference is mainly to the Delhi Sultanate (twelfth to sixteenth centuries) and its successor the Mughal Empire (sixteenth to eighteenth centuries)—was to push its ecological and political frontiers ever outward from the Delhi Doab heartland into Punjab, Kashmir, Gujarat, Deccan, or Bengal. In areas where local Hindu rajahs had already established an agrarian infrastructure by which to extract the surplus wealth of the land, the problem was a political one. Here, the state endeavored to capture the agrarian structure for its own ends by occupying urban centers, establishing garrisons, and perhaps demoting the rajah to a tribute-paying underling (*zamindar*). As the peasantry in such areas was usually already absorbed into the Hindu social and religious order, conversion to Islam was not normally forthcoming, at least on a mass basis. But as the state expanded its power into regions whose agrarian infrastructure was not well-developed—into unirrigated plains or uncleared forest regions—the expansion of the state was ecological and religious as well as political. Here, the religious ideology of the state, Islam, became adopted bit by bit as one aspect of a larger transformation among preliterate inhabitants of lands newly made arable. In a word, indigenous non-Hindu non-agriculturalists were, between the twelfth and seventeenth centuries, gradually transformed into Muslim agriculturalists. To the extent that this was the case, Islam, in India at least, may properly be termed more a religion of the plough than a religion of the sword, as formerly conceived.

Data drawn from both the Punjab and Bengal would sustain this argument. As for the former area, what one finds is, from the thirteenth century, the appearance of huge Sufi shrines, such as those of Farid al-Din Shakargunj in Pakpattan or Baha al-Haqq Zakaria in Multan, becoming the objects of popular devotion by non-Hindu Jat pastoralists as they migrated northward from Sind. By the sixteenth century the Mughal government realized the political potential of these shrines and used them as intermediaries by which to control the turbulent Jat groups. Moreover, it was about this time that these same groups began settling down in the Punjab and taking to agriculture, a development much in line with the Mughal interest in maximizing the revenue-generating capacity of the land. Technologically, this development was made possible by the extention of the Persian wheel into the arid plains of the Punjab in the medieval period. Throughout this period the Jat groups retained their devotional focus on the shrines, gradually becoming ever more closely integrated with their ritual structure. For these groups, then, adhesion to Islam effectively meant adhesion to one of these shrines.[30]

In Bengal an essentially opposite process had the same effect: instead of the people migrating to the land, the arable land migrated to the people. For many centuries the Ganges River had emptied into the Bay of Bengal down the western side of the province so that that area became both the (Hindu) spiritual and agricultural heartland of the region, with the aboriginals in the forests of East Bengal remaining somewhat beyond the pale and only lightly exposed to Brahmanical Hinduism. In the sixteenth century, however, the river silted up its old channels and pushed eastward, opening up huge areas of East Bengal for rice cultivation. River shifts also made possible land reclamation along the lower and eastern delta next to the sea. As these riverine shifts occurred roughly simultaneously with the Mughal conquest of Bengal, many of the colonists moving into the east were Muslim from North India. Significantly, a good many of the saints of East Bengal who had accompanied this colonization are associated with the pioneering of agriculture, and especially with land reclamation in the active delta. In the process, indigenous Bengali peoples who had formerly practiced hunting, fishing, or a crude form of forest agriculture, became gradually transformed into rice farmers. So firmly was rice cultivation identified with Islam, that today, in the value system of peasants inhabiting rural Bangladesh, God is believed to have allowed Adam to exercise his mastery over the earth by farming it; being a good Muslim is closely associated with being a good farmer.[31]

If this was the underlying mechanism of the accretion process, it is clear that the result was far from "total" conversion to Islam. For centuries Punjabis and Bengalis alike had clung to former religious habits and retained long-established social groupings. Basing his observations on nineteenth-century district gazetteers, Mohammed Mujeeb wrote that Punjabi Muslims "were spiritually dependent on miracles and magic to a degree incompatible with genuine belief in any omnipotent God,"[32] while the 1901 census of India reported Bengali Muslims joining in the Durga Puja, worshipping Sitala and Rakshya Kali when disease was present, and making use of Hindu astrologers and almanacs in their everyday life.[33] For peoples of both provinces, as also in other regions of India, Islam was regarded as one technique among many for tapping a "power" which, with the performance of the proper rites known to some local expert, could alleviate one's problems or promote one's mundane concerns.

But this nominal commitment to Islam, made possible by a political and ecological integration into a regional Indo-Muslim state, was followed in many areas of India by a reform made possible by a second order of integration, an integration with the Muslim world. This integration was neither political nor ecological in nature, of course, but affective, as more and more putative Muslims of India became aware of the normative unity of Islam. While members of the ulama and some groups of Sufis had urged his unitary reformist vision at all times of the Indo-Muslim history, sporadic reformist movements appeared in various parts of India or among various communities with visible frequency only from the seventeenth century.[34] It was during the nineteenth century, when vastly improved world transportation systems brought masses of Indians in direct touch with Mecca, that such movements became most widespread of all. These reform movements generally witnessed a Qur'ānic literalism that assumed an increasing sense of urgency as more and more Indian Muslims became aware of the gap between the commands of the Book and the actual practices passing for Islam in their native villages. It was at this point that persons began taking the meaning of their names—for example, ʿAbdallah, "slave of God"—more seriously, if not literally. Finally, insistence on a jealous God to the exclusion of all other superhuman agencies was paralleled by movements for social exclusiveness.

The reform dimension of the conversion process, in India at least, carried with it at least two other important implications, one political, one cultural. The first of these was the demand for a separate Muslim state upon the departure of the British in 1947. In one sense, of course, this was but a logical extension of the reform aspect of the conversion process, which stressed social exclusiveness. The Pakistan movement thus represented a modern reenactment of the Prophet's departure from Mecca and his establishment of a distinct community at Medina; it was a "re-creation" of Medina. The other implication of the reform process was its self-conscious adoption of Arab culture. Here one confronts a central paradox of the reform process. The emphasis upon Islamic unity and universalism as a theoretical model was simultaneously accompanied by an emphasis upon Arab culture and language as a practical model, so that while reform movements sought to lift the focus of religious activity above the Indian regional context, they frequently landed it once again in the Arab cultural context. Accordingly, in the early nineteenth century, Bengalis were urged to eat grasshoppers on the grounds that Arabs ate locusts.[35] And in the 1890s a brillant Bengali writer, Ameer Ali, championed the Islamic reform movement in Bengal by writing such books as *The Spirit of Islam*, glorifying Arab culture and history. From a religious viewpoint, these political and cultural developments may be seen as efforts to perfect a process of conversion having roots deep in the history of the Subcontinent.

To conclude, I must emphasize that this essay by no means attempts to explore all the various processes by which peoples of the subcontinent became drawn into the Muslim community. Clearly this is a complex phenomenon involving a number of distinguishable processes, some of which did not concern conversion at all. There was, for example, the immigration of many thousands of Turks, Afghans, and Iranians into the Subcontinent from the thirteenth century onward, and the slow growth of Muslim communities as a result of intermarriages between Muslim men and non-Muslim women. Even when discussing conversion itself, this essay has passed over the discussion of the conversion of Hindu elites (Brahmans or Kayasthas) in places like Allahabad, Kashmir, or Lucknow. Similarly, a comprehensive study of the conversion of Indians to Islam would have to mention examples of rationally planned, organized conversion efforts such as those of the Shiʿi *daʿwa*, which successfully integrated trading and agricultural castes of Sind and Gujarat into the Muslim community.[36]

Rather, the thrust of this essay has been to draw attention to a dimension of the conversion question not heretofore generally addressed: mass Islamization of the geographical periphery of the Indo-Muslim state and the relationship of ecological change to religious change. I maintain that for India, at least, mass conversion to Islam was a very gradual process involving two discernible aspects, accretion and reform. In a way, these aspects of conversion movements are comparable with Clifford Geertz's "model of" and "model for" dimensions of religious behavior.[37] That is, for those Indians who adhered to Islam, the symbols, rituals, and practices of local religion served as "models of" or descriptions of the social order and its religious life. Thus a Punjabi Sufi might legitimize an ancient, pre-Muslim practice simply by calling it Islamic, and that would be that.[38] In its reform aspect, however, Islam was viewed as a unified set of absolute norms, beliefs, and practices to which one must bend oneself and one's fellows if one is to be saved. Here, as Geertz observed, Islam functioned as a "model for" behavior, and was significant not because it described the social order, but because it shaped it.[39]

In the more vulgar language of social science, religious behavior in the accretion aspect of conversion is a dependent variable since it is a function of socio-political change. It was the migration of Jats into the Punjab and the extension of Delhi's authority there which, along with the introduction of the Persian wheel, attached Jat groups to Sufi shrines and transformed them into agriculturalists. Similarly it was the migration of the Ganges River eastward that caused the ecological transformation of East Bengal, making the aboriginal peoples of the area receptive to a "religion of the plough." In both cases new centers of political and religious authority (local shrines) acquired influence because of changed socio-economic circumstances, and Islamic ritual and belief systems acquired an unconscious foothold in the countryside without necessarily displacing earlier systems.

To stop here would merely reaffirm the Durkheimian position that religion is a reflection of the social order; yet this does not go far enough. For in the reform process it is Islam that is the independent variable inasmuch as it can, and did, cause change in the social and political realms. The political geography of South Asia in the second half of the twentieth century would quite obviously not be what it is if conversion in its reform aspect did not have this capacity to shape the social order. By viewing the double role of Islam as a dependent and independent variable, then, we can see the conversion process as a constantly evolving, dynamic interaction between religion and society.

Part Four

Scholarship and Interpretation

The premise of phenomenology is that the variable cultural manifestations of religion can be reduced to the *eidos* or essence of religious experience. To accomplish this eidetic reduction of cultural phenomena, manifestations of the religious must be considered on their own terms by the suspension of judgment (*epoché*) of the investigator, and this in two senses. The more obvious requirement is to leave aside one's own religious convictions so as not to assess the truth of others on parochial grounds. Equally important, one should not attempt to comprehend cultural phenomena by the categories of the scientific study of natural phenomena. We recognize in this approach the differentiation between *Geistes-* and *Naturwissenschaften* that has been so prominent in humanistic studies since the nineteenth century. In practical terms, the phenomenologists' hermeneutical task of interpreting and understanding textual and archaeological expressions of other religions required approaches that would yield access to original intended meanings of culturally and historically distant data.

Many historians of religion have accepted the assumptions of phenomenology in one form or another, although as I have suggested in Chapter 1, uniformity of methodology and discipline have not yet been achieved. For one thing, as Heidegger, Gadamer, and Ricoeur have argued, the academic and cultural horizon of experience of the interpreting scholar is an important and determining ingredient of understanding religion. For another, the evidence presented by the cultures under analysis contain layers of interpretation that complicate the process of discovering univocal meanings. Clifford Geertz refers to this *reductio* of ethnographic interpretations of native interpretations of still other symbolized experiences as "thick descriptions." Scholarship and interpretation in religious studies, whether we are speaking of textual analysis or social observation, is necessarily an exercise in thick descriptions. Recognition of this aspect of religious studies requires taking stock of our own and others' intellectual horizons, the ways in which a given body of data can be conceived and approached, and the cultural presuppositions inherent in the data.

In Part Four, these three aspects of "thick descriptions" in religious studies are argued successively with regard to Islamic studies. In Chapter 8, Charles J. Adams renders a great service by providing an appreciative yet tough, critical analysis of the life work of Henry Corbin on Iranian Islam. The extensive and often esoteric writings of Henry Corbin about Shiʿi Islam have long baffled many Islamicists, and they are little known among historians of religions. As translator of one of Corbin's major works, Adams provides students of religious studies an evaluation of Corbin's overall accomplishment. Adams's mastery of the fields of Islamic and religious studies shines through every page of his lucid and insightful contribution to this project.

In Chapter 9, Andrew Rippin examines the intellectual horizons of another scholar, John Wansbrough, concentrating on the London scholar's methodologies in interpreting the formation of sacred literature in Islam—especially Qur'ān, *tafsīr*, and *sīra* literature. By so doing, Rippin raises the second question for thick descriptions in religious studies mentioned above, namely, how do we conceive and approach given bodies of data we wish to interpret? The sharpness of Fazlur Rahman's response to Rippin and Wansbrough in Chapter 12 reflects as much the response of Western Islamicists as it does of Muslims to literary/critical analyses of Islamic sacred literature. Rippin might have chosen to have balanced his explanation and appreciation of Wansbrough's methodologies with a critique of his own, thus distancing himself somewhat from that London target of so much recent academic abuse. Yet the very stature of those who have made public refutations of Wansbrough, and the sometimes gratuitous nature of their elaborate verbal assaults, must lend religious studies students outside the field of Islamics the impression that there is more here than meets the eye. The problem of how to assess the literary expression of *Heilsgeschichte*—whether the question be that of the quest for the historical Jesus or the form-critical analysis of the *kerygma* presented in the earliest Muslim literature—remains a difficult one in religious studies scholarship.

In Chapter 10, Azim Nanji turns our attention to the problem of analyzing the cultural symbols and meanings presupposed in religious data, in this case sacred literary materials of the Isma'ili Shi'a. Adams's chapter in Part Four shows that the problem of how to understand esoterism can itself lead to esoteric results in scholarship; the other extreme in Western writing about Islam has been to avoid the task of interpreting this kind of material altogether on the grounds that esoterism is a perversion of the "great tradition" of orthodox Islam. Nanji argues that we must still ask what these symbolic materials mean, however vivid and seemingly heterodox. Like all Muslims, the Isma'ilis constructed a universe of meanings out of Qur'ānic and other symbol systems. Nanji approaches these sacred materials of Isma'ilism with literary theory and themal analysis to determine the more fundamental Islamic message contained in these exegetical works.

8

The Hermeneutics of Henry Corbin

CHARLES J. ADAMS

The work of the French philosopher and student of Islam, Henry Corbin, is important to historians of religion for two principal reasons. First, he was the author of an impressive number of works on religion, and through these has contributed immeasurably to the growth of our knowledge. His studies cover a very wide range of subject matter from ancient Iranian religion to the tradition of "spirituality" in the West. Of primary interest for the present purpose, however, is the fact that the greater part of this production concentrates on the study of Islam. Focusing his work in Islamics on Ithna ʿAshari Shiʿism, Corbin gave attention to matters that had previously been studied but very little, if at all, in the Western world. Corbin is thus a pioneering contributor to the historical knowledge of one of the world's major religious communities. His numerous, weighty, and profound expositions of Shiʿi spirituality deserve to be better known within the scholarly community: they deserve, furthermore, to be celebrated as a monument of original research that has pushed back the boundaries of ignorance.

The second basis of Corbin's importance for historians of religion is his pursuit of a method which he described as phenomenological and through which he sought to make clear the "spiritual" meaning of integral Islam. Our task will be to consider each of these aspects of his work, but especially the latter, for Corbin's hermeneutics raise vital issues for the study of religion. His method is of importance, not only for the relatively narrow field of historical religious expression—Ithna ʿAshari Shiʿism—to which he applied it, but for the study of religion more generally. His phenomenological approach is markedly different from that which has informed the development of the history of religions as an academic discipline; indeed, it challenges the bases of *Religionswissenschaft* as most of us know it. Were his methodological leads to be followed, Islamic studies would be reoriented if not revolutionized, and many of us who profess to be historians of religion would undergo a commensurate personal change. Following Corbin's lead, our historical, philological, and systematic concerns would necessarily recede into the background in favor of a study of Islam that couples philosophical understanding with personal spiritual realization as two inseparable components in the appreciation of the Islamic phenomenon in its true dimension.

Corbin's Contribution to Islamic Studies

Henry Corbin is without doubt one of the giants of Islamic studies in the twentieth century. His first work, published in 1933, some five years after the completion of his doctorate at the Sorbonne, signalled the major concern of his career, for it dealt with a previously unpublished treatise of Shihāb al-Dīn al-Suhrawardī, the Persian philosopher and mystic, known as the Shaykh al-Ishrāq, "Master of Illumination." Suhrawardī was to become the pivotal figure in Corbin's understanding of Islam, and Suhrawardī's philosophy of light was also to provide the categories upon which Corbin would build his hermeneutics of integral Islam. At the time of his death in October 1978, Corbin had published two hundred separate studies,[1] some of them, such as the *summa* in four volumes entitled *En Islam Iranien*, of staggering proportions; and there were still other researches in process but not yet complete. In addition, from 1955 he had regularly engaged in teaching in France and in Iran, given hundreds of lectures, carried the responsibility for the Institut d'Iranologie Franco-Iranien in Teheran of which he was the original organizer, been a pillar of the annual Eranos meetings in Ascona, and had in countless other ways endeavored to forward awareness of the spiritual universes he had discovered. This immense production bespeaks an unfailing industry and a probing intellect, but above all it testifies to a profound commitment to the task of understanding the spiritual life. Among the first and most important things that must be recorded about Henry Corbin is that his scholarship was neither impersonal nor abstracted from life; rather at all times it bore the mark of his personal involvement, evidencing an existential dimension related as much to his own and the universal spiritual problems of humankind as to the particular thinkers, writers, and documents he was studying.

Our principal interest here is the part of Corbin's work devoted to Islam. Here again, we witness a wide range of concerns. The first that may be mentioned is his activity as an editor of texts, and in some cases as a translator as well. His contribution in making accessible a wealth of important textual material unknown outside of Iran, and even there to only a few, is an achievement that alone would make him remembered with gratitude for generations to come. As all who have done it know, the preparation of texts for publication from manuscript materials is an arduous, tedious business requiring formidable linguistic competence and unfailing attention to detail. Corbin's accomplishment is the more remarkable in that he took no satisfaction from the philological work for its own sake; he saw it as an unpleasant but unavoidable first step towards the study of the Islamic philosophy that was the center of his concern. In the prologue to *En Islam Iranien* he complains:

> We do not conceal the uncomfortable predicament, the tribulations, of the Orientalist philosopher in general, or the Islamicist philosopher in particular. From the outset the present state of scholarship requires of him the preliminary labors of the philologist, and these are not really his own. Usually he must edit the texts upon which he will ultimately build his expositions. The philosopher who is privileged to work with texts already edited, even translated, into his own language should compare his colleagues' situation with his own.[2]

Corbin's true launching into his career was marked by his edition of the mystical and philosophical works of Suhrawardī, which emerged as the first tangible product of the years of exile in Istanbul during World War II—years that Corbin spent in exploring the rich libraries of that famous city. His original acquaintance with Suhrawardī he owed to his teacher, Massignon, who in the latter part of Corbin's student days had given him a lithographed edition of one of the works of Suhrawardī, accompanied by a commentary of Mullā Ṣadrā Shīrāzī. The transmission of this text from master to disciple, which Corbin described as a "symbolic act," was decisive in turning Corbin away from a developing interest in the German philosophy of the time towards the study of Islam, Shiʿism, and the Ishraqi philosophy. The first of his textual publications of Suhrawardī appeared in Istanbul in 1945 and the second as part of the Bibliothèque Iranienne in Teheran in 1954. Symbolically again perhaps, the last major work of his scholarly career was a return to the source, a *ta'wīl* in the literal sense, to Suhrawardī, this time in the form of a translation of fifteen Persian and Arabic texts presented under the title *L'Archange empourpré* and published in Paris in 1976.

Although Shurawardī was both the beginning point and center of Corbin's philosophical work on the Islamic tradition, his text editions included a number of other authors. Among them were Nāṣir-i Khusraw (*Jāmiʿ al-Ḥikmatayn*) Ruzbehān-i Baqlī, Mullā Ṣadrā Shīrāzī, and Ḥaydar Āmulī, with the whole of this imposing editorial enterprise culminating in the *Anthology of Iranian Philosophers from the 18th Century to the Present*, a collection of Persian and Arabic texts, prepared in conjunction with the contemporary Iranian scholar, S. J. Ashtiyānī.[3] Corbin was also the general editor and driving force behind the Bibliothèque Iranienne, a formidable series of texts that numbered twenty-six large volumes by the time of his death. Many of the texts which he himself edited were published in the Bibliothèque Iranienne, but the series also afforded opportunity for other students of Iranian thought and mysticism, such as ʿUthmān Yaḥyā, Sayyid Ḥusayn Naṣr, Muḥammad Mukrī, Hermann Landolt, and others to present text editions to the scholarly public.

For Corbin the preparation of texts was only a first step in a larger enterprise. There remained the task of expounding the content of the Islamic philosophy which the texts set forth. In this part of his scholarship Corbin was no less distinguished or impressive than in his work as an editor. A stream of studies flowed from his pen, some of them of massive size. An indication of what he achieved in his analytical and expository studies may be seen in the three major treatises that have been translated into English, *Avicenna and the Visionary Recital*, *Creative Imagination in the Sufism of Ibn ʿArabī*, and *Spiritual Body and Celestial Earth*. These alone amount to 1159 printed pages of densely reasoned argument based on study of difficult texts, many of them all but unknown to the orientalist tradition. These, however, may not be his most important substantive contributions from the standpoint of their influence on subsequent scholarship.

Corbin's *Histoire de la philosophie islamique*, done in conjunction with Sayyid Ḥusayn Naṣr and ʿUthmān Yaḥyā, is a bold effort to strike out on an entirely novel approach to Islamic philosophy. Taking up arms against the prevailing concept of Islamic philosophy which limited it to the writings of Muslim thinkers known to the medieval West through Latin translation, Corbin sought to show that a powerful tradition of philosophical meditation lived on in the Islamic world after the death of Ibn Rushd, finding its greatest flowering on the intellectually fertile soil of Iran. The nature of that philosophical tradition is different, to be sure, from the thought of the Peripatetics of the earlier centuries, but it is both lively and important and continues to be a powerful influence among the philosopher-mystics of Iran in our own day. Unfortunately the promised second volume of this history of philosophy never appeared, but enough of the story is set out in the existing volume that Corbin's intention and basic position are quite clear. The undoubted crown of his analytical studies is the stupendous four-volume *oeuvre* entitled *En Islam Iranien*. This work, organized into seven books, was the fruit of twenty years of inquiry and reflections, much of it done in Iran itself in consultation with representatives of the spirituality it describes. Like all of Corbin's studies, it is copiously annotated with references both to Western and to Oriental language works.

Indeed, for the serious scholar the notes to his many volumes are among the most useful parts of Corbin's contribution, for they are an invaluable and clear guide to a rich literature that is otherwise a *terra incognita*. Some part of Corbin's concern to document his work so thoroughly, as well as the meticulousness with which he did it, is no doubt attributable to the years he spent as librarian in the Bibliothèque Nationale working in the collection of Arabic and Persian manuscripts there. *En Islam Iranien* begins with an exposition of Twelver Shiʿism, and carries the reader through consideration of a mass of thinkers, ideas, books, and movements that constitute the spiritual universe of Islamic Iran. The volumes include pages devoted to figures such as the Shaykh al-Ishrāq, mystics such as Ruzbehān-i Baqlī, ʿAlā al-Dawlah al-Semnānī, and Ḥaydar Āmulī, and to movements and schools such as the School of Isphahan and the Shaykhīs. The work concludes with a comprehensive study of the meaning of the Twelfth Imam and the spiritual chivalry that surrounds this eschatological figure. It is tempting to dwell on the richness that Corbin has bequeathed to us, but we shall content ourselves in this opening tribute by saying that we should know but little if anything of the thought of Muslims such as Mīr Dāmād, Mullā Ṣadrā, Shaykh Aḥmad Aḥsā'ī, and a host of other spiritual adepts in the Iranian tradition were it not for his magisterial efforts.

Corbin's Concept of Islam

While acknowledging a debt of learning to Henry Corbin such as we owe to few others, we must also call attention to his quite unique concept of Islam as a field of study and the strong biases displayed there. Corbin's thought is structured around three poles: philosophy, Iran, and Shiʿi Islam.[4] These three have a rank order, with the concern for philosophy being the most fundamental and the others occupying subordinate positions in the order named. As we shall have reason to emphasize again below, Corbin was primarily a philosopher: all that he has done by way of text editions, analytical studies, and contributions to the study of Islamic philosophy and mysticism is part of a great philosophical quest. For this reason his concern with hermeneutics is of great importance for understanding his thought.

Corbin was secondarily an Iranologue, and it was from the standpoint of his interest in a centuries-old philosophical and mystical tradition in Iranian culture that he came to the study of Shiʿi Islam. What interested him about Shiʿism was its continuity with and its revival and sustenance of motifs that had their origin in pre-Islamic times. The primacy of things Iranian is evidenced in many different ways. One of the foremost is the very title of his *magnum opus*, *En Islam Iranien;* the subject was not Islam as such, certainly not Islam in its multiplicity of modes of expression, but a peculiarly Iranian exemplification of the Islamic phenomenon. In the prologue and elsewhere he says clearly that his intention is to explore the spiritual universes of *Iran* and to make them known to those in other places who share the longing for return from the exile that is our life in this world. Islam happened to have taken strong root in Iran, and having done so, proved through its Ithna ʿAshari branch to be capable of nurturing, expressing, and furthering the profound spirituality of the Iranian soul. On Iranian soil, however, Islam is something different but also something more important, more true, and more real. It is the "Iranian connection" which confers such significance on Ithna ʿAshari Shiʿism and not the other way around.

Evidence of this orientation may also be had from his major study, *Corps spirituel et terre celeste.*[5] The subtitle of this work in the 1977 English translation is "From Mazdean Iran to Shiʿite Iran"; and it begins with discussion of the Mazdean beliefs about the angels (in Corbin's terms its angelology) and proceeds to demonstrate how the cosmological and metaphysical truths represented by this angelology find their reflection in Islamic times in the works of Shiʿi thinkers. The effort is to trace a distinctively Iranian set of themes through both their pre-Islamic and Islamic manifestations down to our time.

More significant, however, than any other indication of the Iranian orientation of Corbin's work on Islam is his preoccupation with Suhrawardī, with whom he began and to whom he returned continually throughout his career. Corbin hailed Suhrawardī's principal contribution as his revival of the ancient Wisdom of Persia, the old Iranian philosophy of Light and Darkness, or the "oriental" theosophy as Corbin prefers to term it. As an Islamic thinker, Suhrawardī was building on something that derived from the Iranian part of his heritage in order to construct a uniquely valuable theosophical and mystical system of universal import. Linking Plato and Zoroaster together as upholders of a common tradition, Suhrawardī interpreted the Platonic ideas in terms of the Zoroastrian angels. He thus was led to introduce the idea of a third world, an intermediate zone lying between the world of the intelligibles and the world of sensible things, a world that is the state of all true spiritual reality. Corbin saw this resurrection of an ancient way of thought which was taken up by many Shiʿi thinkers as the decisive point in the emergence of the tradition of Shiʿi spirituality that reached its flowering in Mullā Ṣadrā and the School of Isphahan. Suhrawardī was the guide, and he led Corbin inevitably and directly to Iran, which was to become Corbin's spiritual home.

The emphasis upon Iran is as significant for what it necessarily excludes from Corbin's realm of interest as it is for the positive orientation that it lends. From the standpoint of a historian of religion the principal exclusion entailed is the study of that great entity known as Sunnism, the religious expression of the vast majority of the Muslim community. One important exception to this exclusion, however, must be noted, namely, the Sufi or mystical element of Sunnism in which Corbin was deeply interested. Sufism attracted him because he perceived it as akin to the spirituality of the Shiʿi tradition, as a force that acted even in the midst of Sunni legalism to draw the mystic into a deeper and more integral spiritual life. Thus, Sufism could be characterized as a kind of proto-Shiʿism or incipient Shiʿism, as a partially developed spirituality on the way to achieving the fullness that would come with the recognition of the Imams and their authority. In disagreement with many other scholars, Corbin held that Sufism is not the sole or even the principal expression of Islamic spirituality; the honor of fulfilling the latter role belonged to Imami Shiʿism. This attitude towards Sufism was, therefore, consistent with the exclusion of Sunnism from his purview, for in studying it he was dealing, as it were, with the Shiʿi dimensions of Sunni experience. The exclusion of Sunnism followed ineluctably from concentration upon Iran whose spirituality, Corbin believed, culminated in Twelver Shiʿism. He turned a blind eye towards Sunnism despite the fact that for most of its Islamic history Iran had had a Sunni majority, having cemented its attachment to Twelver Shiʿism only in Safavid times as a result of the policy of the Safavid Shahs to counter Ottoman claims to the religious leadership of the community.

The concentration upon Iran also excludes any emphasis upon the expression of Islamic experience among other ethnic groups and regional cultures where Islam has flourished. In principle, there is nothing amiss in a scholar devoting his efforts to the study of a particular region as Corbin has done with Iran; such specialization is often the key to profundity and progress in knowledge. In this case, however, there is a disturbing element in the concentration on Iran, for it rests upon the assumption and, indeed, the outright assertion, that Iranian Islam, that is, Ithna ʿAshari Shiʿism, is the very essence of the Islamic experience. In a moment we shall see why it is so, when we come to the Shiʿi pole in Corbin's thought. The concentration on Iran, in other words, is not merely the outcome of some particular attraction that country exerted on Corbin, not is it the accidental product of his having a better acquaintance with Iran than with other parts of the Islamic world. Rather, a judgment and an evaluation were involved; he studied Iranian Islam because there he believed that he had encountered the genuine and true Islam. All else did not merit the same degree of attention.

Corbin was particularly concerned to emphasize the uniqueness and importance of Iranian Islam over that of the Arabs. A large part of *Histoire de la philosophie islamique* is devoted to this theme, and he returns to it elsewhere. Islam is not monolithic, he asserts, and it must not be identified with the Arabs and their culture as Western orientalists have massively tended to do. It would be an exaggeration to say that Corbin was anti-Arab, but he undoubtedly shared some of the sentiment common among Iranians, at least before the recent revolution, that the Arab conquest in the seventh century had been a disruptive intrusion into Iranian history. Even in such a matter as transliteration, he pressed for the primacy of the Iranian element. He insisted that words, Arabic or Persian, be transliterated as they are pronounced in Persian, even Arabic words in an Arabic text. Had he been an Iranian by birth, he might have been accused of xenophobia; and since he claimed spiritually to be an Iranian, the charge may have some justification in any case.

If the attitude toward the Arabs was negative in some degree, that toward other representatives of the Islamic community was simply to ignore them. There are occasional references to Islamic India but most often in connection with Iran's mediating function in passing on certain things from the extreme west to the extreme east of the Islamic world. Note must be taken also of his great study of Ibn al-ʿArabī, though the book is but little concerned with Spanish Islam. There is, however, simply no recognition at all that the vast majority of Muslims are neither Arabs nor Iranians, nor that for centuries the largest concentration of Muslim population has been centered to the east of Iran in the Indian subcontinent and beyond. In short, Corbin had no concern for a comprehensive, systematic, disinterested presentation of historical Islam—the usual goal for a historian of religion. His work rests on a clear value choice, one that deems a certain element of the Islamic tradition supremely significant and others not to be worthwhile in the same degree; this approach we suggest is dictated by the fact that his interests were chiefly philosophical and not historical or scientific.

It is appropriate also to offer some remarks about Shiʿism, the third pole of Corbin's thought. He was interested in both the major branches of Shiʿism, and his works included several important studies of Ismaʿili authors and writings. The center of his concern, however, was undoubtedly the Ithna ʿAshari community whose connection with

Iran we have already indicated. He considered Twelver Shiʿism to be the essence of Islam, and the explanation for this view lies in the emphasis Shiʿism places upon the hidden or esoteric aspect of revelation.

The basic thing in the spiritual reality that we call Islam, Corbin tells us, is the phenomenon of the Book. Islam is a religion of the Book, but not merely in the sense that it possesses a scripture once revealed to the Prophet by God. For the Qur'ān was not meant only for the time and circumstances of seventh-century Arabia; in its larger significance the phenomenon of the Book signifies a continuing guidance, a living and ongoing truth which sustains the spirituality of those with eyes to see. What is important about the Qur'ān is not only what it says, its literal sense in classical Arabic; were that the case, it would now be a dead book, relevant only for the time in which it came and to those who were then alive. No, in addition to the literal sense, it is essential to comprehend the meaning of the Book. There are the Arabic words and their plain sense, but there is also something more, something beyond, to which the words point. To be content with the literal sense is analogous to removing the hull of a nut, keeping the hull, and throwing away the kernel. One receives benefit and nutrition from a nut by eating the kernel. The hull without the kernel is useless, but the kernel cannot be obtained without extracting it from that which covers and protects it. Thus, the two are inseparable. This is the familiar doctrine of the *ẓāhir* and the *bāṭin*, the assertion that the Qur'ān has both an obvious, literal, external, and temporal sense as well as a hidden, spiritual, internal, and transtemporal meaning.

In Corbin's understanding, Sunni Islam with its concern for the Shariʿa, the right modes of conduct on the temporal stage, and *kalām*, the rational expression of religious experience, represents the literal aspect of the Book, whereas Shiʿism searches beyond the external and literal for the deepest hidden secret. The formula then follows: Sunnism stands to Shiʿism as Shariʿa stands to *ḥaqīqa*, or in terms of the analogy just used, as the hull stands to the kernel. Shiʿism is superior because it comprehends the *ẓāhir* but also transcends it to grasp the very hidden heart of reality, the *ḥaqīqa*. Thus, Ithna ʿAshari Shiʿism is integral or complete Islam, for it recognizes, as other expressions of Islam do not, that man's life and reality are not in this world but on another plane which our earthly existence only symbolizes and points to as the *ẓāhir* points to the *bāṭin*. Sunnism in contrast is bound by its legalisms; it is content with following the literal commands of the revelation but does not seek their spiritual meaning. Put in another way what it fails to do, and precisely what Shiʿism does accomplish, is to offer a hermeneutic of the Book.

The key to the capacity of Shiʿism for a spiritual hermeneutic is its acceptance of the Imams, for it is they who through their teaching keep the Book alive and show its hidden secrets. Like all Muslims, the Shiʿa believe Muḥammad to have been the last and the seal of the prophets. But were all to end with prophecy, what then would become of the guidance when there is no longer a guide to mediate it? Is it to be taken only as something pertinent to the past? In the Shiʿi understanding there supervenes upon the cycle of prophecy, brought to its rounded conclusion by Muḥammad, the cycle of the *walāya*, or of the series of Imams who are the heirs, transmitters, and interpreters of the Wisdom hidden in prophetic revelation. The Qur'ān itself speaks of the Wisdom and the Book, thus in its own terms calling attention to its hidden dimension, its Wisdom, of which the Imams are the custodians. Corbin asserts that there is no complete Islam, no full realization of the Islamic truth, without the Imams, for without them the gnosis, the quintessential truth, the *ḥaqīqa* of the Book, could never be known. It is to be emphasized that we are dealing here, not with a description of Shiʿi belief and doctrine, but with the reasons Corbin offers for holding the study of Shiʿism to be the study of integral Islam.

The vehicle which the Imams used to convey the *ḥaqīqa* was their teaching, preserved in the great collections of the *aḥādīth* (Hadiths, canonical sayings) assembled by al-Kulaynī, Ibn-Babūyā, al-Qummī, and Abū Jaʿfar al-Ṭūsī. The core of these teachings according to Corbin is an esoteric truth to which the Imams initiate their followers. The teachings of the Imams culminate in gnosis, in *theo-sophia*, in the literal sense of those words. The real nature of Shiʿism thus shows itself to be mystical, to lie in the creation of a band of *ʿurafā'* (gnostics) or *ḥukamā'* (theosophical philosophers) who constitute a kind of spiritual chivalry clustered about the figure of the Hidden Imam. It cannot be said too strongly that for Corbin this theosophical doctrine and the relatively small number of people who espouse it and live out its consequences *are* Ithna ʿAshari Shiʿism. When he looks at the Shiʿi phenomenon and reads the Shiʿi texts, it is this theosophical tradition he sees, and that alone.

Manifestly such an understanding of Shiʿism is a distortion of the historical reality. There is no doubt a spiritual, mystical, or gnostic tradition within the Ithna ʿAshari community, but there is also a great deal else besides. Exactly like Sunni Islam, Shiʿism has developed the rational expression of its religious experience in a very sophisticated manner, and it is in no way less concerned than the majority community with the details of religious conduct or the minutiae of legal rules. Indeed, were one to weigh the treatises or count the words in them, he would find vastly the greater part of Ithna ʿAshari religious writing to be devoted to subjects that fall into these two fields or into others of the traditional corpus of the Islamic sciences. The meaning of their faith for the majority of Ithna ʿAshari Shiʿa is expressed precisely in the doctrines which they affirm, in the rituals they perform, and in the modes of conduct enjoined by the books of law, in short, in the Shariʿa. In its more straightforward expressions, Shiʿism is every bit as legalistic as the piety of the majority Sunni community; indeed, some would say more so. Even the Hadiths of the Imams, which according to Corbin are the primary source of Shiʿi gnostic doctrine, are filled with statements relating to ritual, theology, and law; just as for the *ʿurafāʾ*, these Hadiths are also the basic source for the Shiʿi *mujtahidīn* (those zealous in their piety).

Corbin's view of Islam ignores this vast sphere of activity empirically and impugns it philosophically. As a self-proclaimed phenomenologist, he follows a method that bypasses the great mass of the phenomena to select only those which speak to his philosophical concerns. Even in respect to representatives of the gnostic tradition Corbin is selective in his treatment, giving attention solely to those elements that bear out his overall thesis about the visionary and gnostic character of true Shiʿism. The point has been documented in Fazlur Rahman's recent book on Mullā Ṣadrā, which shows the thought of this great thinker and mystic to be set essentially within a rational framework, and demonstrates that an approach to Mullā Ṣadrā which emphasizes exclusively the visionary or imaginal aspects of his thought does not do justice to the whole.[6] Corbin is, no doubt, a pioneering student of Shiʿism, and he has put the scholarly world into his debt for his contributions to the subject, but he presents a picture of Shiʿism that is skewed so heavily towards one particular emphasis that it presents a gravely distorted vision of the whole. Thus, there still remains the need for a rounded and systematic study of the Shiʿi phenomenon and its relationship to the other elements in the multiformity we know as Islam.

This criticism of Corbin does not arise because he has been selective, but rather because his selectivity is justified on phenomenological or philosophical grounds. Corbin insists that in pursuing the themes he has chosen he is expounding the real Islam, the integral and complete faith beside which the rest pales into insignificance. Even were he to grant the validity of Corbin's conception of "integral Islam," the historian of religion would continue to be interested in that presumably incomplete and "nonintegral Islam" of daily historical expression, and this for many reasons. Consider for example the light that Corbin's analyses of Shiʿi gnosis throws on present-day events in Iran, where there is unquestionably a great outpouring of religious feelings formed in a Shiʿi mold. Since these events, to the extent that they are religiously motivated at all, involve the expression of Islam in social, political, and generally historical modes, they belong to the realm of the truncated literal and incomplete Islam of history. They fall, therefore, outside the sphere of Corbin's interest and outside what he would consider to be true Shiʿism.

Corbin's Hermeneutics

Of the three poles around which the thought of Henry Corbin revolved, the most important was philosophy. Although on different occasions he may have described himself in various other ways, as an orientalist, an Iranologist, or an Islamicist, Corbin was above all else a philosopher, and the questions to which he addressed himself were universal problems of the human spirit that face all men at all times. Why then, it may be asked, did he evince such a passionate and lifelong interest in matters Iranian and Islamic? On the face of things there is no apparent reason why a philosophical mind should be drawn into the deep study of an alien culture or led to undertake the arduous work of philology; history has witnessed thousands of philosophers who felt no such impulses. Corbin was drawn to Islamic Iran, it would seem, because he found there an expression of spirituality to which he was personally attracted. The Iranian thinkers put forward, as no one else had done with such force and clarity, certain themes which also echo in the spirituality of the West, in Jacob Boehme, in the story of the quest for the Grail, or in Emanuel Swedenborg. The Iranian spiritual philosophy saw no value in analysis for its own sake but insisted that philosophical insight must come to fruition in the personal realization of spiritual truth. Thus, it had two inseparable dimensions, the intellectual and the mystical. Corbin's studies had led him to see philosophy in the Occident from the time of Averroës's rejection of Avicennism to Hegel's philosophy of history[7] as a progressive desacralization of reality and the entrapment of thought in a dilemma which left the choice of assigning spiritual events either to the realm of history or to that of myth. The result was to eliminate the very place of spirituality in the scheme of things and to drive a wedge between life and thought. Having known philosophy in its Occidental pole, he wished through his work to reorient it towards its spiritual and Oriental pole of Light, to point the way towards the end of the "Occidental exile" by a return to the origins. Although as a Western Protestant Corbin held himself at some distance from the Shiʿi spirituality that he described, he had far more than a methodologically conditioned sympathy for it. He found in it things that were true, and he used his work, often in a combative manner, to uphold the philosophical point of view set out by the Shiʿi theosophists. His purpose was to describe but also to advocate, to expound but also to defend and propagate.

The *epoché* of Van der Leeuw's classical statement of method in the phenomenology of religion had little meaning for Corbin; indeed, to the extent that *Religionswissenschaft* seeks to subsume the religious under ordered, systematic categories of understanding, and to impose upon it or see in it some kind of rational scheme, it represented for Corbin the "historicization" of the sacred, a betrayal and degradation of the truly spiritual onto the historical plane. He was no historian of religions, then, but the missionary of a spirituality to which he was himself completely devoted.

Nevertheless, Corbin presented himself as a phenomenologist, a "phenomenologist of the spirit." His use of the word has something in common with the more usual understanding, but also has additional and unusual elements.

Like many others who claim the same designation, Corbin felt it necessary to put himself in the place of those whom he studied, to make their experience, perceptions, and reactions the norms for description of the spirituality in which he was interested. The scholar must become a guest in the spiritual universe of those he studies and ultimately make that universe his own. His attitude was one of sympathy carried to the point of identification. Thus the important thing was the content of Shiʿi consciousness, what was experienced in the

Shiʿi soul without reference to questions of context, social determination, or historical fact. The method is phenomenological insofar as "it involves confronting a religious *fact* by allowing the religious *object* to appear as it appears to those to whom it does appear."[8] The phenomena of spirituality are to be encountered "where they *take place* and where they *take their place*."[9] The place where these events happen is in the souls of the believers, in the inner person on that plane of reality inhabited by the soul, not on the level of history. Phenomenology, then, deals with events of the soul, realities that are neither physical nor intellectual but of a quality all their own. The phenomenologist aims at allowing his work to show what has been shown to the believers in all its nakedness and its fullness without bending it to fit an understanding of reality of his own and without judging it in terms of historical possiblity and veracity. The sole guide, the sole source, and the sole criterion for the study of the Shiʿi consciousness then is the Shiʿi consciousness itself, what it contains, and what it can be made to reveal. The difficulty of following this methodological policy in the academic study of religions is discussed by Martin in Chapter 1 and Rahman in Chapter 12 of this volume.

Phenomenology can thus be defined as "unveiling or exposing to view something that was hidden,"[10] since the life of the inner man and the events of the soul are not open to common sensory observation. Spiritual experience rather is covert, not to be shared even with those who desire to do so unless they themselves participate in a similar spiritual realization. At this point Corbin's concern with the phenomenological method leads directly to the esoterism that he saw as the defining characteristic and great merit of the Iranian Shiʿi tradition. The purpose of the first volume of *En Islam Iranien*, he stated, was to show us Shiʿism "as the sanctuary of esoterism in Islam."[11] Esoterism is concerned with the veiled, hidden, and covert, with the meaning of things that is not apparent from their mere outward and historical form. Phenomenology, it follows, is the key to the esoteric side of Islam, the method that unlocks the otherwise hidden secrets of another plane of reality, and in this role it is equivalent to a hermeneutics of the deep and true nature of Islamic spirituality. Phenomenology in Corbin's sense aims at being precisely the demonstration of the "meaning" of the exoteric reality professed by the common believer of the Shiʿi community. Put in another way the hermeneutics of Islam or the "phenomenology of the spirit" is the teaching of the

Imams, nothing more and nothing less, for it is they who demonstrate, as no others can, the secret, but living, unfolding, and always growing meaning of the Revealed Book. In his own words, "the Imams are the guides to hermeneutics."[12]

In his discussion of the etymology of the word "phenomenology" Corbin points out that the original Greek means "to save or preserve the phenomenon."[13] With Islamic philosophy being a prophetic philosophy in which the vehicle of revelation was the Book brought through the Prophet, one task of phenomenology is to save the Book from the "dead" historical past. The Qur'ān retains no relevance if it is looked upon only from the historicist perspective of the Prophet's time and those who first heard its stirring words, for that time is gone and will not come again. The past is dead and buried. To save the Revelation from this historical "death" the Qur'ān must be made "present" in the experience of the believer. It must thus be wrested from its historical time and transplanted into an existential time where it "lives" and is always contemporary with those who respond to its truth. The meaning of the Qur'ān thus is "open," for it depends upon a decision by the individual to appreciate it. Only by making the literal Qur'ān of the past present to oneself in its inward meaning is one capable of transmitting it to the generations to come. A tradition can be passed on "alive" only in the "time of the soul" as a continually renewed and deepened inspiration.[14] It is this which the teaching of the Imams allows the Shiʿi gnostics to do, and thus the result of the Imams's initiation into the secrets of hidden meaning is to "save the Book."

Phenomenology is salvation of the book in another sense as well, for it insures that the meaning will not be lost in the attention paid to the literal form of the words. The exoteric meaning of the Qur'ān, its *sharīʿa*, taken without its *ḥaqīqa*, its inner dimension of meaning, results in an incomplete Islam, in a failure to grasp and to live what the Qur'ān is truly all about. Further, it may lead to the identification of the Shariʿa with specific institutions, practices, or ideas or with the worldly fortunes of the community—in short, to the "socialization" of Islam. When this identification occurs, it is, in effect, a denial of the existence of all spiritual reality and a capitulation to a purely materialistic view of the universe. Corbin thus has little sympathy for those many Muslims who bemoan the fortunes of the community in the modern era and who seek to reform or rethink Islam as a way of putting right what had gone wrong. In his view they face a false problem because they think in terms of "socialized" Islam. Concentration upon the *ḥaqīqa* that lies behind and above the *sharīʿa* can alone prevent this from happening. Corbin believes the validity of his point to be clearly demonstrated in the development of the more legalistic branch of Islam and in the history of the Christian church in recent times. Both have lost their eschatological dimension, which is to say they have turned their backs on any sphere of reality beyond the mundane and, like the ideologies of our day, have projected all of their hopes and expectations upon the stage of our present life. The *ta'wīl*, or exposition, of its hidden meaning will preserve the exoteric aspect of the Book from this denial of the sacred.

There is, however, a second phenomenon as well which Corbin thinks his own and the hermeneutics of the Shiʿi theosophists to be capable of saving. This he calls the "phenomenon of the mirror." By it he signifies a metaphysics and a cosmology as well as a symbolic relationship among various universes or levels of reality, the most important element of which is an "imaginal world" where the apparitions and theophanies that make up spiritual experience have their reality. Corbin devoted much energy to distinguishing this "imaginal world" from the merely imaginary or unreal realm. While the latter is fleeting and illusory, the former is real and of inexpressible significance though the laws which govern the *mundus imaginalis* (or in Islamic terms the *ʿālam al-mithāl* or the *malakūt*) differ from those of the historical and temporal realm.[15] The human faculty that perceives and responds to the reality of the world of images is also different from the normal sensory faculties. It is clear that in Corbin's view to be a phenomenologist of the spirit means not only to associate oneself personally with a broad spiritual tradition, represented by Shiʿi theosophy (and through it with all of the Abrahamic ecumenism), but also to hold as true and meaningful the metaphysics and cosmology taught by that spiritual tradition. In his words, "We concede the existence of permanent spiritual worlds, which pose perpetual questions for man and offer him an open invitation."[16] Thus, demonstrated here once again is the link between his philosophical concerns and his interest in Islam. They are one and the same. Also demonstrated is the great difference between Corbin's conception of phenomenology and its significance, together with the problematic from which it has emerged as a philosophical approach, and that of most scholars who would call themselves phenomenologists of religion. Whereas for van der Leeuw and those who have followed him phenomenology was a search for a greater objectivity, an attempt to be more rigorously scientific in the understanding of religion, for Corbin its impact was personal and philosophical as the key to religious insight and personal spiritual realization. The two have in common their mutual preoccupation with the problem of knowledge, but their respective ways of integrating religion into the total field of knowledge could scarcely be more different.

We cannot leave the subject of phenomenology without saying something of its implication for Corbin's view of history. At several points above emphasis was laid upon the fact that spiritual events, the events of the soul, those things with which phenomenology and hermeneutics deal, do not happen in mundane chronological history but on another plane, and in another kind of time. Neither do they occur in extended space but "where they *take their place.*" Our normal time is chronological and irreversible, but it is also, according to Corbin, without spiritual meaning. All concern with history in the everyday sense is dealing with the nonspiritual; from this point of view—and Corbin was not reluctant to draw the conclusion—the very term history of religions becomes nonsense if we continue to think of history in chronological and irreversible terms. This negative view of history is significant in the philosophical sphere, but it also had other consequences for Corbin who, as we shall see, firmly refused to permit historical considerations to divert the direction of his thought.

In relation to his study of religions, Corbin's phenomenological method is essentially a refusal of every attempt to reduce the religious experience to something outside itself by attempting to explain it in causal terms. Religious experience, or the sacred, is *sui generis* and must be approached in and through itself. It is a primary or *Urphänomen*, and no grasp of it that assumes something else as its basis can adequately come to terms with its distinctive quality.[17] All studies that deal with religious phenomena through the investigation of social, political, or psychological circumstances touch only the externals, not the reality of religion, according to Corbin. What is forbidden, therefore, is to interpret ideas and thinkers only in relation to their historical time, to explain them causally as the products of their circumstances.[18] One does not study the Shiʿi gnostics in particular in their social contexts because these spiritual heroes were radically alienated from the societies in which they lived, and it would plainly be paradoxical to try to explain them in terms that they themselves rejected.[19] To look at their experience and thought from only a historical perspective is equivalent to confusing philosophy with the sociology of knowledge, and so to deny the truth of philosophy. The historical perspective, in other words, has abolished the line between the sacred and the profane. The great sin of historians when they intrude into the domain of religious studies is their tendency to secularize the sacred and in the process to lose it entirely. Religions transform into knowledge and existence realities that are mystical and thus *directly experienced.* These realities do not subsist on the material plane where all of history occurs, and history, therefore, can neither explain them nor even cast significant light upon them. If they are secularized or historicized, they are lost. To all intents and purposes where the spiritual realities that interest Corbin are involved, normal chronological history at best has no relevance, and if it is pursued too far becomes an obstacle to their realization.

Corbin reacted so strongly against the modern interest in historical studies because he saw in it the hidden danger of a materialistic philosophy. He saw the same result following from the concern with philosophy of history that had been stimulated by Hegel's thought. He held there to be a strong link between the *fides historica* and historical materialism. Every effort to find meaning in history is an effective limitation of the field of vision to the material and sensible, to what occurs between the limits of birth and death. All genuine religion, according to Corbin's pronouncement, is eschatological, with its hope vested in a reality beyond mundane history. The implications of the philosophy of history are the basis of the dilemma of "myth or history" from which modern religious thought has been unable to extricate itself. Because it insists that only those events are true that happen in chronological time on the material plane, the historical approach to religion, when it meets something that it cannot straightforwardly grasp through historical causality, must relegate that thing to the realm of myth with no other alternative available to it. Such an alternative could, of course, be opened up if the historian and the philosopher of history would only raise their eyes beyond the horizon of mundane history as Corbin hopes to persuade them to do. In the choice between myth and history, the preference has clearly been for history, even in theology where the movement of *Entmythologisierung* (demythologizing), to Corbin's horror, has won numerous adherents. Pursuit of the meaning of history, which is characteristic of secularized theologies and the ideologies which are their modern offspring, is an illusion. History has no meaning for Corbin unless it is somehow brought into relationship with and subsumed under a metahistory. In this life we are exiles, banished into the Occident of our beings while our true homes and our origins lie in the Orient of Light (the *mashriq* or place of illumination) which continually beckons us. All possibility for the return of the exile, indeed, all possibility for a spiritual existence of any kind is cut off when one comes to hold that mundane history is the extent of our reality. To believe so is simply to think that the Orient of Light does not exist. In consequence, Corbin describes his philosophical enterprise as a kind of "antihistory."

There is, however, a different kind of history that does have meaning for Corbin, the history of the soul. It is in the soul that spiritual events occur and on that level where they find their proper coordinates, both temporal and geographical. The history of the soul or metahistory stands in relation to mundane history in a symbolic mode. All that happens here finds its counterpart and is reflected there, while everything in metahistory assumes what happens in mundane history and symbolizes it. In one of the neologisms that are sprinkled liberally throughout his writings, Corbin speaks of universes that symbolize *with* one another. Metahistory is to ordinary history what the *bāṭin* is to the *ẓāhir*, the *ḥaqīqa* to the *sharīʿa*, the hidden meaning to the exoteric sense of the Revelation. On the one hand, it is inextricably linked with mundane history, but on the other it is the essence and completion of the latter. For it is in the history of the soul that the Revelation finds its meaning. Revelation derives its true historicity not through the physical coming of the Book but rather by its being made "present" in us, by its continuing to happen in the inner person until the Day of Judgment.[20] The esoteric meaning takes place in the history of the soul. Behind and beneath external history are the essential motifs of a spiritual activity that is the polar opposite of materialistic history. It is on the stage of this metahistory that the Imams appear in their theophanic forms and give their teachings, often in the form of visions.

The rules that govern the happening of events in metahistory are different from those that apply in the realm of the mundane. Time is not irreversible there. Events which happened in the past may be brought back to be made present in the soul of the believer; and both past and present may be transposed into the future. Indeed, even the future may be brought into the present as in the case of the Twelfth Imam, whose future coming every believer achieves in himself. The same event may occur over and over again in metahistory while yet being always contemporary, present, past, and future at the same time. Neither do the normal laws that regulate movement through space have any limiting effect in the realm of the history of the soul. In that visionary kingdom beings are transported over great distances in a moment of time, or they may be present in two different places of that supernatural geography at the same moment. Spiritual events are not situated in that other world in relation to any fixed reference point; rather it is they which are the situating agent around which all else groups itself. Beings there are also capable of having their forms utterly changed, of evolving new and radically different modes of appearance as the secret of that different realm is progressively penetrated.

Perhaps the most significant of the many links between mundane history and the spiritual world (metahistory, and *mundus imaginalis*, *ʿālam al-mithāl*, the *malakūt*) beyond it, at least for the purposes of Corbin's study, is the phenomenon of the visionary recital. Such a recital is an account of an experience (a vision or a dream) which has occurred to a mystic, but it is not merely a story or a tale. Neither is it an allegory. Rather, it is the account of a true and real experience on another plane of reality. When the mystic tells what has happened to him, therefore, he is *re*-citing an event of formative importance, and use of the term "recital" keeps this aspect of such experiences ever before us. In Arabic such a visionary recital is known as "*ḥikāya*," which means both "history" and "imitation." The *ḥikāya* is the history of something that has really happened, but it serves at the same time to lift one into the other world whose history it relates by its function of imitation. Visionary recitals are also, therefore, initiatory, for their basic function is to open out the secret and hidden meaning of an otherwise inaccessible spiritual realm. The events of the *ḥikāya* symbolize what happens on another plane and bring one to participate in the reality of those events. Thus, the *ḥikāya*, like all external history, symbolizes or imitates an internal history, points beyond its literal form to a saving knowledge. In consequence, visionary recitals, such as that of Ibn Sīnā, for example, become vital devices in the hermeneutical process of unlocking the reality of the world of symbols where spiritual reality dwells.

It must be underlined that Corbin is not merely theorizing to establish the existence of a supernatural realm that would provide a philosophical substrate for his gnostic thought. The attitude towards mundane history in his works was as scornful in practice as his theory would imply. Although he did some historical study and expressed the need for historical awareness, he would not allow that issues of historical criticism had any relevance for the study of the spiritual truth of metahistory. Historical criticism was brushed aside in favor of something higher. We have already seen examples of Corbin's tendency to ignore the multiplicity and richness of historical Islam in Iran and elsewhere by compressing it into a mold of his own devising. There are others equally striking that can also be cited. For example, in connection with the Canonical Sayings of the Imams, he mentions the skepticism of many—one may say in fact, the majority—of scholars that the Imams ever actually said many of the things attributed to them. There is no attempt to deal with the issue in terms of the normal criteria for establishing the authenticity of a text or its attribution. In the place of historical analysis of the issue there is a polemic against historicism and repetition of the methodological principle that what ultimately counts is the Shiʿi consciousness.

The Shiʿa believed that the sayings transmitted to them were spoken by the Imams; indeed, in Shiʿi souls the Canonical Sayings are the Imams eternally speaking to the faithful. In the interior lives of the believers these sayings are real events. This fact makes the *aḥādīth*, or Canonical Sayings, valid historical documents without the need for more to be said. A similar argument is mounted in connection with the authorship of *Nahj al-Balāgha*, which the Ithna ʿAshari Shiʿa traditionally attribute to the First Imam. These documents make an equivocal use of the word "history" in their attributions of historicity, and the question of the actual authorship of the sayings or the treatise is never seriously raised. The argument offered is rather *ad hominem*, proceeding on the basis of the evil results that Corbin considers historicism to have produced. Far from elucidating the question of historicity, Corbin's procedure thrusts it into the background and denies its importance. Nonetheless, in full confidence Corbin says of the *aḥādīth* of the Imams, "In my opinion historically and chronologically we cannot go back to any more ancient sources in Islam." One must agree with Corbin that these historical questions are not the fundamental issue in the study of Shiʿi religiosity, but it is not acceptable to relegate critical considerations to the dustbin of insignificance.[21]

Corbin's hermeneutics of Shiʿi Islam is, it will be evident, more than an effort to make the nature of Shiʿi piety understood on the intellectual plane. It is also an exposition and defense of a world view to which Corbin himself was committed. The encounter with Shiʿi gnosticism in Corbin's works is an open invitation to us all to enter and dwell in that realm if only we will "decide" to do so.

9

Literary Analysis of *Qur'ān*, *Tafsīr*, and *Sīra*

The Methodologies of John Wansbrough

ANDREW RIPPIN

That Judaism and Christianity are religions "in history" seems to be a commonly accepted notion among many people today. The view is that history is the "proving ground" of these religions, that the intervention of God in the historical sequence of events is the most significant truth attested by these religions. Whether or not this is theologically valid is a question that must be left for those who pursue such questions; what is of interest here are the implications which this view has had for "secular" historical studies and, most importantly here, for the historical study of religion. The idea that these are religions "in history" has led to an emphasis on the desire to discover "what really happened," ultimately, because of the underlying belief that this discovery would demonstrate the ultimate truth or falsity of the individual religion. Now that may or may not be an appropriate task depending on the particular view of history taken by the historian, but it has led to one important problem in the study of religion—the supposition that the sources available to us to describe the historical foundations of a given religion, most specifically the scriptures, contain within them discernible historical data which can be used to provide positive historical results. In other words, the approach assumes that the motivations of the writers of such sources were the same as the motivations of present-day historians, namely, to record "what really happened."

Whether out of theological conviction or merely unconsciously, modern scholarship has approached Islam in the same way that it has traditionally treated Judaism and Christianity—as a religion of history, that is, as a religion that has a stake in history. Whether this approach is valid or invalid is not the point here. What is relevant is that this view has led to the same sort of attitude toward the sources available in the study of early Islam as that which characterizes the attitude in the study of Judaism and Christianity, namely, that these sources purport to record (and thus provide us with) an account of "what really happened." The desire to know what happened in the past is certainly not unreasonable, nor is it, theoretically, an impossible task; Islam most definitely has a history that needs to be recovered. But the desire to achieve positive results must not lead us to ignore the literary qualities of the sources available to us.

Very little material of "neutral" testimonial quality is available for the study of early Islam; sizable quantities of archeological data, numismatic evidence, even datable documents are all very much wanting. Evidence from sources external to the community itself are not plentiful either and the reconstruction of such material into a historical framework is fraught with difficulties. In *Hagarism*, Patricia Crone and Michael Cook have attempted such a reconstruction and, although they successfully draw attention to the problems involved in the study of Islam, they have not been able to get beyond the limitations inherent in the sources, for they are all of questionable historical authenticity and, more importantly, all are treatises based in polemic. No one has yet expressed the problem better than John Wansbrough: "[C]an a vocabulary of motives be freely extrapolated from a discrete collection of literary stereotypes composed by alien and mostly hostile observers, and thereupon employed to describe, even interpret, not merely the overt behaviour but also the intellectual and spiritual development of helpless and almost innocent actors?"[1] The other sources available to us—the Arabic texts internal to the Muslim community—consist of a limited mass of literature originating at least two centuries after the fact. Such information as this literature contains was written in light of the passage of those two centuries and would, indeed, seem to have a stake in that very history being recounted. These internal sources intended, after all, to document the basis of faith, the validity of the sacred book, and its evidence of God's plan for humankind. These sources recorded "Salvation History."

One brief example may help to clarify the exact dimensions of the problem. Nowhere has the attitude toward the historical character of the sources about the foundation of Islam proved to be more resilient than in the interpretation of the Qur'ān. Muslim exegetes have a category of information available to them called *asbāb al-nuzūl*, commonly translated as the "occasions of revelation," which have been thought by Western students of the Qur'ān to record the historical events concerning the revelation of individual verses of the Qur'ān. Careful analysis of the individual uses of these *asbāb* in exegesis reveals that their actual significance in individual cases of trying to understand the Qur'ān is limited: the anecdotes are adduced, and thus recorded and transmitted, in order to provide a narrative situation in which an interpretation of the Qur'ān can be embodied. The material has been recorded within exegesis not for its historical value but for its exegetical value. Yet such basic literary facts about the material are frequently ignored within the study of Islam in the desire to find positive historical results. A good example of what I mean is found in a recent article on Muḥammad's boycott of Mecca; a *sabab* (occasion) recorded in al-Ṭabarī's *tafsīr*[2] is used to defend and elaborate upon a complicated historical reconstruction about the life of Muḥammad.[3] The desire for historical results has led to an entire glossing of the problems and limitations of the sources.

The Nature of the Sources

John Wansbrough of the School of Oriental and African Studies at the University of London has made a systematic attempt to get beyond the problems involved in trying to understand the beginnings of Islam. In two recent books Wansbrough argues for a critical assessment of the value of the sources from a literary point of view, in order to escape the inherent theological view of the history in the account of Islamic origins. The two works, *Quranic Studies: Sources and Methods of Scriptural Interpretation* (hereafter *QS*)[4] and *The Sectarian Milieu: Content and Composition of Islamic Salvation History* (hereafter *SM*)[5] fit together quite logically, although it should be noted that there is some progression of thought between the two works on some specific topics. *QS* was written between 1968 and 1972 although it was published in 1977; *SM* was written between 1973 and 1977, but published in 1978. Those following Wansbrough's numerous reviews will appreciate that his thought has not stopped there either.[6] Wansbrough emphasizes that the ideas he has put forth in his books are a tentative working out of the problems involved. *QS* deals primarily with the formation of the Qur'ān along with the witness of exegetical writings (*tafsīr*) to that formation; *SM* develops the theme of the evolution of Islam further, through the traditional biographies of Muḥammad (*sīra* and *maghāzī*), and then works through the process of the theological elaboration of Islam as a religious community, examining the questions of authority, identity, and epistemology.

The basic methodological point of Wansbrough's works is to ask the prime question not usually posed in the study of Islam: What is the evidence? Do we have witnesses to the Muslim accounts of the formation of their own community in any early, disinterested sources? The Qur'ān (in the form collected "between two covers" as we know it today) is a good example: What evidence is there for the historical accuracy of the traditional accounts of the compilation of that book shortly after the death of Muḥammad? The earliest non-Islamic source testifying to the existence of the Qur'ān appears to stem from the second/eighth century.[7] Indeed, early Islamic sources, at least those which do not seem to have as their prime purpose the defense of the integrity of the canon,[8] would seem to witness that the text of the Qur'ān may not have been totally fixed until the early part of the third/ninth century.[9] Manuscript evidence does not allow for substantially earlier dating either.[10]

A question for many people still remains, however (and the answer to it evidences Wansbrough's most basic and radical point): Why should we *not* trust the Muslim sources? Wansbrough's answer to this is substantially different from other expressions of similar skepticism, for example as argued by John Burton in *The Collection of the Qur'ān*, where internal contradiction within the Muslim sources is emphasized and then that fact is combined with a postulated explanation of how such contradiction came about.[11] No, Wansbrough's point of departure is more radical: the entire corpus of early Islamic documentation must be viewed as "Salvation History." What the Qur'ān is trying to evidence, what *tafsīr*, *sīra*, and theological writings are trying to explicate, is how the sequence of worldly events centered on the time of Muḥammad was directed by God. All the components of Islamic salvation history are meant to witness the same point of faith, namely, an understanding of history that sees God's role in directing the affairs of humankind. And the difference that makes is substantial. To quote from a work that deals with the same problem, but from the biblical perspective, "Salvation history is not an historical account of saving events open to the study of the historian. Salvation history did not happen; it is a literary form which has its own historical context."[12] Salvation history comes down to us in a literary form and must be approached by means appropriate to such: literary analysis.

At the outset it may be appropriate to pay attention to the use of the term "salvation history" in connection with Islam, especially in light of questions raised about its use outside the Christian context in general. Most recently H. W. F. Saggs has pointed to the fact that although the term "salvation" has a clear meaning in Christian thought—"it is the saving of the individual soul from destruction or damnation by sin, for eternal life"—its application within Judaism would seem to mean "no more than that God maintained a particular religio-ethnic group in existence, when the operation of normal political and social factors might have been expected to result in its extermination."[13] The term "salvation" is ambiguous at best and perhaps only rightfully applied in the Christian case. So that may lead to the question: Are we straitjacketing Islam into a Christian framework by using such a term as "salvation history?" Wansbrough has attempted to make reasonably clear what he means by the term, and what it implies to him (e.g., *SM* ix, 31), making it evident that "salvation," as such, is not the defining characteristic of this history. Indeed, Wansbrough suggests (*SM* 147) that Islamic salvation history may perhaps be more accurately described as "election history" because of the very absence within its early formulation of an eschatological concern. Clearly Wansbrough does not conceive of "salvation" in the term "salvation history" as necessarily laden with its Christian connotations. But further, "salvation history" may be taken on a different level, simply as a technical term referring to literature involved in documenting what could just as easily be called "sacred history," that is, the "history" of man's relationship with God and vice versa. The intellectual baggage of *Heilsgeschichte* may simply be left behind in favor of reference to the literary genre.

Literary analysis of salvation history has been fully developed within biblical and Mishnaic studies; the works of Bultmann and Neusner are obvious prime examples.[14] All such works start from the proposition that the literary records of salvation history, although presenting themselves as being contemporary with the events they describe, actually belong to a period well after such events, which suggests that they have been written according to later points of view in order to fit the purposes of that later time. The actual "history" in the sense of "what really happened" has become totally subsumed within later interpretation and is virtually, if not totally, inextricable from it. The question of whether or not there is an underlying "grain of historical truth" may be thought to be of some concern here, namely, whether or not there must have been some sort of historical event or impetus out of which traditions grew and which, therefore, forms the kernel of the narrative. But the real problem here is that even if one admits the existence of such a "kernel" of history, is it ever possible to identify and extract that information? Wansbrough implies in his work that he feels that it is not, at least for the most part.[15] The records we have are the existential records of the thought and faith of later generations.

This basic insight into the nature of the sources is not totally new to the study of Islam. Goldziher, and Schacht even more so, understood that traditional sayings attributed to Muḥammad and used to support a given legal or doctrinal position within Islam actually derived from a much later period, from times when these legal or doctrinal positions were searching for support with the body of material called the *sunna*. It has become characteristic of Islamic studies after Joseph Schacht, however, either to water down or to ignore totally the implications of such insights. This was clear to Schacht himself toward the end of his life.

> One thing disturbs me, however. That is the danger that the results achieved by the Islamic scholars, at a great effort, in the present generation, instead of being developed and being made the starting point for new scholarly progress might, by a kind of intellectual laziness, be gradually whittled down and deprived of their real significance, or even be turned inside out by those who themselves had taken no part in achieving them. This has happened in the past to the work of Goldziher . . . and it has happened again, recently, with regard to the conclusions of the history of Islamic law achieved by critical scholarship.[16]

The "intellectual laziness" is, it seems to me, a counterpart to the desire to produce positive historical results—to satisfy that internal yearning to assert "what really happened."[17] The works of three people can be cited as the most obvious examples of the latter trend: in "The materials used by Ibn Isḥāq," W. M. Watt distorts the work of Schacht and attempts to use Schacht's results against the latter's own position,[18] and in the works of Sezgin[19] and Abbott[20] elaborate schemes are set forth to contradict the insights of Schacht, but are based on no *tangible* evidence. Sezgin especially displays an overt tendency to date works to the earliest possible historical period, with no apparent justification thereof, for example, in the case of the works of Ibn ʿAbbās.[21]

Wansbrough's argument, however, is that we do *not* know and probably never can know what really happened; all we can know is what later people *believed* happened, as has been recorded in salvation history. Literary analysis of such sources will reveal to us the components with which those people worked in order to produce their accounts and define exactly what it was that they were arguing, but literary analysis will not tell us *what* happened (although the *possibility* of historical implications of such studies cannot be, and certainly are not within Wansbrough's work, totally ignored).

The point of Islamic salvation history as it has come down to us today, Wansbrough argues, is more specific than merely to evidence the belief in the reality of the theophany; it is to formulate, by adopting and adapting from a well-established pool of Judeo-Christian religious themes, a specifically Arabian religious identity, the inception of which could be placed in seventh-century Arabia. At the beginning of *QS* Wansbrough brings forth a multitude of evidences from the Qur'ān which point to the idea that the very notions in that book demand that they be put within the total Judeo-Christian context, for example, the prophetic line ending in the Seal of the Prophets, the sequence of scriptures, the notion of the destroyed communities, and the common narrative motifs. This notion of extrapolation is, in a sense, the methodological presupposition that Wansbrough sets out to prove within his books by posing the question: If we assume this, does the data fit? At the same time he asks: What additional evidence appears in the process of the analysis to corroborate the presupposition and to define it more clearly?[22] This kind of approach to the material is similar to that of Harry A. Wolfson in his use of the scientific method of "conjecture and verification."[23] So the question raised by some critics concerning whether it is accurate to view Islam as an extension of the Judeo-Christian tradition cannot be considered valid until the evidence and the conclusions put forth in Wansbrough's works have been weighed. The point must always be: Is the presupposition supported by the analysis of the data? To attack the presupposition as invalid is to miss the entire point. To evaluate the work one must participate within its methodological presuppositions and evaluate the final results.

Wansbrough's Approach to the Sources

Charles Adams has summed up the common feeling of many students of the Qur'ān in the following words: "Such matters as the formation of the Qur'ān text, the chronology of the materials assembled in the text, the history of the text, variant readings, the relation of the Qur'ān to prior literature, and a host of other issues of this kind have been investigated thoroughly."[24] Wansbrough, however, has made it clear that we have really only scratched the surface of these studies. All previous studies, he states, have involved an acquiescence to the normative data of the tradition and are characterized by "a distinctly positivist method: serious concern to discover and to describe the state of affairs after the appearance of Islam among the Arabs . . ." (*SM* 2). What Wansbrough has done has been to bring to the study of Islam and the Qur'ān the same healthy skepticism developed within modern biblical studies (and modern historical studies in general) in order to supplant such positivism. At this point it is worth noting that the highly praised work of Richard Bell,[25] although supposedly using the biblical methodology consequent on the Documentary Hypothesis, has, in fact, progressed not one iota beyond implicit notions in the traditional accounts of the revelation and the collection of the Qur'ān; he took the ideas of serial revelation and the collection after the death of Muḥammad (the common notions accepted by most Westerns students of the Qur'ān) and applied them literally to the text of the Qur'ān. However, the primary purpose of employing modern biblical methodologies must be to free oneself from age-old presuppositions and to apply new ones. This Bell did not do; in fact, he worked wholly within the presuppositions of the Islamic tradition. Wansbrough's claim that "as a document susceptible of analysis by the instruments and techniques of Biblical criticism [the Qur'ān] is virtually unknown" (*QS* ix) can certainly not be questioned, least of all by adducing the work of Bell.[26]

Wansbrough has also tried to show a way to free the study of the Qur'ān from the uniquely fundamentalist[27] trend of the vast majority of modern treatments of the book in which the idea of an "original" meaning or intention is pursued relentlessly but ultimately meaninglessly. Such a position in scholarship has been reached especially because of two factors inherent in previous methodologies in the study of Islam. One, the basic historico-philological approach to Islam has become trapped by the consequence of narrow specialization on the part of its proponents. For the most part, there are few scholars active today who can move with equal agility throughout the entire Western religious framework and its necessary languages.[28] Scholars have come to feel that competent knowledge of Arabic and of seventh-century Arabia are sufficient in and of themselves to understand the rise of Islam.[29] No different are the views of such people as Serjeant, who attempt to champion the notion of the influence of pre-Islamic southern Arabia on Islam, but do so to the virtual exclusion of the Jewish element in the population there.[30]

The philological method has been affected also by a second method which within itself has produced the stagnation of Islamic studies within its fundamentalist framework. The irenic approach, which according to Charles Adams aims toward "the greater appreciation of Islamic religiousness and the fostering of a new attitude toward it,"[31] has led to the unfortunate result of a reluctance on the part of many scholars to follow all the way through with their insights and results. The basic problem of an approach to Islam that is concerned "to understand the faith of other men"[32] is confronted when that approach tries to come to grips with the historical dimensions of a faith that conceives itself as having a stake in that very history.[33] The irenic approach to Islam, it would seem, in order to remain true to the "faith of other men," is doomed most of all to avoid asking the basic question: How do we know?

Wansbrough's analysis of the basic character of the Qur'ān reveals his assessment of the extent of the problem involved in the use of these two approaches to the Qur'ān. Wansbrough isolates four major motifs of the Qur'ānic message, all from the "traditional stock of monotheistic imagery" (*QS* 1): divine retribution, sign, exile, and covenant. These motifs, Wansbrough notes, are "repeatedly signalled but seldom developed" (*QS* 1), a fact which leads him to emphasize throughout his works one of his major insights concerning the Qur'ān: its "referential" style.[34] The audience of the Qur'ān is presumed able to fill in the missing details of the narrative, much as is true of a work such as the Talmud, where knowledge of the appropriate biblical citation is assumed or supplied by only a few words. Only later, when

"Islam" as an entity with a fixed and stable identity (based on a political structure) comes into being after the Arabs' expansion out of their original home, does the Qur'ānic material become detached from its original intellectual environment and need written explication—explication that is provided in *tafsīr* and *sīra*.

Two of the examples discussed by Wansbrough will clarify his notion of the referential character of the Qur'ān. Most evident is the example of Joseph and the mention of the "other brother" in S. 12:59 (see *QS* 134, *SM* 24–25), parallel to the biblical account in Genesis 42:3–13; knowledge of this latter story is assumed on the part of the Qur'ānic audience, for within the Qur'ān no previous mention has been made of Benjamin and his being left at home due to Jacob's fears for his safety. Joseph's statement in the Qur'ān, "Bring me a brother of yours from your father," comes out of nowhere within the context of the Qur'ān, although not if one comes first with a knowledge of the biblical story. The second example is one which deals with Abraham's willingness to sacrifice his son and the removal within the Qur'ān of the dramatic impact contained in the biblical story, where the son does not know that he is the one to be offered (see *SM* 24). The question is far more complex because the Jewish exegetical tradition may play a role here; the study of Geza Vermes[35] makes it clear that many Jewish (and Christian) traditions adjust the story to let Isaac know he is to be sacrificed well before the actual event in order to emphasize the willingness of Isaac to offer himself. The Jewish exegetical tradition is referential as well; it already assumes that the basic story of the sacrifice is clear to its audience and that the significance of Abraham in the story will be evident to all who read the Bible; thus, the emphasis is on Isaac but certainly not to the exclusion of the role of Abraham. The position of the Qur'ān is similar. The knowledge of the biblical story is assumed; reference is made to developed traditions concerning the sacrifice. The referential character of the Qur'ān should make clear the insufficiency of an approach to the Qur'ān which looks at the so-called "exclusively Arabian" (whatever that may be!) character of the book and tries to ignore the total Judeo-Christian background.[36]

The notion of the referential style of the Qur'ān also leads Wansbrough to the supposition that what we are dealing with in Islam is a sectarian movement fully within the Judeo-Christian "Sectarian Milieu" (*QS* 20, also *SM* 45). The parallels between Qur'ānic and Qumranic literature, while not necessarily displaying an interdependency, *do* demonstrate a similar process of biblical-textual elaboration and adaptation to sectarian purposes.[37] The inner workings of the sectarian milieu are to be seen in both literary traditions.

The Qur'ān as a document, according to Wansbrough, then, is composed of such referential passages developed within the framework of Judeo-Christian sectarian polemics, put together by means of literary convention (for example, the use of *qul* ["say"] (*QS* 12 ff., also 47–48), narrative conventions (*QS* 18 ff.), and the conjunction of parallel versions of stories called by Wansbrough "variant traditions" (*QS* 20 ff.), which were perhaps produced from a single original tradition by means of variation through oral transmission within the context of liturgical usage (*QS* 27). Here, clearly enough, a variety of individual methods (e.g., form analysis, oral formulaic analysis) which have been worked out in fields outside Islam, primarily the Bible, are used by Wansbrough in his analysis of the nature of the Muslim scripture.

Significantly, Wansbrough's analysis reveals that the Qur'ān is not merely "a calque of earlier fixed forms" (*QS* 33), that is, it does not merely seek to reproduce the Bible in Arabic, adapted to Arabia. For one thing, the Qur'ān does not follow the fulfillment motif set as a precedent by the New Testament and its use of the Hebrew Bible. Rather, and, indeed, because of the situation of polemic from which the Qur'ān derives, there is a clear attempt made to separate the Qur'ān from the Mosaic revelation through such means as the mode of the revelation and the emphasis on the Arabian language of the Qur'ān.

Canonization and stabilization of the text of the Qur'ān goes hand in hand with the formation of the community, according to Wansbrough (*QS* 51). A final, fixed text of the scripture was not required, nor was it totally feasible, before political power was firmly controlled; thus the end of the second/eighth century becomes a likely historical moment for the gathering together of oral tradition and liturgical elements leading to the emergence of the fixed canon of scripture and the emergence of the actual concept, "Islam."[38] This time period, Wansbrough several times points out, coincides with the recorded rise of literary Arabic.[39] Further evidence for this position is derived in *QS* from a "typological analysis" of *tafsīr* (see *QS* 44 and ch. 4). The basic inspiration and thrust of Wansbrough's approach may once again perhaps be traced to modern biblical studies; such people as Geza Vermes and Raphael Loewe have been drawing attention to the need to stop plundering exegetical works, Greek and Aramaic translations of the Bible, and so forth, in order to find support, somewhere, for one's own argument. Rather, they suggest, such works must be studied as a whole with attention given to the historical context of their writing and to their literary context.[40] The analysis of Qur'ānic *tafsīr* literature into five genres—haggadic, halakhic, masoretic, rhetorical, and allegorical—once again sets the basic insight. The genres display an approximate chronological development in the above sequence and display a historically growing concern with the textual integrity of scripture and then with the community function of scripture.[41]

The *sīra*, while partly exegetical as Wansbrough explains in *QS*, has a much greater role in Islam: it is the narrative witness to the Islamic version of salvation history. Most significant here is Wansbrough's analysis (*SM* ch. 1) of much of the contents of the *sīra* into elaborations of twenty-three polemical motifs traditional to the Near Eastern sectarian milieu—items such as the prognosis of Muḥammad in Jewish scripture, the Jewish rejection of that prognosis, the role of Abraham and Jesus in sectarian soteriology, and resurrection. All these themes are elaborated within a narrative framework set in seventh-century Arabia but yet all are themes that had been argued so many times before among sectarian groups in the Near East. The analysis of the *sīra* underlines Wansbrough's main contention in both of his books that "by its own express testimony, the Islamic kerygma [is] an articulation . . . of the Biblical dispensation, and can only thus be assessed" (*SM* 45).

It will be clear to any attentive reader of *QS* and *SM* that Wansbrough's work still leaves much to be done with the basic data in order to work out fully the implications of his kind of study. Close and detailed analyses of the many texts involved are still needed in order to demonstrate and, indeed, to assess the validity of his approach. What Wansbrough has accomplished, it seems to me, is to point to a new direction that Islamic studies could take in order to revitalize itself; Wansbrough has marked a path in broad outlines, but the road must still be cleared.[42]

Several reviewers have seized upon (and, indeed, Wansbrough himself has emphasized the point)[43] various statements in *QS* with regard to methods determining one's results. I. J. Boullata, in his review of *QS*, put the matter this way: "To quote him from page 91 'Results are, after all, as much conditioned by method as by material.' If this is true and his material is given credence in spite of its selectivity, there remains a big question about his method and the extent to which it conditioned his results."[44] Fazlur Rahman in his book *Major Themes of the Qur'ān* makes a similar point about method.

> My disagreements with Wansbrough are so numerous that they are probably best understood only by reading both this book and his. (I do, however, concur with at least one of his points: "The kind of analysis undertaken will in no small measure determine the results!" [p. 21]) I do believe that this kind of study [i.e., the comparison with Judaism and/or Christianity] can be enormously useful, though we have to return to Geiger and Hirschfeld [! not Speyer?!] to see just how useful it can be when done properly.[45]

What does Rahman mean here concerning method? Does he mean to imply: Well, Wansbrough has a method and that has been his downfall; I have no method so I have imposed nothing upon the material? I doubt that Rahman wants to urge methodological naiveté. More likely, perhaps, Rahman means: Wansbrough has his method and I have mine, but mine is right. That the methods which Rahman (and virtually every other student in the field) imposes upon his study happen to be, for the most part, the traditional theologico-historical methods is a fact that needs to be recognized, just as does the fact that Wansbrough imposes literary methods. If the study of Islam is to remain a scholarly endeavor and retain some sense of intellectual integrity, then it must, first, become methodologically aware and, second, be prepared to consider the validity of other methods of approach to the subject. This means that Islamic studies must differentiate between the truth claims of the religion itself and the intellectual claims of various methods, for ultimate "truth" is not susceptible to methodological procedures. To remain within the search for the "true" meaning of Islam and not to be prepared to free oneself from, for example, the priority of history[46] within the study of Islam, will surely sound the death-knell for a potentially vital and vibrant endeavor of human intellectual activity.

10

Towards a Hermeneutic of Qur'ānic and Other Narratives in Isma'ili Thought

AZIM NANJI

Studies of the Shi'a Isma'ili have gone through several stages within the study of Islam as a whole. Since the bulk of early Western scholarship depended primarily on non-Isma'ili sources—sources which for the most part were hostile to the movement—they inherited the biases already present in such accounts. In this initial stage, the particular Islamic visions reflected in Shi'i and Isma'ili texts came either to be neglected or considered as being on the periphery of the Sunni interpretations which were accepted as representing normative Islam. The late Marshall Hodgson among others has traced this process particularly as it applies to the study of Shi'ism in general.[1]

In its second stage, Isma'ili studies faced another problem, a sort of variation on the methodological issues inherent in the previous stage. Here, scholars of the esoteric traditions of Islam, including Isma'ilism, came to regard such traditions as embodying the real heart of Islam. Perhaps the best example of this approach was the great French scholar of Shi'i Islam, the late Henry Corbin. In Chapter 8 above, Charles Adams analyzes Corbin's assumptions and their implications for the study of Islam. Vladimir A. Ivanow, who with Corbin and Hodgson must surely rank among those pioneers of Western scholarship who have done much to advance Shiʿi Ismaʿili studies, reflected, in contrast, a discomfort with "esoteric" elements, and he often discarded or adjusted such data to fit what was for him "classical" Ismaʿilism.[2]

When we consider the fact that more recent scholarship has tended to go beyond the prejudices and assumptions of the two stages mentioned above, then one can hope that we are entering a third stage in Ismaʿili Studies. In this new stage historians of religion dealing with Islam can begin to study and take account of Ismaʿilism utilizing research tools and scholarly perspectives that are applied within the study of religions as a whole.

Among the better known doctrinal principles associated with Shiʿite Ismaʿili thought is the concept of *ta'wīl*. Primarily a tool applied specifically to the exegesis of the Qur'ān, ta'wil has by extension also come to signify the hermeneutical basis of analysis for most esoteric thought in Ismaʿili writings. Such a notion of ta'wil has come to be applied in traditional Ismaʿili thought to Qur'ānic narratives, and it establishes a framework for an understanding of Ismaʿili cosmology, the main features of which are by now well known to most students of Ismaʿilism. In addition, over the period of its intellectual history Ismaʿili thinkers have also extended the principles of anagogic hermeneutics to include narrative material. Such narrative material as that of cosmology has its roots in Qur'ānic accounts of the Creation and of the various prophets.

This essay is an attempt to develop a basis for understanding Ismaʿili hermeneutics around two types of narratives. First, it will consider the foundational Qur'ānic narratives related to Adam, and it will establish a framework for relating cosmological and symbolic motifs within those accounts. Second, it will focus on several selected narratives from the Ginan tradition in Nizari Ismaʿili literature and develop a framework for analyzing them.

Literary Theory and Ta'wil

It is clear that what we have called ta'wil is essentially a tool for analysis. By relating such a tool to developing methodologies in the area of literary and structural analysis, it is hoped that this essay can help move current discussions toward a definition of an Ismaʿili hermeneutic. Current literary theory, as with other fields of inquiry, has many divergent schools. Among these schools two broad positions can be identified. One supports a more formalist, text-oriented approach while the other espouses a more reader-oriented one. For the former, the text and not the context constitutes a relevant object of study whereas the latter chooses to emphasize the element of the text "received" contextually by the readers. Within these two perspectives there are obviously several subsystems.[3]

What is of interest to the student of Muslim anagogic literature is the relevance of a tool such as ta'wil in providing a means of literary analysis that can do justice to the text with respect to the assumptions of its creator, as well as help us to refine our methods of literary criticism in the field, so that we can show that in the understanding of the texts it is necessary to go beyond a mere formal analysis. It is perhaps in this context that ta'wil may best be rendered as "hermeneutic interpretation" where the word hermeneutic does not simply mean "related to the art of interpretation" but carries a far more extensive connotation of increasing certitude about, rather than mere knowledge of, the text.

Jean Pépin in analyzing the original Greek word *hermēneuein* came to the conclusion that

> as used generally the word has come to signify 'interpretation' and that hermeneutics today commonly has as its synonym 'exegesis'. However, the original meaning of *hermeneuein* and of related words—or, in any case their principal meaning—was not that at all, and was not far from being its exact contrary, if we grant that exegesis is a movement of penetration into the intention of a text or message.[4]

In the above context the word ta'wil—to go back to the first or original meaning—can then be said to designate a similar interpretive function. The goal of ta'wil as set forth in Ismaʿili writings is to enable the reader to penetrate beyond the formal literal meaning of the text and to create in the reader a sense of certitude regarding the ultimate relevance and meaning of a given passage in the Qur'ān or in other sacred texts.

Ta'wil and the Qur'ānic Narrative of Creation

The overall thrust and methodology of Ismaʿili interpretation is best set out by Nasir-i-Khusraw, the eleventh-century Ismaʿili philosopher who explained the nature of revelation, and by inference, religion.[5] Scripture has two parts, *tanzīl* and *ta'wīl*, which are reflected in the Haqiqa (*ḥaqīqa*), where the Shariʿa is like a symbol (*mithal*) and the

Haqiqa is that which is symbolized (*mamthūl*). The *sharʿi* aspect has changed during the various cycles of history; the *ḥaqīqī* aspect consists of eternal divine virtues that are not subject to change. In Nasir-i-Khusraw's understanding then, the tanzil defines the letter of the Revelation embodied in a "coming down" of the values of the Shariʿa and is therefore amenable to the type of exegesis defined as "ta'wil," which has the sense of returning to the origin, that is, of going back to the original meaning or sense of revelation. More specifically, ta'wil aims at reaching the interior (*bāṭin*) beneath the exterior (*ẓāhir*), both representing the dual aspects of scripture as well as of religion. Qāḍī al-Nuʿmān, the famous Fatimid jurist and writer of the tenth century, wrote the classic juristic formulation of the Ismaʿili understanding of Islam in a work called *Daʿā'im al-islām*, in which he wrote in detail about the Shariʿa. Then, however, he wrote a complementary work entitled *Ta'wīl al-daʿā'im* where the interior aspect of the previous work is discussed.[6] This duality of exterior/interior meanings is reflected in most of the writings of the Fatimid period and in fact the two works cited above reflect two different but complementary genres of literature that developed among the Ismaʿilis: the Haqa'iq literature, whose main concern was with ta'wil, and other forms such as those on Shariʿa, whose primary thrust was in the areas of law and history.

The background of the concepts with which I have chosen to illustrate the Ismaʿili interpretation of scripture is their understanding of the doctrine of Creation. More specifically, I will discuss briefly the interpretation by al-Mu'ayyad fī-al-Dīn al-Shīrāzī, the eleventh-century Ismaʿili thinker, of the Qur'ānic verse: "God created the Heavens and the Earth in six days" (S. 7:54).[7]

Al-Shīrāzī starts by demonstrating somewhat pointedly that the reference to "days" has nothing to do with the conception of a day measured by the rising and setting of the sun; since there was no sun before creation, it would be ridiculous to suppose such a measure of time in relation to God's creative power. He then refers to other Qur'ānic references where God is said to create things faster than the twinkling of an eye, and so on, and he concludes that the reference to heaven and earth, and to days, has, in reality, nothing to do with the heaven, earth, and days as we conceive of them. The ta'wil of the verse according to al-Shīrāzī reveals that the reference to "six days" connotes the six cycles of prophecy, each of which reflect a time cycle. These prophets or *nuṯaqā'* are Adam, Nūḥ (Noah), Ibrāhīm (Abraham), Mūsā (Moses), ʿIsā (Jesus), and the Prophet Muḥammad. The mission (*daʿwa*) of each of these six prophets is referred to at the completion of God's Creation and in the Qur'ānic verse, "Today I have perfected your religion for you and called it Islam" (S. 5:4), which refers to the fulfillment or consummation of this creative process embodied in the mission of the six prophets.

Such an interpretation of Creation implies a sense of "history," but more so of the "sacred" nature of such a history, which reveals the development of prophetic cycles, each of whose prophets provides a Shariʿa, a pattern of life revealed to those who are living, leading to the ultimate goal, which, of course, in the Qur'ān is the salvation of humankind. This concept of salvation history is linked to the concept of God communicating with his creatures through the prophets and books. In the Ismaʿili conception this is extended to include in history the successors of the prophets—the Imams, whose function it is to explain the inner meaning of the Shariʿa and lead the believers to the Haqa'iq (and who, of course, among the Shiʿa are "those firmly rooted in knowledge (*rāsikhūn fī l-ʿilm*)," referred to in the Qur'ān, S. 3:7.

Such a cyclical concept of history patterned in cosmic frameworks of time is linked to the notion of human destiny. The Qur'ānic account of the "Fall of Adam" illustrates best this linkage in Ismaʿili writings, and helps situate "history" within a larger cosmological framework.[8] The ta'wil of the account of Adam in the Garden, his Temptation by Iblis, and his subsequent Fall are all interpreted on a cosmic plane, that is to say, as taking place in a preexisting nonmaterial world which is called *ʿĀlam al-ibdāʿ*. Adam is called the "spiritual Adam" *Ādam rūḥānī*. Within this preexisting universe of *ibdāʿ*, there were seven "Intelligences" or *ʿuqūl*. Adam was of the order of the Third Intelligence after what in Ismaʿili thought are generally referred to as *al-ʿaql al-awwal* (the First Intelligence) and *al-ʿaql al-thānī* (the Second Intelligence). The good aspect of the Tree which he was not to approach is *al-ʿaql al-awwal*. Adam's fallen angel or Iblis is his own refusal to accept his divinely appointed status, and this caused him to commit the sin of being ambitious in wanting to attain equality of rank with those above him. The expulsion of Adam from the Garden denotes the loss of his rank and preeminence over other Intelligences below him. Adam, in fact, became (that is, he fell or descended to the level of) the Tenth Intelligence. It is by returning through the Intelligences above him that Adam can, in the sense that he symbolizes all humankind, recover his original status. It is for this reason that the *ʿĀlam al-ibdāʿ*

has as its correspondence a series of figures embodied in the "hierarchy of faith" (*ḥudūd al-dīn*) here on earth. Collectively, they stand for the da'wa with each representing a step in an ascending process. The Prophet Muḥammad is at the head of this Hudud, and by extension he is the *mithal* or representation of al-'Aql al-Awwal. 'Ali, the Imams after 'Ali, and the representatives of the Imams who conduct their individual da'was, all constitute the other steps in the process. For Adam, as the symbol of humankind, such a hierarchy represents the path he would have to traverse (the ladder he would have to climb), in order to reach the First Intelligence. Such a return would represent the potential goal he could attain, through which he could recognize the principle of divine cosmic unity (*tawḥīd*).

The mode of exposition reflected in these writings has come to be regarded as a product of the "classical" period of Isma'ili thought, and by extension, as "normative" within the Isma'ili tradition. Such an attitude led to a sorry neglect of other literary traditions in Isma'ilism, particularly those that might be considered "popular" in the sense of being deviations from normative doctrines. It is such traditions, however, that help us to understand more clearly how continuities within esoteric modes are sustained and how such modes mirror variations within the exegetical processes of the tradition. The narrative material that I have chosen to illustrate these same cosmological concepts is contained in the *ginān*s preserved among the Nizari Isma'ilis of the Indo-Pakistani Subcontinent.[9]

Ginan Narratives on Creation

The Ginans belong to a literary category which is generally defined as "anagogic," that is to say, "mystical or esoteric in its broadest sense." Like the Haqa'iq literature of classical Isma'ilism, the Ginans thrive on the use of ta'wil aiming to penetrate the inner (*bāṭin*) signification of the Qur'ān rather than the external (*ẓāhir*) aspects. On this basis the Ginans comprise a whole system of hermeneutics, metamorphosing positive religion with its external rules and obligations into a theosophy which constitutes the *satpanth* or "True Religion," leading the adept through a process of intellectual and spiritual initiation to the truth of the Haqa'iq.

The literary approach most suited to analyzing the Ginans is that of themal analysis. Such themal description helps to focus on the intent of the Ginans and allows for an analysis of the mode of transformation by which the Ginans have transposed focal Ismaʿili themes within a new framework. Lévi-Strauss, in reference to mythologically oriented thought, compares this symbolic transposition to what he defines as "intellectual bricolage."[10] At the bottom of his argument lies the conviction that the heterogeneous repertoire of this type of thought uses images and signs to lead to concepts that are being continually reconstructed. For the analysis of the Ginans in the context of Ismaʿili literature such a theory implies that both structuralism and hermeneutics may be helpful in deepening our understanding of Ismaʿili texts. First, this approach prevents us from regarding such texts as fixed entities that merely follow an established structure. Rather, within Ismaʿili literature, the structure of ta'wil interpretation reflects a constant reworking and rearrangement of focal themes. Within such a reworking we may discern a fusion of symbols or themes. Because the Ginans belong to the category of esoteric literature, the themes do not appear as literal statements. Rather, they appear in a mythical state or are couched in symbolism. Hence, the aim is to synthesize the import behind these symbols, and in the final stages of synthesis to describe the interrelationship between the main themes, the ways they interact, and the processes by which such standard Ismaʿili themes are evolved in the Ginans. Such an approach by no means exhausts the possibilities of further textual and themal analysis, but it does suggest ways in which the more formal and structuralist approaches may add new dimensions of understanding to the hermeneutic approach denoted by "ta'wil." It can only offer for the time being a partial view—a perspective for understanding the import of the Ginans.

The Ginans also contain as a major theme narratives on Creation.[11] The initial act of Creation results, as told in these narratives, from a desire, an act of self-contemplation by the Divine Being who is described as having the quality of *nirakar* (i.e., he is "formless"). A foam-like substance emerged from his mouth and took the form of an egg. Through additional acts of contemplation on this egg, the Divine Being created the ten heavens and the seven skies. This was followed by a long period of inactivity, a lull of many *yugas*, after which the Divine Being created out of his light four forms. He, too, took a form, thus bringing into existence a pentad: Muḥammad, Faṭima, Ḥasan, Ḥusayn, and ʿAli. This is, of course, the Shiʿi doctrine of the *panj-tan-i-pāk*, "the Five Companions of the Mantle."[12] The Ginans make no attempt to elaborate a systematic theory of Creation. All the same this does not mean that there is indiscriminate and chaotic integration of elements from Hinduism. This is rather a selection of ideas and symbols which are, however, presented in mythical form. This mythopoeic mode of explanation in the Ginans can best be described as inspirational rather than expository.

Returning to the cosmogonic outline elaborated in the Ginans, we find that one of the Hindu concepts integrated into this framework is that of an initial, remote, and transcendent Supreme Being. The Supreme Being is not identical, however, with any of his creations. The symbol of the foamlike substance emerging out of the mouth of the "formless" being is significant and echoes, however remotely, the verbal Qur'ānic command (*amr* or *kalima*) by which in previous Isma'ili doctrine God brings into being his Creation. Another factor of great significance is the image of light (*nūr*) out of which the five preeternal figures of the *panj-tan-i-pāk*, are created. The concept of light does not play as important a role in Hindu cosmogony, though it is not entirely unknown there as a progenitive cosmic power. In the Ginans, however, the image of light takes on central importance because the pentad is, in fact, seen as emerging from this one Light and this constitutes, in essence, a Unity. Having established the primacy of these given preeternal forms in the cosmogony, the Ginans continue the dramaturgy to elaborate the epiphanic representations of this pentad to include also the gods of Hindu theogony.

After the creation of the pentad there elapses again, according to the Ginans, a long period of inactivity. But after that, in a series of creations, the five preeternal forms become metamorphosed. Out of the form of Muḥammad, issues the epiphany of Brahmā. The Divine Being already personified in the epiphany of 'Ali takes the form of Vishnu. Ḥasan (whom the Ginans also make homologous with Adam), takes the form of Maheśvara, that is, Śiva. Faṭima is made analogous with Śakti and also Sarasvati who in Hindu tradition was often considered the daughter of Brahmā. Brahmā, Vishnu, and Śiva form a well-known triad in Hinduism called the *trimurti;* their roles are described as those of Creator, Sustainer, and Destroyer, respectively. The notion of *trimurti* has also been interpreted to represent a concept of three images reflecting the same essence.[13] The integration of Hindu symbols into the cosmogony of the Ginans, elaborated above, reveals a pattern which could be reconciled with the basic Isma'ili concepts. The chief concept here is of a Supreme Being who transcends his Creation and yet is able to bring all of Creation into existence through the creation of preeternal cosmic principles. The principles in the Fatimid and Nizari works were made to correspond with Muḥammad, ʿAli, and the Imams, all playing key roles as the earthly epiphanies of the highest cosmic principles. The mode of mythopoesis inherent in the Ginans transposes the earlier schemes, but retains the epiphanies of the Hindu theogony.

When we consider the cosmogony in the Ginans as the background for the development of the doctrine of *Dasa Avatāra*, that is, the "ten descents,"[14] we see a much clearer instance of symbols fused in the narrative. The "Universe of the Intelligences" in the earlier Ismaʿili schemes had as its manifestations the prophets and their *wāṣīs* (executors). In the post-*Qiyāma* (resurrection) doctrine of Nizari Ismaʿilism these *wāṣīs* had reached the fullness of their potential roles by becoming the Imam-Qa'im figures. In the Ginans there is evident a similar dimension, only it is the ten avataras of Vishnu, the representation of the preeternal ʿAli, who are considered the most significant manifestations during the period of the Four Yugas. As the tenth avatara, the historical ʿAli and, after him, the Imams become these manifestations on earth.

By the inclusion of names from both Hindu and Ismaʿili traditions, a chain of figures was established that ties together the two traditions in a combination that accentuated the timeless and ageless nature of the doctrine of the remote and supreme divinity manifesting himself to all human beings at all times. As an interesting postscript to the theme of divine manifestation, the Ginans refer to the "four revealed books" of the Islamic tradition and make them analogous to the four Vedas, the primary scriptures of Hinduism. All the various chords, however, merge and center upon the single feature of the "Imam of the Age."

The ta'wil of the Qur'ānic story of Creation and the analysis of the Ginan narratives are rooted in two essentially Islamic themes—a cosmos mirroring "Unity" and a sacred history reflecting the working out of divine purpose and human destiny. Although the materials from Ismaʿili literature discussed in this chapter include the philosophical and poetical genres, underlying both strains is a common hermeneutical trait. One effect of this common trait is that we are reminded to distinguish constantly between symbols employed in poetical and philosophical discourse and to be aware of a constant restructuring and metamorphosis of these symbols.

A final question might be raised as to whether or not the methods of literary analysis and their relationship to ta'wil do indeed deepen our understanding of such texts. More properly, the question ought to be put somewhat differently—do ta'wil and the mode of hermeneutical analysis lead us to those elements in the text that not only increase our knowledge about the subject, but create a sense of certitude about what is worth knowing in these texts? There are no simple answers to such questions but textual analysis, at least in the case of Isma'ili Haqa'iq literature, should not be merely descriptive. Such writings are meant to engage the readers in an experience in which they, in responding to the texts, do not merely recreate an established, given meaning, but rather embark on a quest in which they are called upon to create and to verify a meaning within themselves. In some of the Ginans and in the ta'wil of Qur'ānic verses, such a quest culminates in the experience within the human self of the Light (*nūr*), the prime Qur'ānic and Ginanic symbol of divine unity and knowledge. The point of this essay is that to understand this experience better, the application of structuralist and other types of literary analysis can lead to more productive results.

Part Five

Challenge and Criticism

The conduct of academic studies of religion in the company of persons belonging to religious communities is a contemporary fact of life which is nowhere more troubled than in the case of Islam. The American Academy of Religion and the Society of Biblical Literature are not innocent of the problems that attend the critical study of Judeo-Christian beliefs, practices, and sacred texts. Yet, the problem of the nonconfessional academy versus the seminary or yeshiva pales in comparison to the experiences of Western and Muslim scholars who prescribe how to interpret and understand Islam. The issue is often exacerbated by frustration on both sides, leading to conferences and literary efforts where each side prefers to speak *to* the other rather than to speak one *with* the other in a mood of mutual trust and cooperation in search of common truths.

Part Five concludes the present volume with two essays by Muslim scholars who, in quite different ways, have had a considerable impact on the academic study of Islam in North America and on the final result of this book. In Chapter 11, Muhammad Abdul-Rauf seeks to establish some bridges between Muslim and non-Muslim students of Islam by offering irenic remarks about the value of some Western linguistic and historical studies of Islamic materials. He finds much else in Western Islamic studies to be prejudicial and harmful, however. Most significantly, perhaps, he establishes boundaries around the Qur'ān and Sunna of the Prophet. These are for him—as indeed for many Muslims—matters upon which he is unwilling to agree to disagree even in scholarly realms of discourse. Such boundaries obviously place serious qualifications on the academic study of Islam as religion; this is indicated by the attempt of virtually every contributing author in this volume to address Abdul-Rauf's concerns in one way or another.

In Chapter 12, Fazlur Rahman conducts a limited review of the volume as a whole. He analyzes several of the issues raised by Abdul-Rauf and others—particularly the boundaries raised when the insider/outsider dichotomy is hailed—arguing that all sides fail to clarify the real issues. Rahman's use of philosopher John Wisdom's reflections on what we can claim to know of "other minds" illuminates the logical nature of the difficulties that arise when Muslims and non-Muslims attempt to talk about the Muslim religious experience. Rahman holds that an outsider's report about an insider's report of his own religious experience can be just as valid as the insider's report. Whether or not Rahman's approach to the problem can be applied to the problem of *interpreting* what insiders say and do remains to be tested, but his attempt to clarify the problem is surely helpful and welcome. Rahman's sharpest critique is leveled at Andrew Rippin's discussion in Chapter 9 above of the methodologies of John Wansbrough. Indeed, Chapters 9 and 12 constitute an interesting and important debate at the heart of the academic study of religion more nearly than the insider/outsider issue.

The authors in Part Five find unanimity with other authors in the volume on the point that prejudice against Islam is counterproductive and sympathy or empathy toward Islam is productive if not essential to sound scholarship. Probably most historians of religion and Islamicists would agree on the point that "sympathy for" is better than "prejudice against," although both attitudes of mind are forms of bias that can lead to distortions. The present near consensus that Western orientalism has not been without anti-Muslim biases may warrant making special attempts to avoid further negative biases. Sympathy and empathy are still forms of bias, however, though at times helpful ones and at times, perhaps, like prejudice, distorting ones. Much more needs to be said about this as a methodological issue by those who insist upon it in the pursuit of the academic study of religion.

11

Outsiders' Interpretations of Islam

A Muslim's Point of View

MUHAMMAD ABDUL-RAUF

The purpose of this essay is to present a Muslim perspective on the relation of the Islamic faith to the scholarly disciplines that study it. Since historians of religions who write about Islam have gleaned their information mainly from Western experts in "Islamic studies," the focus of this paper will be on Islamic studies as such. The essence of the problem that needs airing is: Does the term "Islamic studies" designate an intellectual pursuit discovered and maintained only by Western scholars? This view, common though it seems to be in the West, ignores the study of Islam by Muslims themselves since the rise of Islam. Is the Western study of Islam, then, intrinsically misguided and harmful? This, too, is an attitude that is blind to obvious achievements, many by non-Muslims. Wherein lie the problems many Muslims experience with "Islamic studies?" The following anecdote illustrates a point that needs to be made.

On December 7, 1979, *Al-Ahram*, the leading daily Egyptian newspaper, carried an interesting story by a renowned contemporary writer. The writer told of his late friend, Salah Saljuke—former Afghani Ambassador to Cairo and an accomplished scholar and authority on Sufism—who about twenty years prior had paid him a visit one day and had looked very disturbed. "Saljuke told me," the author related, "to rise up and struggle to prevent a great disaster! America and Russia have now joined hands, this time to undermine al-Azhar University. The Representative of the Soviet Union and the American Ambassador have counseled our President (of Egypt) to modernize al-Azhar and make it more relevant to modern times."

Moved by this appeal, the writer told his readers that he sent a letter to Egypt's President, warning of the disastrous consequences of such a step. He also wrote letters to all the newspapers criticizing the idea of "modernizing" the Muslim world's center of religious and intellectual training. He reminded the President and the media of the great prestige of al-Azhar and its fundamental mission especially to preserve the Qur'ān and the religious and traditional sciences.

The writer received no response to his appeal, however, and none of his letters were published. Meanwhile, he learned from the press that a committee formed by official decree to reform al-Azhar was chaired by an acquaintance of his, the president of Cairo University, whose departure to Spain as Egypt's ambassador had been announced a day earlier. The press report stated that while he was chairman the committee had decided it was time to transform al-Azhar University into a modern university that would include schools of agriculture, medicine, business, and engineering. It was only when the ambassador had returned from Spain that the writer learned from him, contrary to the earlier media announcement, that the committee had rejected the proposed reforms. The ambassador added that the chancellor of al-Azhar, in a poignant moment during the committee meetings, broke down in tears because he greatly feared the harm that would come to al-Azhar and to Islam as a result of the proposed reforms.

Before commenting on this story, let us go back to the time of our Prophet, Muḥammad—God's blessings and peace be upon him—and trace the origins of that broad subject, Islamic studies.

The Origin and Growth of Islamic Studies in the Muslim World

During the Prophet's mission, his concern was to ignite men's souls with the torch of knowledge, and he discouraged his companions from certain kinds of speculation, most notably speculation on the essence of God and the unseen realities. Since the finite mind is unable to grasp the infinite, any attempt to operate beyond these limits can only lead to error.

As a result of the Prophet's mission, many questions were raised, and through means found in the Qur'ān and the Prophet's Sunna they were answered. The Prophet was the Guide. At his death, the momentum of his mission nonetheless continued to guide his companions, who collectively and individually maintained the glow of divine passion within their hearts and souls. After the passing of this first generation of Muslims, and with the development of Islamic civilization to include non-Arabic speaking peoples, new pressure began to weigh upon this growing society. An important goal was to help non-Arab peoples assimilate Islam into their lives without distorting it. Considering the fact that strong remnants of ancient and well-entrenched civilizations, such as the Persian and the Egyptian, were now encompassed by the Muslim polity, the assimilation of Islam was no mean task.

The organic unity of this growing Islamic civilization was fractured by an ordinance of fate. The question of the nature of the Islamic state and the issue of succession led to the cleavage between Muslims who thereafter identified themselves as either Sunni or Shiʿi. The painful experience attended by this cleavage led to another simultaneous separation of components within Islamic society, namely, the concentration of worldly concerns in the hands of those in pursuit of power politics and the concentration of spiritual concerns among those devoted passionately to the faith of Islam. This led to the rise of Sufism, many of whose proponents sought to differentiate themselves from established institutions.

With the growth of Islamic civilization, an educational system evolved that expressed the basic Islamic impulse of personal salvation. Since education is the means by which society safeguards and transmits its cherished values and heritage, the goal of education in Muslim lands was never divorced from a belief in God or from the basic elements of the Islamic faith. This is true in spite of different opinions about some peripheral aspects of the content of this belief. Significantly, until this time, a clear definition of "Islamic studies" per se did not exist, since the notion of an "Islamic versus a "non-Islamic" subject of study had not occured to early Muslim scholars. All divisions of knowledge were regarded as "Islamic."

ISLAMIC STUDIES EAST AND WEST

The awareness of Muslim versus non-Muslim subject matters was consciously at stake in the conflict between the Muslim East and the Christian West during the Middle Ages. As the Muslim lands declined in power and came under the colonial rule of the West in more recent centuries, two simultaneous concepts of Islamic studies emerged, one outside the Muslim world and one within. Most Western readers will be somewhat familiar with the works and criticisms Western Islamists have penned about Islam. They will be less familiar, perhaps, with the impact this has had upon Muslim scholars who have sought to maintain their own tradition according to sources, standards, and criteria derived from the Qur'ān and the Prophet's Sunna.

Western Islamic studies were given impetus by the need for the colonial powers to learn about and understand the people they ruled. As such, the complete heritage of Islamic culture, whether in the field of Islamic religion per se, or philosophy, or art, came under the one rubric of Western scholarship: "Islamic studies" (originally called "oriental studies"). It was promulgated by European scholars in European universities for European students.

Within the Islamic world, the colonial rulers established "secular" systems of education patterned after their own. As a result, the traditional Muslim educational systems came to be labeled "religious." Traditional Muslim academic centers became, in very short order, schools of "Islamic studies!"

With the eventual achievement of political independence, Muslim countries entered a transitional stage of working toward a political, economic, and social identity that would conform once again to their religious and cultural heritage. This is the state of development as of the 1980s. Although political independence was the first and easiest to achieve, economic and cultural independence have been less easy to effect. Western perceptions of an Islamic revolution all too often fasten on political rather than the internal economic, religious, and cultural dimensions of what I here refer to as a "transition."

The rapid increase in global communications is the result of unprecedented technological growth. More people today travel widely and come into contact with cultures that are quite different from their own. One result is that most of the technocrats of Muslim countries have been educated in the West. There was a time when the majority of them were infatuated with technology and with Western culture as a whole. As time passed, however, the "foreign" became less appealing, and this infatuation began to be replaced by cautious appreciation of technological rewards, with awareness of the drawbacks and, more importantly, the limitations.

Even in the West faith in science and technology as paths to human salvation appears to be on the decline. There is an increasing realization that values as much as material growth are a crucial aspect of the good and happy life. The search for bigger and better material standards of living only serves to heighten spiritual appetites. Recent discussions in psychology have pointed out the inadequacies of behavioristic and purely physiological theories of human nature. There is more to being human than we currently know. The growing hunger in the West for spiritual forms created a surge of interest in oriental philosophies and religions as possible avenues to personal fulfillment, if not personal salvation.

As the world continues to grow smaller there is growing pressure for all of us to try to live as one community of humankind. The pressure to become one is, in reality, a pressure exerted upon cultures and nations outside the big powers to conform to their ways of life. In reaction to this pressure Muslim intellectuals have sought to adapt what is valuable and necessary in the modern age to Islamic principles. This is *the* great challenge facing Muslim scholars today. We cannot yet claim that their attempts have succeeded. We can, however, affirm that with sincere attempts progress is being made. Examples include the creation of Islamic banks, whose express purpose, in keeping with Islamic law, is to obviate the need for fixed interest rates; resistance to the secularization of al-Azhar University, mentioned above; and the creation of the state of Pakistan. These are merely a few tangible examples, and by no means isolated ones, demonstrating three different fronts: economic, educational, and political. *The* challenge facing "Islamic studies" within the Muslim world, then, is to create and maintain viable *Islamic* systems to cope with current realities.

THE PROBLEMS WITH THE TWO BASES OF ISLAMIC STUDIES

To return to the story quoted at the beginning of this essay, it indicated the deeply felt Muslim desire to undo much of the 1961 Reform

Law of al-Azhar. This reflected concern on the part of many Muslims about the status and conditions of the Islamic schools in the Muslim world whose traditional scope has been the perpetuation of Islamic Studies *par excellence*. For example, instead of attempting intelligently and sensitively to bring al-Azhar into line with modern curricular needs in both method and content, the new law sought to change the age-old curriculum—highly venerated by Muslims throughout the ages—by adding technical curricula in medicine, agriculture, engineering, and business. The sacred center of learning would become secularized. Even worse, traditional requirements were to be rescinded and the traditional curriculum itself drastically amended. The former prerequisite for admission to the first level of preparatory classes—knowing the entire text of the Holy Qur'ān by heart (which provided pupils with ready sources of all Islamic knowledge)—was to be eliminated or reduced. This could only lead to immediate and serious compromise of Muslim academic standards. A complicating factor was that by introducing secular subjects into the curriculum, traditional textual and theological studies were in the same measure squeezed out.

Reform should have aimed at fostering independent thinking and critical reasoning rather than learning only by memory. There was room for reform by going back to classical texts as opposed to using the dull and colorless digests and the compendia culled from them in less creative times. Why continue to treat works and forms rather than content and substance? Reform might also have focused on the library with its precious volumes and thousands of manuscripts. Rather than allowing it to turn into a museum, which only serves to highlight the distance and antiquity of its holdings, the library could be so organized as to improve its reading facilities and encourage reader usage. Microfilming facilities could have been made available to scholars wanting copies of rare works and journals from all over the world on Islamic subjects added to collections of publications from the Muslim world. Departmental libraries could be similarly equipped. Students could be encouraged to acquaint themselves with the scholarship of non-Muslims, and taught how to approach these materials appreciatively yet with discrimination, so that horizons might be widened and stereotyped suspicions challenged. In short, the need for reform is not here disputed; the question is what reform should be sought and how it should be accomplished.

On the other side, Islamic studies in the West also needed to be examined. With inquisitive minds and speculative methods, Western savants were stimulated by their contacts with oriental cultures, looking beyond cultural phenomena to the social and historical forces behind them. The studies produced thus far have been less descriptive and analytical, more historical and conjectural. This has been especially true of works written about Islamic religion. Questions about the origins of Islam, the derivation of the Prophet's knowledge and ideas, the chronological order of Qur'ānic passages, the authenticity of Hadith, and other matters, became major topics of investigation. Yet much has been left to guesswork, and methods worked out far from the "field" have been conjured up to explain Islam. Socialists turned to Marxist interpretations, finding in the theory of class struggle a solution to questions about historical causes, and they ignored the possibility of Islam's originality. In western Europe and America, the roots of Islam have been presumed to reach down into the Judeo-Christian soil. The given truths accepted and upheld by all Muslims for the past fourteen centuries—the life of the Prophet, his Sunna, the text of the Holy Qur'ān, virtually the entire sacred content of the faith of Muslims—have been subjected to misguided critical analysis, sometimes ruthless and usually insensitive. The situation is further complicated by a legacy of unhappy past political experience and continuing cultural prejudices.

Interest in the study of Islam in Western institutions has not been without its salutary effects, however. It has indeed enriched the library on Islam in many respects, and it has posed a beneficial challenge to Muslim scholarship. Fairminded orientalists have been instrumental in exposing some of the achievements of Islamic civilization to Western society. And yet it is dangerous when, in the name of being scientific, the origins of Islam are explained as arising out of economic or other cultural phenomena. Whatever may be said about Islam in relation to the place and time in which it arose, its unique and well-testified claim upon its adherents cannot be explained away.

We have as historical fact that Muḥammad's contemporaries, after years of resistance, mockery, rejection, and oppression, accepted the Prophet's teachings as divinely given truths, by means of the compelling forces of the miracles he achieved under their own eyes. The roots of Islam, as of Judaism and Christianity, are divine revelation. How can we now come, fourteen centuries later, and pretend that

Muḥammad got it all from Jews or Christians? There is no substantial evidence of Jews or Christians living in Mecca where Muḥammad was born and spent the formative years of his life. He traveled to Syria twice on busy commercial trips, the last time being some fifteen years prior to his calling as Prophet. Even if he could have learned so much under these circumstances, why would he have waited so long to proclaim it? If his supposed teachers had the wisdom to enlighten Muḥammad earlier, why did they not come forth later when the fruits of their labors began to change the world around them? Muḥammad, who demonstrated abundant gratitude to all those with whom he had been involved in his early life, would surely not have concealed a sense of gratitude to any teacher he might have had. Could the inimitable noble text of the Holy Qur'ān be simply a trading of words and ideas from the Bible? Even Muḥammad's enemies, who refused to acknowledge God but who were endowed with a sense of stylistic appreciation, recognized that the Qur'ān was not the product of a human mind.

As for the life of the Prophet, why look so hard for presumed weaknesses of character and evidence of moral turpitude, ignoring relevant information about his wisdom and integrity? For example, up to the age of fifty-three, including twenty-five years of happy marriage, Muḥammad maintained a monogamous marriage to his first wife, Khadijah. Only after her death and after he had achieved a new social and political status following his invitation to help the citizens of Yathrib (later called Medina) attain civil order did he become polygamous. Why is it so difficult to see as reasonable the factors leading to his polygamy in this newly acquired status? What compels some to believe stories about Muḥammad's excessive sensuality in his later years? Again, when the Prophet decided to emigrate from Mecca, he hinted to his companions that they should precede him to Yathrib in order to avoid the certain wrath of the Quraysh once his own departure became known. Why must some "analysts" find in this a reason to impute to the Prophet mistrust of the pledge from Yathrib, or cowardly assurances that his Meccan followers would surround him in Yathrib?

Muslims of all generations have believed that the entire text of the Holy Qur'ān was revealed by God to the Prophet and transmitted to his contemporaries, the vast majority of whom entrusted it to memory *tout à fait* within the lifetime of the Prophet. It was also written down during his lifetime according to his wishes. Being the Word of God to man recited in prescribed diction and sounds, the Holy Qur'ān is inimitable and not subject to the limiting dimensions of space and time. The order of its verses in each of its 114 chapters, which are mutually and closely related, cannot be subjected to limits imposed by conceptions of finitude.

Even now, fourteen centuries later, serious attempts are still being made to advance accusations, often based on linguistic errors and inappropriate assumptions, claiming that some parts of the text of the Holy Qur'ān were added or altered as a result of a putative process of editing. Evidence for this is purely hypothetical. Why have certain orientalists wasted so many precious years of their lives trying to reorder the text of the Qur'ān chronologically under the assumption that a human hand played a role in the formation of the text? Such programs of research are not merely an offense to the consciences of millions of Muslims, but are also misleading and thus unworthy to be considered as scholarship. The pursuit of knowledge about the contexts and circumstances in which the various parts of the Qur'ān were revealed, a genre called "the occasions of revelation" (*asbāb al-nuzūl*), represents a well-known discipline among early Muslim scholars who were engaged in Qur'ānic exegesis and the legal sciences. These works present a "history" of revelation that stands in conformity with the life of the Prophet, not a *destructio* of the tradition.

I should like to close by restating my respect for the serious undertaking by many Western scholars who have helped us learn more about Islam. Through painstaking efforts many have made useful contributions to our knowledge without demeaning the substance of Muslim faith, the Prophet, or the meaning of the Qur'ān. Such scholars regard Muslims as a people in their own right, not as colonial subjects or objects of curiosity. The challenge now facing Islamic studies in the West, particularly in the United States, is to seek to become an effective bridge between the West and the Muslim world. Difficult questions must be faced. To what extent do Islamic scholars play a role in helping formulate United States foreign policy *vis à vis* Muslim nations? How could Western Islamicists serve to lessen rather than heighten misunderstandings about a part of the world that now affects the West so profoundly?

Within the Muslim world, Islam is very much a twentieth-century way of life. When our Prophet Muḥammad began preaching fourteen centuries ago, Islam was here to stay. In spite of the Sunni-Shiʿi division arising from early political differences (and not atypical of major religious traditions) Islam has remained intact. Within the Muslim world, it will remain so. As an academic discipline in our American universities, Islamic Studies is therefore by no means an irrelevant subject. This is all the more reason, then, to go about it accurately and sensitively.

12

Approaches to Islam in Religious Studies

Review Essay

FAZLUR RAHMAN

In this volume, many contributors have discussed methodological problems of various kinds in the study of the history of religions, as relevant particularly to Islam. Some also suggest approaches to the solution of methodological problems, or clarify their nature, notably Earle H. Waugh (Chapter 3) and Frederick Denny (Chapter 4). Some authors, notably Andrew Rippin (Chapter 9) and Marilyn Waldman (Chapter 6), recommend the application of particular methods to the study of Islam. My basic purpose in this brief review is not to consider all the important things said in this variegated and rich volume, but rather to address myself to certain issues raised by Abdul-Rauf's sensitive protest against the way many Western scholars of Islam have handled their subject and his contention that non-Muslims may study Islamic history, for example, if indeed they can study it with fairness, but that they may not study the nature and origins of Islam, for they can never truly understand it. My aim is to focus on the meaning of this contention in order to make it more precise; in doing so, I expect that certain conclusions will follow which may affect specific methods in the study of religions, notably, the historical, phenomenological, personalist, and so-called literary methods.

The problems of misunderstanding and misinterpretation are universal in all human experiences, including the natural sciences, where a scientist may misconceive or misinterpret his or her experiments. The corrigibility of wrong scientific results, however, is relatively easy in principle because of easy access to verification. This ease of data gathering and verification is basically facilitated by the fact that the object of study is not esoteric but public, and the subject of study is "unprejudiced" and open-minded, while the instruments are "trustworthy." Almost none of these conditions is available quite in this sense when we come to the study of human affairs. Leaving aside the question of instruments, here the subject is neither so unprejudiced nor the object so public. By "prejudiced" I do not necessarily mean consciously or willfully prejudiced, but rather preconditioned in a manner that is not conducive to the study of the object as it is. Yet it is a fact that many human affairs can be studied, if not absolutely correctly, certainly satisfactorily. A marriage may, in some respects, be an esoteric affair, yet it has an important public aspect that can be witnessed, compared, and contrasted, and brought under certain generalizations even if already existing generalizations have to be adjusted in order to apply them to a certain given case.

When we pass to the realm of religion, however, we are confronted with a phenomenon that consists in values, convictions, and feelings that involve the utmost depths of the human mind or, rather, the human psyche. Religions certainly have observable expressions and measurable vehicles or institutionalized manifestations, as Jacques Waardenburg has pointed out, but, as he has also said, it is precisely the meaning of these expressions, vehicles, and manifestations that is at issue.[1] Can an outsider understand their meaning adequately if not fully? Or must his or her attitude be, to an extent, empathetic or participatory? If participation is demanded the question must be asked whether or not all believers in or followers of a given religion, that is, all members of a given religious community, understand their religion adequately if not fully. If they do not, as I think it is fair to conclude, then in what sense is *their* attitude to their religion participatory in a meaningful way? Wilfred Cantwell Smith has suggested that a statement about a religion by an outsider would be correct (or adequate?) if the followers of that religion say 'yes' to it. This principle is excellent and will be discussed a little later to make its meaning more precise. But in the meantime we should take notice that especially among religions with well-defined orthodoxies or concrete traditional cores some followers continuously make statements that others—perhaps a majority—reject. Can such phenomena be treated only as family feuds? We should also note in this context that what many Muslims may have regarded as being of great importance to Islam in one period may differ from what they may have emphasized in an earlier or later period. Such historical differences are quite separate from regional differences within a broad and basic framework of belief and practice.

Insiders and Outsiders

In *Other Minds*, John Wisom argued that the owner of an experience has privileged access to his or her experience, which cannot be shared by any other person. When A says (truthfully), "I have a toothache," and when B then reports to C, "A has a toothache," B is obviously not sharing A's toothache. At least B, if he has previously suffered a toothache, can analogize on the basis of that experience and understand A's statement, and so also with C. But can we, on this account, go on to say that when A says (truthfully) "I have a toothache," and B says to C "A has a toothache," these two propositions do not have the same meaning? Wisdom rejects this conclusion absolutely, for the meaning of a proposition cannot be made relative to having or not having a certain experience. A's having a toothache is a fact that is universally true (or false) regardless of who states the case.[2]

The picture is not as simple as that, however. Facts, of course, are not private; their meanings are universal. That is why in the above example the fact of the experience of a toothache will be equally true even if A is not having a toothache at the time he asserts the proposition to B but had it in the past. In this case, there would appear to be hardly any difference between A's statement to B and B's report to C, particularly if B also had experienced a toothache in the past. Indeed, the meaning of this proposition would remain unchanged even if B never had a toothache in his lifetime. Having said this, however, we must go on to say that although the meaning of this proposition is universally true, this does not imply that the *understanding* of that meaning is also universal. That Muslims are monotheists and that Christians are trinitarians are universally known facts, but are they universally *understood?* Before answering, the statement just made needs to be amended; instead of saying Muslims are monotheists and Christians are trinitarians, one should say, "Muslims say they are monotheists," and "Christians say they are trinitarians." The distinction is important for reasons that will follow shortly with the discussion of the question of internal differentiation within religions.

For a meaning to be "understood," it has to become *meaningful to someone*, so that it ceases to be purely impersonal. Now, being "meaningful" can have more than one sense. In one sense something can be meaningful in an inimical way. In this sense, for example, Ṣalāḥ al-Dīn Ayyūbī and Richard the Lionhearted were highly "meaningful" to each other, and few would deny that they "understood" each other in some definite sense of the word. So, too, a fanatical Christian believer and his or her Muslim counterpart can "understand" each other. But this is obviously not the sense of understanding in the present context. Why? Because this kind of being meaningful is equivalent to "not understanding" in a real or more ultimate sense. Shall we say that real understanding comes about when, say, a non-Muslim shares, or identifies himself, however temporarily, with Muslim beliefs? This is what Jane Smith has asked non-Muslims to do.[3] Now, although it is a noble ideal to try to see things from another person's point of view, I am afraid that it must be admitted that this is impossible in the final analysis. The reason is that an observer of an experience would have to become the owner or at least the sharer of that experience, and we have already seen that this is not a legitimate demand. Further, an observer does not *need* to have an experience in order to make sense of propositions about it. The search must, therefore, be for some other sense of "understanding" and of "being meaningful to someone." In the case of the study of a religion such as Islam, it seems more appropriate to aspire to "intellectual understanding or appreciation," and it will be shown that this is possible both for Muslims and for non-Muslims to a degree that one can learn from the other.

The first condition for this understanding is that the investigating subject not be inimical to or prejudiced against the object of his or her study, in this case Islam, but rather be open-minded and, if possible, sympathetically attuned. Prejudice is not confined to religious or other emotional conditions. Intellectual prejudice may come in the form of preconceived notions or categories. Scholars trained in certain disciplines are specially liable to this kind of prejudice. Honesty is the sole remedy for this, that is, to admit that one's categories have broken down. Again, some ways of intellectually constructing reality are such that even when they are grossly inadequate the subject cannot often easily recognize those inadequacies. Historical reductionism is one such method when, for example, a scholar may attempt to "explain" Islam's genesis and even its nature with reference to Jewish, Christian, or other "influences."

Now, what Abdul-Rauf is protesting against is precisely this brazen-faced cultural superiority—whether in the form of religious prejudice, cultural prejudice, or some form of intellectual prejudice. Pre-nineteenth-century Western treatments of Islam suffered from the first while nineteenth- and early twentieth-century scholarship suffered particularly from the last two. And it was this cultural and intellectual superciliousness which the Turkish modernist Namik Kemal bitterly attacked in his *Refutation of Renan* and which in our own day has been dealt with analytically by Edward Said.[4] I think it is because of this that Wilfred Smith laid down the principle referred to above, namely, that for a statement to be valid about a religion it must be not only acceptable to outside scholars but also true or valid for those inside that religion. On the other hand, as we pointed out earlier, there are many statements made all the time by some insiders that are repudiated by other insiders. Indeed, there are many statements made about Islam by outsiders such as H. A. R. Gibb and Wilfred Smith which are rejected by many Muslims but which are regarded as highly meaningful by many other Muslims. In Chapter 5 of this volume William Roff, referring to Smith, rightly observes that it can be asked "how many—or how few—Muslims may in such circumstances constitute a court" when an outsider seeks insider approval of his or her statements about Islam. The present writer must acknowledge that he has learned a great deal about Islam from the insights of several Western scholars just as he has learned much and gained fundamental insights into Islam from his Muslim teachers, particularly his father. And about some of their own statements concerning Islam, Muslims themselves are sharply divided. What does this mean?

Before going further, let us emphasize that the kind of intellectual understanding being considered—given concern, sympathy, and lack of prejudice—is a sort of scientific knowledge. It is not a religious experience but a quasi-scientific (intellectual) knowledge of a religious experience, where the normativeness or authority of the experience vanishes, but something of its direct effect upon the experiencing subject (including the latter's report of it) can be preserved and made accessible to others. The experience as a living and integral whole, therefore, cannot be conveyed by a historian or social scientist; such scholars nonetheless can appreciate it intellectually and convey it so that it becomes a part of "scientific knowledge."

An interesting discussion of the insider/outsider question is to be found in Robert Merton's *Sociology of Science.*[5] Merton studies groups and their group-centered claims and ideologies; his approach is, therefore, that of a structural-ascriptive analyst. Now, groups and their cultures are amenable to this treatment but religious phenomena with universalist truth claims are not. In the present context, therefore, we must distinguish between the religious communities as bearers of religious cultures and the normative truths or transcendent aspects of religions, as in the case of Islam in this volume. Even when a social group claims normative quality for its "truth"—for example, the truth claim of Aryan science versus the falsehood of Jewish science made by the Nazis—this may sound like a religious truth claim, but it is not. That it is not is evidenced by the fact that it is dismissed as false or as dangerously stupid or as amusing—depending on who the respondent is—by all outsiders in a manner in which these latter cannot dismiss a religious claim of universal validity. This may be despite the fact that the group in question (the Nazis in this case) makes its claim with a fervor and sincerity of commitment that is not less than that of any Muslim or other religious person. Muslims do not claim a "Muslim" truth for Islam, but a transcendent, universal truth.

Indeed, that part of Islam which has become the property of Muslims and has become part of the culture of the Muslim community is precisely amenable to the structural-ascriptive analysis Merton is talking about. In this area, the experience of the Muslim community is something unique, non-transferable, and cumulative. It is cumulative because it is inherited and ongoing, and in this sense it cannot be shared by an outsider historian or social scientist; this is what Merton holds when he quotes Claude Lévi-Strauss to the effect that a historian or an ethnographer can generalize an experience *as experience.* I must repeat that an experience as an integral whole cannot be transferred but, through intellectual appreciation of it, the historian or social scientist can convey something of the immediate effect the experience had upon the subject or its significance for the subject. Not only that. When the historian or social scientist generalizes about the experience, he can also illuminate it by making comparisons, contrasts, and analyses in a way the insider cannot, unless the latter becomes a historian or social scientist. Both the insider and the outsider can learn from one another in this sense.

But surely to Islam there also belongs a transcendent aspect, an aspect which has not yet been appropriated and which is still an open book. The Muslim community may appropriate it in the future and make it part of its cumulative tradition; or anyone else may appropriate it if one cares to. Whether Muslims have an advantage over others because they are already committed to Islam, or others have an advantage over Muslims because the latter are limited by an already solidified tradition is an open and highly interesting question. In any case, however, it is in this respect that a genuine religion differs from group ideologies such as White truth or Black truth, and from the pseudo-religious group claim for such things as Aryan truth and Aryan science.

To return to the question posed above, while it is obviously the Muslims' task to propound Islam, Muslims and non-Muslims can certainly cooperate at the level of intellectual understanding. Such statements as grow out of this cooperation ought to be valid for both Muslims and non-Muslims. Further, in the face of disagreements within Islam, one cannot view this affair only from the perspective of the insider or the outsider. Given honesty, open-mindedness, and fairness of mind on the part of the outsider, the intra-Islamic differences may cut across outsider-insider differences at the intellectual level. The intra-Islamic differences are of various types. We have mentioned earlier that most of these are differences of time and place. There was a time when Sufism was unheard of in Islam. Then there was a time when Sufism arose and was generally opposed by the *'Ulamā'*. Then Sufism multiplied into various types and engulfed the entire body-social of Islam. Lastly, we witness a time when the attempt has been to reform and reinterpret Sufism, and it may well be in the process of transformation. Indeed, the differences of opinion within the "orthodox" community are such that no single voice can hope to carry the entire community with it. Then there are differences between regions where forms of Islam are colored by ecological conditions—some local conditions being not antagonistic to Islam while others are incompatible with it.

Although there will always be legitimate differences in interpretation, the spectacularly wild growth of interpretations is surely not all a product of Islam. Social scientists divide Islam into a "great tradition" and a "little tradition." We have just noted that the great tradition itself is not monolithic—quite apart from Shiʿi-Sunni differences. Further, the social scientist regards all manifestations in the name of Islam as genuine and valid manifestations of Islam. For one thing, throughout Islamic history, the "orthodoxification" of the little traditions has been going on, sometimes at a quicker pace than at others, and not the least rapid at the present in certain cases. This suggests that the distinction between great and little traditions is not a divinely ordained imperative. But secondly, and far more importantly, this phenomenon does call for a criterion-referent, that is to say, a normative Islam. Even the social scientists' distinction of a great and little tradition assumes such a normative criterion and cannot simply rest on literate/nonliterate distinctions. Witness the phenomenon of the Muslim philosophers—al-Fārābī and Ibn Sīnā—whose major theses in the realm of religion were virulently rejected by the Shariʿa orthodoxy but who nonetheless cannot be classed as members of a little tradition. This criterion, which must judge between the differences among Muslims and those among Muslims and non-Muslims as to what normative Islam at the intellectual level is, must remain the Qur'ān itself and the Prophet's definitive conduct. Among non-Muslims, primary thought is of the Islamicist scholar who deals with the great tradition. As for the social scientist, particularly the anthropologist, he studies the little tradition as an empirical reality without talking about normative Islam. The wish is not to decry the work of those who study actual Muslim societies; on the contrary, their work is not only highly useful but an essential prerequisite even for any would-be Muslim reformer. Criticism is due because when social scientists study "Islam as it is actually lived," they tend to believe and also to induce others to believe that this situation is static and even perhaps "normative for those people."

I think these remarks have relevance to a problem raised by Earle Waugh in the opening lines of his paper in Chapter 3 of this volume on "The Popular Muḥammad," where he contends that many devout Muslims refuse to accept outsiders' descriptions of their beliefs. Waugh expounds the idea that treatments of Muḥammad should be done "at all levels." As said above, a criterion-referent is needed not only for little traditions but also for the great tradition(s), and indeed equally for outsiders' judgments about Islam; further, this criterion can only be the Qur'ān and the Prophet's definitive conduct, for the following reasons. Not only do the people of the great tradition(s) but also those of the little traditions claim, and claim sincerely, that it is these two sources that constitute the norm of Islam; but the people of the great tradition(s) go further and claim they are trying to follow that norm and that if they consciously or in ignorance deviate from it that would constitute a sin, even a grave sin. Here, too, the two traditions do not actually differ. Indeed, in the great tradition itself there have been elitists and populists. For example, while the Ashʿarite theologians asserted that one cannot be a real (as opposed to a nominal) Muslim unless one rationally understands the basis of Islam, particularly monotheism, their contemporaries, the Māturidi theologians in Central Asia, were saying that the actual Islam of the common Turks was good Islam whether the Turks had any rational knowledge of their religion or not.

Generally modern scholars (social scientists in particular) believe that normative Islam is the Shariʿa. There is no doubt, however, that the Shariʿa has only a derivative status—both in concept and content—since it is the historical product of lawyer-theologians. It is purportedly deduced from the Qur'ān and Sunna. Indeed, some scholars even hold the normative to be that which Muslims or some learned Muslims believe to be "correct Islam." Now a Muslim, of course, may well say that what he believes is what he thinks to be correct or even true Islam, but he will never claim it is normative Islam for he will readily admit that what he considers true or correct Islam is to be judged (solely) by the Qur'ān and Sunna. This normative anchoring point, namely, the Qur'ān and Sunna, must modify the phenomenological approach which otherwise tends to be incurably relativistic. We are often invited to accept scholarship which is very tight and neat (even dogmatic) so far as its methods and categories go, but which indulges in a free-for-all Islam at the same time. I think these remarks should clarify my position *vis à vis* say, those of Richard C. Martin as found in chapter one above.

To sum up the main points I have attempted to make so far, an intellectual understanding and appreciation of Islam is quite possible for a non-Muslim who is unprejudiced, sensitive, and knowledgeable; I would say such understanding is as possible for a non-Muslim as for a Muslim. Abdul-Rauf's remarks are effective only against those non-Muslims who lack these conditions. I think that Wilfred Smith's principle of verifying interpretations of Islam with Muslims is also intended as a safeguard against failures to meet any of these conditions and also perhaps as a sort of additional verification. I find historical reductionism to be a result of the failure to meet these conditions. I welcome the phenomenological approach with the provision that its users recognize the Qur'ān and Sunna as normative criterion-referents for all expressions and understandings of Islam. In the introduction to this author's book, *Islam and Modernity*,[6] an effort is made to enunciate a satisfactory hermeneutical method for the Qur'ān.

Historical Versus Literary Criticism

It is with this background that I take notice of Andrew Rippin's paper in Chapter 9 of this volume dealing with the exposition and justification of John Wansbrough's methodologies as expounded in the latter's *Quranic Studies* and *The Sectarian Milieu*.[7] Rippin's paper and the documents on which it is based are undoubtedly among the kinds of works against which Abdul-Rauf protests in his paper. The strategy adopted by those who uphold Wansbrough's methods is, in effect, to negate history and then apply what they call the "literary method." Rippin begins by observing that it is a commonly accepted notion that Judaism and Islam are religions "in history." Now, unless the phrase "in history" has some mystical meaning, *all* religions are in history. It has, of course, been commonly held that Judaism, Christianity, and Islam are historical religions because in the view of these religions God intervened in history in order to fulfill purposes. It is obvious that such statements are not historical in the sense that they can be proved or disproved through historical inquiry. What historical inquiry can prove or disprove is whether or not these religions, in fact, have made such claims and at what point in time. Rippin, who does draw similar distinctions, nevertheless seems to confuse these two issues, namely, a religious view of history and a historical view of religion. This is the reason why, after rejecting the claims of these religions, he goes on to reject the historical inquiry into "what really happened." For whether or not one agrees with the claims of these religions, the fact that these religions make such claims can and should be historically investigated. We want to know, for example, when these claims were made, who made them, and so on. How can the rejection of a theology of history obviate the necessity of a history of that theology?

Also, why have these three religions been called historical and not, say, Hinduism and ancient Greek religion? This question is particularly relevant since Rippin goes on to try to prove his thesis of the non-historicity of Islam by asserting that no extra-literary corroboration in terms of archaeological data are available for Islam; were this all there was to say, he should accept Hinduism and Buddhism as historical religions, because a great deal of such data is available in their cases. Again, there is confusion between two very different types of questions, the theological and the historical. And so, we are told that in order to cure this theological problem of the origins of Islam, Wansbrough embarked upon a new method. This method is not a new historical approach, for a historical approach cannot get rid of the theological problem (we wonder why); instead, one must turn to the approach of literary analysis, to which we now turn.

Rippin says that this "classic insight" into the early Islamic sources is not new but that Goldziher and Schacht had pioneered this approach in connection with their critiques of Hadith. What our author does not see, however, is that Goldziher and Schacht had primarily relied on a historical method to show that certain Hadiths had, in fact, originated after certain other Hadiths. They did not rely on literary analyses like Wansbrough's. Indeed, this author has done historical criticism of many of the "fundamental Hadith" in *Islamic Methodology of History*.[8] It would seem that the efficacy of the historical method is proof enough that Muslim historical materials are basically genuine and do not need recourse to a purely literary-analytical method. Neither is it clear by what logic Rippin adduces the historical method of Goldziher and Schacht to support Wansbrough's methods of literary analysis, for, as will be shown, the latter are so inherently arbitrary that they sink into the marsh of utter subjectivity.

The greatest consequence of giving up on history so easily is that the upholders of the literary method cannot seem to make sense of the Qur'ān. Wansbrough would have us accept his notion of different (Judaic) background traditions rather than chronological Meccan and Medinan periods to explain certain differences within the Qur'ān. This is not the place to go into details,[9] but just consider the following. The Qur'ān, in narrating the story of Abraham's dispute with his father, says (19:47, Meccan) that Abraham, while parting company with his father, told him he would continue to pray for his forgiveness. In Medina, however, when it became imperative to wean off the Muslim immigrants from members of their close relatives in Mecca who were still pagans and were engaged in active hostilities against Muslims, the Qur'ān tells them (9:114) "Abraham prayed for his father's forgiveness only because he had made a promise" (i.e., otherwise he had completely cut off all relationship with him). Now, my point is that each of these passages fits exactly into the Prophet's historical circumstances respectively in Mecca and Medina. There may be one, two, or a thousand traditions—they are all related in the Qur'ān to Muḥammad's situation. Again, compare Qur'ān 11:27–29 where the prophet Noah is asked by "big ones" among his people to give up his low-class followers before they will join him—which was Muḥammad's own situation in his later years in Mecca (cf. 6:52ff.). Or see Qur'ān 11:84 and 7:85 where the prophet Shuʿayb is represented as admonishing his people to desist from committing fraud in commerce, which was again, of course, a problem in Muḥammad's society. What else can these and innumerable other examples lead us to conclude except that the Qur'ān is intimately related to the Prophet's activity?

Having unanchored the Qur'ān from its historical moorings in the Prophet's life, one basic task of Wansbrough and Rippin is to anchor it historically elsewhere. For, as we have already seen above, the necessity of historical relocation cannot be obviated by a simple rejection of the historicity of the early sources themselves. We must know where the Qur'ān belongs and to which person or groups. It appears, however, that the whole idea of rejecting traditional history without further ado was to divest oneself at a single stroke of all historical responsibility. Rippin tells us in his essay (in a slightly different context which applies *a fortiori* to the Qur'ān, however): "But we do *not* know and can probably never know what really happened; all we can know is what later people *believed* happened. . . ."

Coming now to the content of the principle of literary analysis, four themes are put before us as especially characteristic of Jewish prophetical literature which must illustrate the salient characteristics of the Qur'ān as well, namely, retribution, sign, exile, and covenant. The most fundamental question to be asked here is: On what basis has Wansbrough selected these four topics as being of salient importance to the Qur'ān? Why is there no talk, say, of socio-economic justice or Jihad as major themes of the Qur'ān? Neither the Muslims (who, according to Wansbrough, eventually formed the Qur'ān out of the diverse Judeo-Christian traditions) nor yet the Western tradition of Islamic scholarship (which Wansbrough accuses of having succumbed to the claims of the Muslim tradition) regard Wansbrough's four themes as the most prominent ones in the Qur'ān. If the Qur'ān was the result of a conspiracy which Wansbrough now claims to have unearthed, then at the very least he should clarify why these four themes—so prominent in his analysis—did not gain prominence in Islam. If Muslims are asked about the most salient teachings of the Qur'ān, I suggest that most replies will include monotheism, prayers, alms, fasting, and pilgrimage. Wansbrough's thesis, then, requires more than one conspiracy: One to hide the very origins of the Qur'ān and to attribute it to a prophetic revelation, and a second (not necessarily inconsistent with the first) to underplay the importance of Wansbrough's four themes (the real themes of the first conspiracy) and to replace them with what Muslims regard as the "Pillars of Islam."

It was on some of these methodological grounds that I criticized Wansbrough's *Quranic Studies* in the introduction to *Major Themes of the Qur'ān*, to which Rippin replies toward the end of his paper. He suggests that my criticism of Wansbrough boils down to the fact that I simply regard my method to be better than his. The fact is, however, that I have advanced, both here and elsewhere (see note 9), several basic considerations to show that my method makes sense of the Qur'ān—as a body of doctrine that is coherent in itself and that fits into the life of the Prophet. Wansbrough's method makes nonsense of the Qur'ān, and he washes his hands of the responsibility of explaining how that "nonsense" came about.[10]

As for Rippin's complaint that several scholars have emphasized the Arab background of Islam at the expense of the Jewish or Judeo-Christian, it appears to me that Wansbrough has gone beyond any reasonable limits in making the Qur'ān a completely Judeo-Christian sectarian manifestation. The facts are that in Arabia itself Judeo-Christian ideas were fairly widespread. The Qur'ān affirms that there had been attempts to proselytize the Meccans but that these had been unsuccessful. The Meccans and the Arabs, however (and not just the Prophet as is commonly believed), had come to know a fair amount of the biblical tradition. Thus, a great deal of this tradition had already been Arabized; witness the prophetology which, along with the biblical personages, included certain Arab prophets—and the tradition that the Kaʿba had been built by Abraham and Ishmael. Now, the starting point of the Qur'ānic teaching was not biblical controversies but existential problems within Meccan society itself. During its course, no doubt, the Qur'ān picked up a great amount of Judeo-Christian tradition. To insist, however, that the Qur'ān is purely or even basically a result of that tradition is a manifest travesty of truth, for basically the Qur'ān remains Arab to the core.

Although it has not been possible for me to discuss every contribution to this volume, I believe the problem I have elaborated—the insider/outsider dilemma—points to the complexity of the historical/comparative study of religion, in particular Islam. In his comprehensive introduction, Richard C. Martin has given an overview of the study of Islam as it has developed in the West, underlining in particular two different approaches, the "classical" orientalist and the newer social scientific, thus suggesting the need to bridge and combine the two with history of religions. Western orientalist scholarship had, of course, itself started to develop a certain self-critique at the hands of certain scholars, including Jacques Waardenburg.[11] One hopes that after a *bouleversant* (though rather sweeping) work like Edward Said's *Orientalism*,[12] healthier, richer, and more synthetic studies of Islam may gradually emerge. Islam is an area of study which has been notoriously neglected by historians of religions, perhaps because it has not been amenable to their pet categories and methodologies. The Arizona State University symposium on "Islam and the History of Religions" from which this volume has resulted has proved to be a unique forum for the underlining of problems and opportunities. It is important now to apply and test many different ideas, approaches, and methods and, indeed, to demonstrate that Islam is a very complex and rich phenomenon. The study of Islam is a challenge to the human mind—a challenge as rewarding as it is difficult. It is certain that Islam in history has changed and that it will continue to change at an even more rapid pace. This change appears to have a double dimension: The changing of "little" traditions in relation to the "greater" ones, which can be characterized as the "orthodoxification" of the tradition, and secondly, the modernization of the great tradition. Yet, basically, Islam will remain the same.

What the present volume highlights is the need for an interdisciplinary approach, not just in terms of the "orientalist" and "social scientist" of whom I have spoken above, but in terms of several disciplines with defined methods of research. For the former without the latter remain myopic, resulting in dangerous generalizations, while the latter without the former become abstract, in fact, chimerical.

Part Six

Reference Material

Notes to the Chapters

Chapter 1. Islam and Religious Studies

1. See P. Joseph Cahill, *Mended Speech: The Crisis in Religious Studies and Theology* (New York: Crossroad, 1982), chapter one.

2. Charles J. Adams, "The History of Religions and the Study of Islam," in *The History of Religions: Essays on the Problem of Understanding*, ed. Joseph M. Kitagawa with Mircea Eliade and Charles H. Long (Chicago and London: University of Chicago Press, 1967), pp. 177–93.

3. Ibid., pp. 178–80.

4. The most obvious and convenient example of the impact of religious studies is the historical- and textual-critical studies of the Bible since the late-nineteenth century, with noticeable changes in the Western self-understanding of the Judeo-Christian traditions. A good assessment of this problem is Van Harvey, *The Historian and the Believer: The Morality of Historical Knowledge and Christian Belief* (New York: Macmillan, 1966).

5. The reference is to the symposium on "Islam and the History of Religions" held at Arizona State University, January 1980 (see the Preface).

6. Much has been written on hermeneutics and religious studies in recent years. On hermeneutics generally, see David Cousins Hoy, *The Critical Circle: Literature and History in Contemporary Hermeneutics* (Berkeley: University of California Press, 1978).

7. The following pages about history of religions rely on Eric J. Sharpe, *Comparative Religions: A History* (New York: Scribner's, 1975). See also Jacques Waardenburg, *Classical Approaches to the Study of Religions*, 2 vols. (The Hague: Mouton, 1972).

8. Wilfred Cantwell Smith, "Comparative Religions: Whither—and Why?" in *The History of Religions: Essays in Methodology*, ed. Mircea Eliade and Joseph Kitagawa (Chicago and London: University of Chicago Press, 1959), pp. 31–58.

9. See Willard Gurdon Oxtoby, "*Religionswissenschaft* Revisited," in *Religions in Antiquity: Essays in Memory of Erwin Ramsdell Goodenough*, ed. Jacob Neusner (Leiden: E. J. Brill), pp. 590–608.

10. See, for example, Robert D. Baird, *Category Formation and the History of Religions* (The Hague: Mouton, 1971). An entertainingly critical but unfortunately unconstructive discussion of Baird and other recent books on methodology is the review article by Hans Penner, "The Fall and Rise of Methodology: A Retrospective Review," *Religious Studies Review* 2 (1976):11–16.

11. Bernard Lewis, "The State of Middle Eastern Studies," *The American Scholar* 48/3 (1979):365–81.

12. Leonard Binder, "Area Studies: A Critical Reassessment," in *The Study of the Middle East: Research and Scholarship in the Humanities and Social Sciences* (New York: Wiley, 1976), pp. 1–28.

13. Richard D. Lambert, *Language and Area Studies Review*, Monograph 17 of the American Academy of Political and Social Science (Philadelphia, 1973).

14. Binder, "Area Studies," pp. 9–13.

15. Edward W. Said, *Orientalism* (New York: Pantheon, 1978).

16. Said, *Orientalism*, p. 2.

17. Ibid., p. 239.

18. Jacob Neusner, "Judaism Within the Disciplines of Religious Studies: Perspectives on Graduate Education," *The Council on the Study of Religion Bulletin* 14/5 (1983):141.

19. Ibid., p. 143.

Chapter 2. Qur'ān as Spoken Word

This study is dedicated to Wilfred Cantwell Smith. It grew out of a shorter paper presented at a conference in honor of Smith at the Center for the Study of World Religions, Harvard University, 15–17 June 1979. The shorter paper was published in revised form in *Die Welt des Islams* as this article was being revised for the present volume. The present study reflects and is indebted to Smith's own deep interest in the Qur'ān and the study of Scripture, which is evidenced in a variety of his publications. Cf. "The True Meaning of Scripture", *International Journal of Middle Eastern Studies*, 11 (1980):487–505; *Islam in Modern History* (Princeton: Princeton University Press, 1957), pp. 17–18, nn. 13–14; "Some Similarities and Differences Between Christianity and Islam," in *The World of Islam: Studies in Honour of Phillip K. Hitti*, ed. J. Kritzeck and R. B. Winder (London: Macmillan, 1959), pp. 47–59, esp. pp. 52, 56–58; "Is the Qur'ān the Word of God?," in *Questions of Religious Truth* (New York: Scribner's, 1967), pp. 39–62; "Koran," *Encyclopedia Britannica* (1966), *s.v.*; and "The Study of Religion and The Study of the Bible," *Journal of the American Academy of Religion*, [hereafter, JAAR], 39 (1971):131–140.

1. "Study of religion" is used here as an "umbrella" term for all those studies concerned primarily with religion and "the religions" as opposed to one particular religious

tradition or one particular dimension of religion (e.g. the psychological). Thus distinctions among *Religionswissenschaft*, *Religionsgeschichte*, comparative religion, and the like are subsumed under this general rubric. The key element is the generic or global interest in the study of religion, not whether the emphasis is on hermeneutical, comparative, or historical problems. Concerning the use of various terms for different kinds of generic study of religion, see Willem A. Bijlefeld, "Islamic Studies within the Perspective of the History of Religions," *Muslim World* 62 (1972):1–11, esp. p. 2, n. 6.

2. The best-known statement of this problem is that of Charles J. Adams, "The Study of Religions and the Study of Islam," in *The History of Religions: Essays on the Problem of Understanding*, ed. J. M. Kitagawa (Chicago and London: University of Chicago Press, 1967), pp. 177–93.

3. A point that is made specifically for biblical studies by Andrew Rippin in chapter 9 in this volume.

4. According to the *Oxford English Dictionary*, the generic use of "scripture" in English as "sacred writings or records" (the fourth meaning given) is attested as early as 1581, but the reference is to noncanonical, presumably Christian, works; the first unambiguous reference to non-Jewish, non-Christian texts (in this case, the Vedas) is only from 1764. At least one older example has come to my attention: George Sale, in his "Preliminary Discourse" to his 1734 translation of the Qur'ān, speaks of the Qur'ān as sharing things with "other books of Scripture." "Holy writ," according to the *Oxford English Dictionary* (*OED*), appears to have been used very early to refer to noncanonical as well as biblical texts, but it is first clearly used for non-Jewish, non-Christian texts in 1805 (again for the Vedas). For "canon" as an accepted collection of scripture outside the Christian tradition, the *OED* can cite no one before Max Müller in 1873, who speaks of a "canon of sacred books." Finally, "bible" as a generic term for a holy scripture is attested, again in the *OED*, only from 1883, although it does occur early in the nonreligious sense of simply "a large book, a tome, a long treatise." It would be interesting to do a serious search for the beginning, not only in English but other European languages, of the use of such Judeo-Christian conceptual terms to apply to other traditions.

5. Discussion of the history of these and related terms for Judeo-Christian writings can be found in: *Encyclopaedia Judaica* (Jerusalem, 1971) [hereafter, *EJ*], s.v. "Bible," and W. F. Adeney and F. C. Grant, "Scripture," in *Dictionary of the Bible*, ed. James Hastings. Rev. ed. (1963) F. C. Grant and H. H. Rowley [hereafter *HDB*]. For the names applied in particular to the emerging "canon" of Hebrew scriptures, cf. James Hastings, "Bible," *HDB*, and F. Maass, "Bestand und Zusammensetzung des AT," *Religion in Geschichte und Gegenwart* [hereafter, *RGG*], 3rd ed., 1:1122.

6. A. Jepsen, "Sammlung und Kanonisierung des AT," *RGG*³, 1:1123–25; *EJ*, 4:817–19, 821–27. James A. Sanders, *Torah and Canon* (Philadelphia: Fortress, 1972), deals at length with the "origins and function" as well as the "structure" of the Torah canon; he would argue for an exilic date (by the end of the sixth century B.C.E.) by which a rudimentary "canon" was emerging (pp. 91ff.). See also H. F. D. Sparks, "Canon of the Old Testament," *HDB*, and W. F. Aveney and B. M. Metzger, "Canon of the New Testament," *HDB*.

7. Hans Freiherr von Campenhausen, in "Das Alte Testament als Bibel der Kirche," in his *Aus der Frühzeit des Christentums* (Tubingen: J. C. B. Mohr, 1963), pp. 152–96, gives a clear interpretation of the importance of Hebrew scripture in early

Christianity. (The title of this chapter is apparently a phrase coined by the author.) See also Ferdinand Hahn, "Das Problem 'Schrift und Tradition' im Urchristentum," in *Evangelische Theologie*, 30 (1970):449–68.

8. Synopses of the history of modern biblical scholarship can be found in *RGG*³, vol. 1: "Bibelkritik: AT" (F. Baumgärtel), "Bibelkritik: NT" (Erich Dinkler), "Bibelwissenschaft des AT" (C. Kuhl), and "Bibelwissenschaft des NT" (W. G. Kümmel). For fuller treatment the standard works are: Han-Joachim Kraus, *Geschichte der historisch-kritischen Erforschung des Alten Testaments*, 2nd ed. (Neukirchener Verlag, 1969) (on Wellhausen and his influence, see esp. pp. 255–94) and Werner Georg Kümmel, *Das Neue Testament: Geschichte der Erforschung seiner Probleme* (Freiburg and Munich: Karl Alber, 1958) (on F. C. Baur, the "Tübingen school," and their ideas, see esp. pp. 145–230). Studies of the wide range of work on nonbiblical sacred literatures are harder to find, but some impression can be gained by referring to J. Waardenburg, *Classical Approaches to the Study of Religion: Aims, Methods and Theories of Research*, 2 vols. (The Hague and Paris: Mouton, 1973), and Eric J. Sharpe, *Comparative Religion: A History* (New York: Scribner's, 1975). (On Max Müller, see 1:85–95 of Waardenburg and pp. 35–46 of Sharpe.)

9. These points about the focus of previous scriptural study were persuasively made by W. C. Smith in *JAAR*, 39 (1971):131–40. To my knowledge the first to enunciate this problem, Smith has stimulated considerable discussion in textual fields, as witness in W. A. Bijlefeld, *MW*, 62 (1972):5ff.

10. Witness the dearth of articles on scripture as a general category even in major reference works (e.g., the *EJ* and the *Encyclopaedia of Religion and Ethics*, ed. James Hastings). The *RGG*³ has an article by Siegfried Morenz, "Schriften, heilige", but it is allotted only a column and a half. The only substantial historical study of scripture on a cross-cultural basis is the fine work (limited in scope to the pre-Islamic Mediterranean world) by Johannes Leipoldt and Siegfried Morenz, *Heilige Schriften: Betrachtungen zur Religionsgeschichte der antiken Mittelmeerwelt* (Leipzig: Otto Harrassowitz, 1953). Cf. also Morenz's article, "Entstehung und Wesen der Buchreligion," *Theologische Literatur-Zeitung* 75 (1950):709–16. Mention should also be made of the various studies of the "heavenly Book" idea in the Semitic and Iranian world by Geo Widengren (*Muḥammad, the Apostle of God, and his Ascension*, Uppsala Universitets Årsskrift, 1955:1, and *The Ascension of the Apostle and the Heavenly Book*, Uppsala Universitets Årsskrift, 1950:7. There is also a rather disappointing colloquium collection, *Holy Book and Holy Tradition*, ed. F. F. Bruce and E. G. Rupp (Manchester: Manchester University Press, 1968). As is the case with the latter volume, there seem to be otherwise only works that treat every individual scriptural tradition separately: e.g., Gunter Lanczkowski, *Heilige Schriften: Inhalt, Textgestalt und Überlieferung* (Stuttgart: W. Kohlhammer, 1956).

11. Cf. Mircea Eliade, *Traité d'histoire des religions* (Paris: Payot, 1953), and its English version, *Patterns in Comparative Religion*, trans. Rosemary Sheed (Cleveland and New York: World Publishing Co., 1963), in which "scripture," "book," etc., are not treated, nor even listed in the indices. Still more striking is the absence of any such rubric among the themes of Eliade's *From Primitives to Zen: A Thematic Sourcebook of the History of Religions* (New York: Harper and Row, 1967), and the use of only the terms "document," "text," or "sacred text" in the Introduction to the collection, which consists of many selections from scriptures of the world.

12. E.g. Friedrich Heiler, *Erscheinungsformen und Wesen der Religion*, 2nd rev. ed. (Stuttgart.: W. Kohlhammer, 1979; orig. ed., 1961), in which chs. A:VII and A:VIII treat "Das heilige Wort" and "Die heilige Schrift," respectively. Cf. Geo Widengren, *Religionsphänomenologie* (Berlin: Walter de Gruyter, 1969), ch. 19, "Heiliges Wort und Heilige Schrift"; Gustav Mensching, *Das heilige Wort* (Bonn: L. Röhrscheid, 1937), ch. II:4, "Das gehörte und geschriebene Wort"; G. van der Leeuw, *Religion in Essence and Manifestation*, trans. J. E. Turner, with additions from the 2nd German ed. by Hans H. Penner [New York and Evanston: Harper & Row, 1963 (orig. German ed. 1933)], ch. 58, "The Sacred Word," and ch. 64, "The Written Word."

13. Gustav Mensching, *Die Religion. Erscheinungsformen, Strukturtypen und Lebensgesetze* (Stuttgart: Curt E. Schwab, 1959), pp. 328–29; Robert Will, *Le culte: Étude d'histoire et de philosophie religieuses*, 3 vols. (Strasbourg and Paris, 1925–1935), 2:363; and Alfred Bertholet, "Schriften, Heilige," *RGG*², 5:266, cited in Heiler, *Erscheinungsformen*, p. 356.

14. Cf. above, p. 2–3. To the Greek and Latin terms may be added the Hebrew *kitve* and *sifre* (cf. *EJ*, 4:816–17). The Hebrew *miqrā'* (above, p. 31) is the significant exception.

15. On the typographic or "chirographic," visual orientation of our modern Western culture, see esp. Josef Balogh, "'Voces Paginarum'. Beiträge zur Geschichte des lauten Lesens und Schreibens," *Philologus* 82 (1926–27):83–109; 202–40; J. C. Carothers, "Culture, Psychiatry, and the Written Word," *Psychiatry* 22(1959):307–20; Marshall McLuhan, *The Gutenberg Galaxy: The Making of Typographic Man* (Toronto: University of Toronto Press, 1962); H. J. Chaytor, *From Script to Print: An Introduction to Medieval Vernacular Literature* (Cambridge: W. Heffer, 1945), esp. chs. I, II, VI; Walter J. Ong, *The Presence of the Word: Some Prolegomena for Cultural and Religious History* (Minneapolis: University of Minnesota Press, 1981; orig. ed., Yale University Press, 1967); *idem*, *Orality and Literacy: The Technologizing of the Word* (London and New York: Methuen, 1982). On the objectification associated with print culture and writing generally, see, in addition to the above: David Riesman, "The Oral and Written Traditions," *Explorations* 6 (1956):22–28; George Steiner, "The Retreat from the Word" (1961), in *Language and Silence: Essays on Language, Literature, and the Inhuman* (New York: Atheneum, 1982), pp. 12–35.

16. Cf. the comment of Sergius Bulgakov, describing the relationship of scripture and tradition in Eastern Orthodoxy: ". . . the Word of God, while being studied as an historical document, can never become *only* a document, for its exterior form, although bearing the character of a certain historical epoch, nevertheless encloses the word of eternal life; in this same sense it is a symbol, the meeting place of divine and human" [*The Orthodox Church*, trans. E. S. Cram, ed. D. A. Lowrie (New York and Milwaukee; Morehouse and London: Centenary Press, c. 1936), p. 22].

17. "The tradition of the sacred word is originally oral; it lives in being recited, and only later did oral tradition give place to graphic . . ." (van der Leeuw, *Religion*, p. 435); "Das Aufzeichnen und Rezitieren der heiligen Schriften geht [*sic*] also Hand in Hand, und dasselbe gilt ganz allgemein im Vorderen Orient: *Lesen ist lautes Lesen, Rezitation*" [ital. mine] (Widengren, *Religionsphänomenologie*, p. 559). Cf. A. Bertholet's examples from around the world of the power of reading aloud from scripture, in "Die Macht der Schrift in Glauben und Aberglauben," *Abhandlungen der deutschen*

Akademie der Wissenschaften zu Berlin, phil.-hist. Klasse, 1948, no. 1, pp. 38–40; and also the contribution by Marilyn Waldman in Chapter 6 in this volume.

18. I am currently engaged in a book-length project in which I attempt to document this; its projected title is *Scripture as Spoken Word.* A shorter version of my arguments ("Beyond the Written Word: The Oral Dimensions of Scripture") is included in a forthcoming volume entitled *Rethinking Scripture*, Miriam Levering, ed.

19. On Torah-reading, see Leipoldt and Morenz, *Heilige Schriften*, pp. 100–106; Ismar Ellbogen, *Der jüdische Gottesdienst in seiner geschichtlichen Entwicklung*, 3rd ed. (1931; 4th repr. ed., Hildesheim: G. Olms, 1962), pp. 155–205; Paul Glaue, *Die Vorlesung heiliger Schriften im Gottesdienste: I. Teil, Bis zur Entstehung der altkatholischen Kirche* (Berlin: A. Duncker, 1907), esp. pp. 1–12. On *lectio divina*, see Jean Leclercq, *L'amour des lettres et le désir de Dieu* (Paris: Éd. du Cerf, 1957), pp. 20–23. Eng. trans. Catherine Misrahi (New York: New American Library, 1962), pp. 23–26. On *meditatio* as oral recitation, see Heinrich Bacht, "'Meditatio' in den ältesten Mönchsquellen," *Geist und Leben* 28 (1955):360–73, and the further literature cited there.

20. Or has it? It would be interesting to investigate the degree to which, even back as far as medieval times, contact with and awareness of Islam, however limited, suggested to European minds an analogy between Muslims' possession of a Book (however false it may have appeared to Christians and Jews) and that of Christians and Jews. Given the historical contacts and early translations of the Qur'ān (e.g., that of Robert of Ketton, in 1143), it would seem logical that Muslim concern with scripture would have impinged upon Western consciousness even before awareness of Indian scriptural texts. If this was the case, then the fact of the existence of a Muslim scripture, rather than any specifically Muslim concept of scripture, would have been the key influence on Western generalizing of the idea of scripture.

21. The qur'ānic idea of a history of scriptural revelations of which it is itself the culmination has a precedent (and possible source of influence?) in the ideas of Mani, who speaks of "Scriptures . . . in the earlier religions" (Widengren, *Muḥammad*, p. 132). Cf. the comments about Mani's consciousness of producing "scripture" in W. C. Smith, *The Meaning and End of Religion* (New York: Macmillan, 1963), pp. 95f.

22. Concerning *al-kitāb*, *umm al-kitāb*, *ahl al-kitāb*, see J. Pedersen's review of E. Meyer, *Ursprung und Geschichte der Mormonen* (1912), *Der Islam* 5 (1914):110–15; Frants Buhl, "Die Schrift und was damit zusammenhängt," in Cyrus Adler and Aaron Ember, eds., *Oriental Studies* (Paul Haupt *Festschrift*) (Baltimore: Johns Hopkins; and Leipzig: J. C. Hinrichs, 1926), pp. 364–73; D. Künstlinger, "Kitāb und Ahlu-l-kitāb," *Roznik Orientalistyczny* [hereafter, *RO*] 4 (1928):238–47; Geo Widengren, *Muḥammad*, esp. pp. 115–39; Tilman Nagel, "Vom 'Qur'ān' zur 'Schrift'—Bells Hypothese aus religionsgeschichtlicher Sicht," *Der Islam* 60 (1983):143–65. NB that "book," "prescript," and "scripture" are all possible renderings of *kitāb* in its scriptural contexts.

23. The Muslim view of the history of the collection of the Qur'ān, as well as the modern Islamicist agreement with the basic outlines of this understanding, have been radically questioned by some, notably John Wansbrough in *Quranic Studies: Sources and Methods of Scriptural Interpretation* (Oxford: Oxford University Press, 1977). Wansbrough argues that several different styles of explanatory gloss and "exegesis" (all based on Jewish antecedents) are evident in the text of the Qur'ān itself. His conclusion, based on his own rhetorical analysis and unsupported by historical evidence, is

that there was a long process of "canonization" (at least two centuries) in the Islamic as in the Jewish and Christian cases. Cf. the similar scepticism about the traditions surrounding the ʿUthmānic redaction and its variant traditions on the part of John Burton, in *The Collection of the Qurʾān* (Cambridge: Cambridge University Press, 1977). Burton, however, reaches different conclusions, preferring to see the traditional accounts as a smokescreen hiding the fact that the *textus receptus* was already fixed under Muḥammad's direction well before ʿUthmān's caliphate. While both of these interpretations place the issue of "canonization" in a different light, neither can be said to be proven and accepted at present.

24. An exception to this is the title "Qur'ān karīm" that appears on many editions, especially but not exclusively those published outside the Arab world, (rather than "al-Qur'ān al-karīm"), apparently as a quotation from Sūra 56:77.

25. But cf. n. 23 above. On the *qurrā'*, see G. H. A. Juynboll, "The Qurrā' in Early Islamic History," *Journal of the Economic and Social History of the Orient* 16 (1973):113–29, and the earlier literature cited there. To this add: Paul Kahle, "The Arabic Readers of the Koran," *Journal of Near Eastern Studies* 8 (1949):65–71.

26. Al-Bukhārī, *al-Ṣaḥīḥ*, 9 vols. (Beirut, n.d.), book 66, sect. 16; Ibn Ḥanbal, *al-Musnad*, 6 vols. (Cairo, 1313/1859), 1:415.

27. Frants Buhl, "Ḳoran," *Encyclopaedia of Islam* [hereafter, *EI*[1]]. His discussion of this point is the clearest in the literature; but see also Th. Nöldeke, *Geschichte des Qorāns*, 2nd rev. ed. (3 vols.) by F. Schwally (vols. 1, 2) and G. Bergsträsser and O. Pretzl, vol. 3, (Leipzig, 1909–1938 [hereafter *GdQ*]), 1:31–34.

28. "The Earliest Meaning of 'Qur'ān'," in *Die Welt des Islams* 23/24 (1984).

29. R. Payne Smith, *Thesaurus Syriacus*, 2 vols. (Oxford, 1883–1901), 2:3716b, citing several occurrences in the first sense in pre-Islamic Christian sources, beginning with I Tim. 4:13, and several in the second sense in sources as early as St. Cyril's commentary on Luke. Clear attestation of *qeryānā* as a technical term in liturgical contexts is to be found in sixth- and seventh-century manuscripts of liturgical texts such as the *Qeryānā d-yom bāʿwātā* ("Reading for the Day of Supplications"), according to a 1980 personal communication from Alford T. Welch, which I have since been able to confirm with his source, Sebastian Brock at Oxford. For previous discussions of *qeryānā*, see my forthcoming article (above, n. 28), esp. n. 18. See also the very convincing article of John Bowman, "Holy Scriptures, Lectionaries and Qur'an," in A. H. Johns, ed., *International Congress for the Study of the Qur'an* (selected papers from the meeting of 8–13 May 1980, Australian National University), Series 1, 2nd ed. (Canberra: Australian National University, 1982), pp. 29–37, in which the author argues for the strong influence of Syriac Christian usage on the conception of the Qur'ān and its function in early Islam.

30. J. Horovitz, "Qur'ān," *Der Islam*, 13 (1923):67, does not distinguish between the two, calling both "Schriftverlesung"; cf. *GdQ*, I:32, where it is noted that *miqrā'* can be used for parts as well as the whole of scripture. Cf. Ellbogen, *Der jüdische Gottesdienst*, pp. 158ff. Arthur Jeffery, *The Foreign Vocabulary of the Qur'an* (Baroda: Oriental Institute, 1938), p. 234, notes that Marracci and Geiger had long ago argued for the Hebrew as the source of *qur'ān*, but he prefers the Syriac. Cf. "Bible Canon," *The Jewish Encyclopedia* (New York and London: Funk and Wagnalls, 1901–1906), 3:141a. A personal communication from Judith Wegner at the Harvard Law School also stresses similarity of the *miqrā'* usage to that of *qur'ān* (Nov. 1979).

31. *EJ*, 4:816. Cf. Künstlinger, "Kitāb," p. 239; *idem*, "Die Namen der 'Gottes-Schriften' im Qorān," *RO*, 13 (1937):76, n. 2; *GdQ*, 1:32; *EJ*, 4:816.

32. Geo Widengren, *Die Religionen Irans* (Stuttgart: W. Kohlhammer, 1965), p. 197.

33. Tor Andrae, *Mohammed. Sein Leben und sein Glaube* (Göttingen: Vandenhoeck & Ruprecht, 1932), pp. 78–79 (= p. 96 of Eng. trans. by T. Menzel, rev. ed. [New York, 1960] which is wholly inadequate in its rendering of the original passage here); cf. Bowman, "Holy Scriptures."

34. I.e., gets up in the night to perform extra, supererogatory devotions, a common pious practice in Islam: see A. J. Wensinck, "Tahadjdjud," *Shorter Encyclopaedia of Islam* (Leiden and London, 1961) [hereafter, *SEI*].

35. *Kitāb al-Mabānī*, ed. Arthur Jeffery, in *Two Muqaddimas to the Qur'anic Sciences* (Cairo, 1954), p. 58; al-Ṭabarī, *Tafsīr*, vols. 1–16 [incomplete], ed. by M. M. Shākir and A. M. Shākir (Cairo, n.d.), 1:97 (where *qur'ān* is glossed as *qirā'a*, the more common verbal-noun form). Also cited by Josef Horovitz, *Koranische Untersuchungen* (Berlin and Leipzig: W. de Gruyter, 1926), p. 74, n. 1, and in *GdQ*, 1:34.

36. Ibn Ḥanbal, *Musnad*, 4:159.

37. *Ibid.*, 2:285.

38. Al-Tirmidhī, *Ṣaḥīḥ*, 13 vols. (Cairo, 1350/1931–1353/1934), book 46, sect. 25; al-Dārimī, *Sunan*, ed. ʿAbdallāh al-Yamanī al-Madanī, 2 vols. (Cairo, 1386/1966), book 23, sect. 6.

39. Rudi Paret, "Ḳirā'a," *Encyclopaedia of Islam. New Edition* [hereafter, *EI*²]; Régis Blachère, *Introduction au Coran* (Paris: G. P. Maisonneuve, 1947), p. 103.

40. On the science of *qirā'a* generally, with primary emphasis on the *qirā'āt*, see *GdQ*, 3 ("Die Geschichte des Korantexts"); Blachère, *Introduction*, pp. 103–35, 199–210; Otto Pretzl, "Die Wissenschaft der Koranlesung (*ʿIlm al-qirā'a*)," *Islamica* 6 (1933–34):1–47, 230–46, 290–331 (esp. 1–47); Ignaz Goldziher, *Die Richtungen der islamischen Koranauslegung* (1920; 2nd photogr. repr., Leiden: E. J. Brill, 1970), pp. 1–54; Frederick M. Denny, "Exegesis and Recitation: Their Development as Classical Forms of Qur'ānic Piety," in Frank E. Reynolds and Theodore M. Ludwig, eds., *Transitions and Transformations in the History of Religions: Essays in Honor of Joseph M. Kitagawa* (Leiden: E. J. Brill, 1980), pp. 91–123, esp. 109ff.; further literature may be found in the bibliography of Paret, "Ḳirā'a." The traditional Muslim source is Ibn al-Jazarī, *al-Nashr fī al-qirā'āt al-ʿashr*, ed. ʿAlī Muḥ. al-Ḍabbāʿ, 2 vols., (Cairo, n.d.). See also Labīb al-Saʿīd ["Labib as-Said"], *The Recited Koran: A History of the First Recorded Version*, trans. and ed. Bernard Weiss, M. A. Rauf, and Morroe Berger (Princeton: The Darwin Press, 1975), pp. 15–60.

41. Labīb al-Saʿīd, *Recited Koran*, pp. 19–50.

42. Kristina Nelson, "The Art of Reciting the Qur'an," University of California diss. (Berkeley, 1980) [forthcoming publication by University of Texas Press], pp. 21–22.

43. Al-Bukhārī, *Ṣaḥīḥ*, book 44, sect. 4; 59, 6; 66, 5; 88, 9; 97, 53; for other occurrences of this Ḥadīth in the classical collections, see A. J. Wensinck *et al.*, *Concordance et indices de la tradition musulmane*, 7 vols. (Leiden: E. J. Brill, 1936), 1:448b. Cf. Goldziher, *Richtungen*, 3ff, 36ff.; *GdQ*, 1:48–52; K. Nelson, "Art of Reciting," Appendix B, "The Seven *Aḥruf* and the *Qirā'āt*."

44. Fuat Sezgin, *Geschichte des arabischen Schrifttums*, vol. 1 (Leiden: E. J. Brill, 1967) [hereafter *GAS*], pp. 4–11.

45. *Ibid.*, pp. 8–13; Paret, "Ḳirā'a," pp. 127b–128a; Pretzl, "Wissenschaft der Koranlesung," pp. 4ff.

46. *GAS*, p. 14; Blachère, *Introduction*, pp. 127–29.

47. On the "seven," "ten," and "fourteen" *qirā'āt*, see Blachère, *Introduction*, pp. 116–32; *GdQ*, 3:186–89; Labīb al-Saʿīd, *Recited Koran*, pp. 53–56, 127–30. On the actual variations on particular passages, see *inter alia* Goldziher, *Richtungen*, pp. 4–32; Arthur Jeffery, *Materials for the History of the Text of the Qur'ān: The Old Codices* (Leiden: E. J. Brill, 1937); G. Bergsträsser, "Die Koranlesung des Hasan von Basra," *Islamica* 2 (1926–27):11–57; *idem*, ed., *Ibn Hālawaih's Sammlung nichtkanonischer Koranlesarten*, Bibliotheca Islamica, ed. H. Ritter, vol. 7 (Leipzig: Brockhaus, 1934); O. Pretzl, ed., *Das Lehrbuch der sieben Koranlesungen von Abū ʿAmr ʿU̱tmān ibn Saʿīd ad-Dānī*, Bibliotheca Islamica, ed. H. Ritter, vol. 2 (Istanbul, 1930). Further literature in bibliography of Paret, "Ḳirā'a."

48. See K. Nelson, ch. II; Frederick M. Denny, "The *Adab* of Qur'an Recitation: Text and Context," in Johns, ed., *International Congress*, pp. 143–60.

49. On *tartīl*, see E. W. Lane, *An Arabic-English Lexicon*, 8 vols. [incomplete] (London, 1863–1893), 3:1028.

50. K. Nelson, "Art of Reciting." This fine study shows how both in theory and practice a variety of skills and disciplines are involved in *tajwīd* (see esp. chs. II, IV, V, VII, VIII).

51. See above, nn. 40, 47. Of works on *tajwīd*, see esp. the two most well-known Muslim works (to which Denny, "The *Adab*," provides good brief introductions): Abū Zakarīyā al-Nawawī (d. 676/1277), *al-Tibyān fī ādāb ḥamalat al-qur'ān* (Cairo, 1397/1977, *inter alia*), and Muḥammad al-Ghazālī (d. 505/1111), "Ādāb tilāwat al-qur'ān," book 8 of *Iḥyā' ʿulūm al-dīn*, 5 vols. (Beirut, n.d), 1:272–93. In modern scholarly study of *tajwīd* before the recent work of Nelson and Denny, note esp. G. Bergsträsser, "Koranlesung in Kairo," *Der Islam* 20 (1932):1–42; 21 (1933):110–40 (includes a discussion and musical settings of sample recitations contributed by Karl Huber, pp. 113–31); O. Pretzl, "Wissenschaft," pp. 290–331; Jean Cantineau and Léo Barbès, "La récitation coranique à Damas et à Alger," *Annales de l'Institut d'Études Orientales* (Algiers), 6 (1942–47):66–107; M. Talbi, "La qirā'a bi-l-alḥān," *Arabica* 5 (1958):183–90; Habib Hassan Touma, "Die Koranrezitation: eine Form der religiösen Musik der Araber," *Baessler-Archiv* (Berlin) n.f. 23 (1975):87–120. Cf. also H. G. Farmer, "The Religious Music of Islām," *Journal of the Royal Asiatic Society* (1952): 60–65.

52. *Recited Koran* (above, n. 40).

53. "Art of Reciting" (above, n. 42).

54. "Exegesis and Recitation" (above, n. 40); "The Adab" (above, n. 48). See also his "Types of Qur'ān Recitation Sessions in Contemporary Cairo," unpublished paper delivered at the annual meeting of the American Research Center in Egypt, Detroit, Michigan, 1 May 1977. I am particularly grateful to Professor Denny for sharing this latter paper with me. Also of interest is the perceptive article by Richard C. Martin, "Understanding the Qur'an in Text and Context," *History of Religions* 21 (1981–82):361–84. Martin's emphasis on the oral force of the Qur'ān in Muslim life, based on modern hermeneutical and speech-act theory, is noteworthy.

55. Both terms are used to refer to recitation of the Qur'ān in general, but *qirā'a* is the term used in compounds referring to a particular style (e.g., *al-qirā'a bil-alḥān*),

while *tilāwa* "is always general" [K. Nelson, "Art of Reciting", p. 139; cf. pp. 137–44]. Note especially the ethical dimension lent to *tilāwa* by its double sense "to follow" and "to recite" (cf. Sūra 2:121; 35:29; 27:91, and Ghazālī, *Iḥyā'* 1:272, lines 21–22).

56. Above, n. 35. The *Mabānī* was written in 425/1033. Its author is unknown because the unique Berlin manuscript is without the first folio. See Jeffery's preface to the edition.

57. *Al-Mabānī*, p. 89.

58. Constance E. Padwick, *Muslim Devotions. A Study of Prayer-Manuals in Common Use* (London: S.P.C.K., 1961), p. 108. Cf. Ghazālī on *qirā'a* in the *ṣalāt: Iḥyā'*, 1: 153–54.

59. Bukhārī, *Ṣaḥīḥ*, book 10, sect. 94. Cf. Ghazālī, *Iḥyā'*, 1:154.

60. Ibid., 1:276. Cf. Ibn Baṭṭūṭa's descriptions of the joining of recitation sessions to the regular performances of *ṣalāt* in fourteenth-century Egypt, a practice popular still today (H. A. R. Gibb, trans., *The Travels of Ibn Baṭṭūṭa*, 3 vols. (Cambridge: The University Press, for the Hakluyt Society, 1958–71), 1:44–45, 65–66).

61. Sūra 12:2; 20:113; 39:28; 41:3; 42:7; 43:3.

62. M. Yvan, *Voyages et récits*. Vol. 2: *Six mois chez les Malais* (Brussels: Meline, Cans, 1853), p. 76. The entire anecdote is found on pp. 75–76; the translation is my own, as I have been unable to obtain a copy of the English translation apparently published in London in 1855. I am grateful to William Roff of Columbia University (personal communication, 14 July 1980) for the reference to the English version and a citation of part of the passage in question, from which it appears that the English translation is rather free.

63. Cf. the *ḥadīth* in which the Prophet is cited as saying that when the Qur'ān is recited, there descends with the reciting the divine presence (*sakīna*): Bukhārī, *Ṣaḥīḥ*, book 65, sect. on *tafsīr* of S. 48; book 66, sect. 11; al-Tirmidhī, *Ṣaḥīḥ*, book 46, sect. 25; cf. William A. Graham, *Divine Word and Prophetic Word in Early Islam* (The Hague and Paris: Mouton, 1977), pp. 20–21, esp. n. 13.

64. *Al-Muqaddima*, ed. [Etienne] Quatremère, 3 vols. (Paris, 1858), 3:260. On memorizing and recitation as the heart of Muslim education, see Dale F. Eickelman, "The Art of Memory: Islamic Education and its Social Reproduction," *Comparative Studies in Society and History* 20 (1978):485–516.

65. Cited by al-Ghazālī, *Iḥyā'*, 1:273. According to Wensinck, *Concordance*, 1:275b, the ḥadīth does not occur in the classical sources; the Muslim editorial note in my edition of the *Iḥyā'* calls the tradition "weak" and says it is cited in Abū Nuʿaym's *Faḍā'il al-qur'ān* also.

66. The thirtieths are not, of course, the only divisions of the Qur'ān used for recitation: see al-Ghazālī, *Iḥyā'*, 1:276; cf. Edward Sell, *The Faith of Islam*, 3rd ed. (London, 1907), Appendix A, "ʿIlmu't-tajwīd."

67. Such retreats in Ramaḍān are known as *iʿtikāf* (lit. "withdrawing"). Cf. Th. W. Juynboll, "Iʿtikāf," *SEI; Kitāb al-fiqh ʿalā al-madhāhib al-arbaʿa: Qism al-ʿibādāt* (Cairo: Wizārat al-Awqāf wal-Shu'ūn al-Ijtimāʿīya, 1387/1967), section "al-Iʿtikāf", pp. 551–60.

68. Louis Gardet, "Dhikr," *EI²*; "Zikr," in Thomas Patrick Hughes, *A Dictionary of Islam* [Lahore: Premier Book House, n.d. (orig. ed., 1885)]; Kojiro Nakamura, *Ghazali*

on Prayer (Tokyo: Institute of Oriental Culture, University of Tokyo, 1973), pp. 10–18 (further literature, p. 11, n. 4).

69. Denny, "The Adab" (above, n. 48), and esp. "Qur'ān Recitation Sessions" (above, n. 54). There is also much information on public recitation in Cairo throughout K. Nelson, "Art of Reciting," esp. in ch. IV.

70. Ibid., pp. 120ff.

71. On the importance of *tajwīd* for accurate transmission, see the comment of Nelson, ibid, p. 168.

72. For an extremely informative survey of such popular use of the Qur'ān, see J. Jomier, "La place du Coran dans la vie quotidienne en Égypte," *Institut des Belles Lettres Arabes* (Tunis), 15 (1952):131–65. See also Padwick, *Muslim Devotions*, pp. 108ff.

73. C. Snouck Hurgronje, *Mekka in the Latter Part of the 19th Century*, trans. J. H. Monahan (1931; photogr. repr., Leiden: E. J. Brill, 1970), p. 29; Hughes, *Dictionary*, pp. 45–46; R. Paret, "Fātiḥa," *EI*²; Jomier, "Place du Coran," p. 141, 149.

74. Jomier, "Place du Coran," esp. pp. 148–65, for diverse examples of the popular use of particular sūras and verses; see also Padwick, *Muslim Devotions*, pp. 109–20, and esp. 117ff. on S. Yā Sīn. On the *Laylat al-Barā'a*, the 15th of the month of Shaʿbān, see *ibid.*, pp. 117–18; Hughes, *Dictionary*, p. 570 (*s.v.* "Shab-i-Barāt"); "Mrs. Meer Hasan Ali," *Observations on the Mussulmauns of India*, 2 vols. (London, 1832), pp. 300–3; Jaʿfar Sharīf, *Islam in India, or the Qānūn-i-Islām: The Customs of the Musalmans of India*, ed. and trans. G. A. Herklots. Rev. ed. William Crooke (1921; repr. ed. New Delhi: Oriental Books Reprint Corp., 1972), pp. 203–4; Snouck Hurgronje, *Mecca*, p. 61.

75. Al-Ghazālī, Iḥyā', 1:272.

76. Padwick, *Muslim Devotions*, p. 119.

77. "Entstehung und Wesen der Buchreligion," note 10 above.

Chapter 3. The Popular Muḥammad

1. Joachim Wach, *Sociology of Religion* (Chicago: University of Chicago Press, 1954), p. 331.

2. See Joseph Kitagawa, "Kukai as Master and Saviour," in *The Biographical Process*, ed. Frank E. Reynolds and Donald Capps, (The Hague: Mouton, 1976), pp. 319–41.

3. Wach seems to have recognized this when he places Muḥammad in the founders column, despite his prophetic characteristics (*Sociology* p. 347), and sees al-Ghazzali as an example of a cultus prophet (p. 349). Although other scholars, such as Tor Andrae (*Mohammed: The Man and His Faith*) have attempted to apply history of religions categories to the biographical literature about the Prophet, our concern here is with other dimensions of the problem.

4. Ibn Isḥāq, *The Life of Muhammad*, trans. A. Guillaume, (Lahore: Oxford University Press, 1967), p. 81 [hereafter, *The Life*].

5. *The Life*, p. 230.

6. As we see in the work of Charles C. Torrey, *The Jewish Foundation of Islam* (New York: Jewish Institute of Religion Press, 1933).

7. For example, legal structures find little space in Eliade's work. In a revealing note in his *Journal* of 1942 when speaking of his novels, he says: 'I should point out, at

this juncture, the total absence of the moral dimension in these books. The characters do as they wish without the least resistance, the women give in easily, no one marries, no one has children. . . . The truth is, that, for me, the metaphysical and biological concentrations do not leave room for any other problematic. Eros, with me (that is, since I was about 8 or 10 years old) has had a metaphysical function. Love engages and sanctions without any indispensable presence of society or institutions. . . . Another thing: I am living markedly by the textual and symbolic expression of Hindu mysticism (Vaishnavism) which expresses mystical love in terms of adultery and not marriage; therefore, to signify the transcendence of all mystical experience, one sees its essence as estranged from the world.' *Mircea Eliade*, comp. Constantin Tacou, et al., (Paris: L. Herne, 1977) p. 328, nt. 56, my translation. Just about everything he says would put him beyond the pale according to Islam.

8. This historical data is based upon Yuen Ren Chao, "Models in Linguistics and Models in General," *Logic, Methodology and Philosophy of Science*, ed. Ernest Nagel, Patrick Suppes, and Alfred Tarski, (Stanford, Calif.: Stanford University Press, 1962), pp. 558–66.

9. Charles Francis Hockett, "Two Models of Grammatical Description," *Word* 10/2–3 (1954):210.

10. Hockett, "Two Models," pp. 563–64.

11. Max Black, *Models and Metaphors* (Ithaca, New York: Cornell University Press, 1962), pp. 219–43.

12. See Stephen Coburn Pepper, *World Hypotheses: A Study in Evidence* (Berkeley: University of California Press, 1948), especially chapter 5.

13. Ibid., p. 241.

14. Ibid., p. 232.

15. Among them: Ian T. Ramsey, *Religious Language* (London: Oxford University Press, 1957); *Freedom and Immortality* (London: Oxford University Press, 1960); *On Being Sure in Religion* (London: Oxford University Press, 1963); *Models and Mystery* (London: Oxford University Press, 1964); *Religion and Science* (London: Oxford University Press, 1964).

16. Ibid., p. 1.

17. Ibid., p. 45.

18. Ibid., pp. 10, 11, and 13.

19. Ibid., pp. 57–58. There are two reasons which he says take him beyond Black. One is that an object "declares its objectivity by actively confronting us" (*Models and Mystery*) and two is by the special meaning of religious utterances. See also *Religious Language*, pp. 51ff.

20. *Models and Mystery*, pp. 21, 66.

21. *Models and Mystery*, p. 67.

22. Ewert Cousins, "Models and the Future of Theology," *Continuum* 7 (1969): 78–92.

23. Ibid., p. 83.

24. Ibid., pp. 85–86.

25. Ibid., p. 87.

26. For an outline of this literature see Ibn Isḥāq, *The Life*, introduction, xiv ff.

27. Ibid., p. xvii.

28. John Wansbrough, *The Sectarian Milieu: Content and Composition of Salvation History* (Oxford: Oxford University Press, 1978), p. 103 (hereafter *SM*).

29. Walter Bauer, *Rechtgläubigkeit und Ketzerei im ältesten Christentum*, 2nd ed. G. Strecker (Tübingen: Mohr, 1964) and Julius Wellhausen, *Das arabische Reich und sein Sturz* (Berlin, 1960 [1902]), Eng. trans. Margaret Graham Weir, *The Arab Kingdom and Its Fall* (London: Curzon Press, 1973).

30. Wansbrough, *SM*, p. 125–26. For an appreciative assessment of Wansbrough's methodology, see Andrew Rippin's contribution to this volume, Chapter 9; in Chapter 12 Fazlur Rahman offers a sharp criticism of Wansbrough and Rippin.

31. Ibid., p. 128.

32. Ibn Isḥāq, *The Life*, p. 6.

33. Ibid., pp. 20–33. But see p. 34 where the Quraysh are squarely rulers with Himyar, the Abyssinians, and the Persians.

34. Ibid., p. 27.

35. Ibid., p. 28.

36. Ibid., pp. 35–36.

37. Ibid., pp. 596–97.

38. E.g., see Aḥmad al-Sharabāṣī, *Min adab al-nubūwwa* [Selections from the Literature of Prophecy] (Cairo: The Higher Council of Islamic Affairs, 1971); Aḥmad Ḥusayn, *Nabī Al-insanīyya* [The Prophet of Humanity] (Cairo: The Higher Council of Islamic Affairs, 1970). Remarkable, too, is a collectively authored volume entitled *Muḥammad: Naẓra ʿaṣriyya jadīda* [Muḥammad: A New Modern Viewpoint] (Beirut: Foundation of Arabic Studies and Publication, 1972).

39. Ṭāhā Ḥusayn, *Fī l-shiʿr al-jāhilī* [on Pre-Islamic Poetry] (Cairo: Dar al-Kutub al-Miṣriyya, 1926), p. 12.

40. *ʿAlā hāmish al-sīra* [On the Margin of (the Prophet's) Biography] 3 vols. 22d ed. (Cairo: Dar al-Maʿārif, 1973).

41. *ʿAlā hāmish*, vol. 1.

42. It was even more baffling when I learned that he had published a book on Ibn al-ʿArabī that very nearly was banned by the parliament in 1978. Conservatism must have felt greatly threatened.

43. ʿAbbās Muḥmūd al-ʿAqqād, *ʿAbqariyya Muḥammad* (Cairo: Dār al-Kitāb al-ʿArabī, 1969).

44. Ibid., pp. 55–57.

45. Ibid., pp. 61–63.

46. Ḥusayn, *ʿAlā hāmish*, vol. 3, p. 242. Quoted in Pierre Cachia, *Ṭāhā Ḥusayn*, (London: Luzac and Co., 1956), p. 97, emphasis added.

47. Aḥmad Tālib, *Lettres de Prison, 1957–61*, trans. Kenneth Cragg (Algiers: Editions Nationales Algériennes, 1966), pp. 109–16. Selection quoted in Kenneth Cragg and Marston Speight, *Islam from Within* (Belmont, Calif.: Wadsworth, 1980), p. 228.

48. Cragg, *Islam from Within*, p. 229.

49. Khālid M. Khālid, *Kamā taḥaddatha al-rasūl*, (Beirut: Dār al-Kitāb al-ʿArabī, 1974), vol. 3, p. 129.

50. Ibid., p. 131.

51. Ibid., p. 130.

52. Ibid., p. 130.

53. Perhaps even beyond the language of the "secularist" and "religionist." See the argument of Hisham Sharabi, *Arab Intellectuals and the West: The Formative Years, 1875–1914*, (Baltimore: Johns Hopkins Press, 1970), pp. 86ff.

54. From Ibn Hishām's notes, attributed to Ḥassān b. Thābit, *The Life*, pp. 796–97.

Chapter 4. Islamic Ritual

1. Wilfred Cantwell Smith, *Islam in Modern History* (Princeton: Princeton University Press, 1957), p. 20.

2. *Encyclopaedia of Islam*, new ed., s.v. "ʿIbādāt."

3. The first Hadith is from Muslim, the second from Aḥmad b. Ḥanbal; for the original texts see M. M. Ali, *A Manual of Hadith* (Lahore, n.d. [1944]), pp. 41–42.

4. See J. D. J. Waardenburg, "Official and Popular Religion as a Problem in Islamic Studies," *Official and Popular Religion as a Theme in the Study of Religion*, ed. Vryhof and J. Waardenburg (The Hague: Mouton, 1979), pp. 340–86.

5. Clifford Geertz, *Islam Observed: Religious Development in Morocco and Indonesia* (New Haven: Yale University Press, 1968).

6. S. F. Nadel, *Nupe Religion: Traditional Beliefs and the Influence of Islam in a West African Chiefdom* (New York: Schocken Books, 1970; first published in 1954).

7. Sir Richard F. Burton, *Personal Narrative of a Pilgrimage to Al-Madinah and Meccah*, 2 vols. (London, 1893; New York: Dover Publications, 1964); C. Snouck Hurgronje, *Mekka in the Latter Part of the 19th Century*, trans. J. H. Monahan (Leiden: E. J. Brill, 1931), a translation of the second volume of *Mekka* 2 vols. (The Hague, 1888–1889). See nt. 16 below.

8. See Hortense Powdermaker's discerning reflections of this in *Stranger and Friend: The Way of an Anthropologist* (New York: W. W. Norton, 1966), especially pp. 111–13; 289–96.

9. Clifford Geertz, "Religion as a Cultural System," in Michael Banton, ed., *Anthropological Approaches to the Study of Religion*, A. S. A. Monographs, no. 3 (London: Tavistock Publications, 1966), pp. 28–29, 40.

10. George Santayana, *Reason in Religion*, vol. 3, *The Life of Reason, or the Phases of Human Progress* (New York: Scribners, 1905; repr. 1926), pp. 5–6. Quoted as the epigraph to Geertz, "Religion as a Cultural System," p. 1.

11. See Claude Lévi-Strauss, *Tristes Tropiques* (New York: Atheneum, 1963), especially pp. 381–92.

12. For sensitive and wise reflection on this see Wilfred Cantwell Smith, "Comparative Religion: Whither—and Why?" in *The History of Religions: Essays in Methodology*, ed. Mircea Eliade and Joseph M. Kitagawa (Chicago: University of Chicago Press, 1959), pp. 31–58, especially 34ff.

13. See Mircea Eliade, "A New Humanism," in *The Quest: History and Meaning in Religion* (Chicago: University of Chicago Press, 1969), pp. 1–11. Eliade stops just short of calling the history of religions a "new humanism," but instead sees it as being the most promising avenue to a "philosophical anthropology."

14. Edward William Lane's classic, *An Account of the Manners and Customs of the Modern Egyptians* (New York: Dover Publications, 1973; first pub. 1836), continues to

serve as a mine of information on ritual, customs, superstitions, etc., both because of its excellence and its lack of rivals. Apparently less well known but far more exhaustive and scientific, is Edward A. Westermarck's stupendous *Ritual and Belief in Morocco*, 2 vols. (London: Macmillan and Co., 1926). For a basic orientation, see Frederick M. Denny and Abdulaziz A. Sachedina, *Islamic Ritual Practices: A Slide Set and Teacher's Guide*, Asian Media Resources 7 (New Haven: Yale Divinity School Paul Vieth Center, 1983).

15. See Waardenburg, "Official and Popular Religion," especially pp. 342–60.

16. The earlier study is *Het Mekkaansche Feest* (Leiden: E. J. Brill, 1880); the lengthy work which resulted from his field work in Mecca is *Mekka*, vol. 1, *Die Stadt und ihre Herren*, vol. 2, *Aus dem heutigen Leben* (The Hague: 1888–1889).

17. See J. Chelhod, "A Contribution to the Problem of the Pre-eminence of the Right, Based upon Arabic Evidence," in *Right and Left: Essays on Dual Symbolic Classification*, ed. Rodney Needham (Chicago: University of Chicago Press, 1973), pp. 239–62.

18. Mary Douglas, *Purity and Danger* (Baltimore: Pelican Books, 1970), ch. 3, "The Abominations of Leviticus."

19. Ibid., p. 72.

20. Chelhod, "Pre-eminence of the Right," is an exception and he provides a useful bibliography, particularly of classical sources. See also A. J. Wensinck, "The Ideas of the Western Semites Concerning the Navel of the Earth," *Verhandelingen der Koninklijke Akademie van Wetenschappen te Amsterdam*, Afdeeling Letterkunde, n.s., vol. 17, no. 1.

21. Various calendars have been used by Islamic peoples. For a review of those of ancient times, see Al-Bīrūnī, *Chronology of Ancient Nations*, trans. and ed. C. Edward Sachau (London: W. H. Allen, 1879). Westermarck, *Ritual and Belief*, vol. 2, pp. 58–158, provides exhaustive data on observances connected with the Islamic calendar in Morocco.

22. William A. Graham, *Divine Word and Prophetic Word in Early Islam* (The Hague and Paris: Mouton, 1977), p. 213.

23. See, for example, Joseph Williams McPherson, *The Moulids of Egypt: Egyptian Saints Days* (Cairo, 1941); Taufik Canaan, *Mohammedan Saints and Sanctuaries in Palestine* (London: Luzac and Co., 1927); and R. Kriss and H. Kriss-Heinrich, *Volksglaube im Bereich des Islam*, 2 vols. (Wiesbaden: Otto Harrassowitz, 1962); contains excellent materials on popular pilgrimages, magic, divination, and amulets; copiously illustrated.

24. Victor Turner, *The Ritual Process* (Chicago: Aldine, 1969). See William Roff's discussion of Turner in Chapter 5 of this volume.

25. See Seyyed Hossein Nasr, *Islamic Science* (London: World of Islam Festival Publishing Company, 1976), pp. 91–93 and *passim*.

26. Theodor Gaster, *Thespis: Ritual, Myth and Drama in the Ancient Near East* (New York: Harper Torchbooks, 1966; repr. of rev. ed. 1961).

27. Ibid., p. 23.

28. See McPherson, *Moulids*, pp. 285–93.

29. See, for example, Ignaz Goldziher, "Veneration of Saints in Islam," in *Muslim Studies*, vol. 2, trans. C. R. Barber and S. M. Stern (London: George Allen and Unwin, 1971), pp. 307–10; originally published as two volumes in one, *Muhammedanische Studien* (Halle: Max Neimeyer, 1889–90).

30. Nadel, *Nupe Religion*, chs. 3 and 4.

31. See Muhammad U. Memon, *Ibn Taimiya's Struggle Against Popular Religion* (The Hague and Paris: Mouton, 1976).

32. Unpublished lecture delivered at the University of Colorado, October, 1979, titled "Saint Cults in Southwest Arabia." See Serjeant's "Haram and Hawtah, The Sacred Enclave in Arabia," *Mélanges Taha Husain*, ed. Adburrahman Badawi (Cairo: Dār al-Maʿārif, 1962), pp. 41–58, for a suggestive overview of sacred space in Arabia and its social as well as military ramifications.

33. Arnold van Gennep, *The Rites of Passage*, trans. M. B. Vizedom and B. L. Caffee (Chicago: University of Chicago Press, 1960; orig. pub. 1909).

34. W. Montgomery Watt, "Conditions of Membership in the Islamic Community," *Studia Islamica* 21 (1964):5–12.

35. Mischa Titiev, "A Fresh Approach to the Problem of Magic and Religion," *Southwestern Journal of Anthropology* 16 (1960):292–98.

36. See Lane, *Manners and Customs* (New York: Dover Publications, 1973), pp. 57–58. The donning of girl's clothing is to deflect the "evil eye" from the boy's person. Westermarck, *Ritual and Belief*, vol. 2, pp. 416–33, provides much information from various Moroccan locales. A discerning psychoanalytic study of circumcision and other genital operations is Bruno Bettelheim, *Symbolic Wounds: Puberty Rites and the Envious Male* (New York: Collier Books, 1962; orig. pub. 1954), which is worth consulting with reference to Islamic practices.

37. Seyyed Hossein Nasr, *Ideals and Realities of Islam* (Boston: Beacon Press, 1972), p. 51.

38. Muḥyi l-Dīn Abū Zakarīyā' Yaḥyā al-Ḥizāmī al-Dimashqī, a famed Shāfiʿī jurist (A.H. 631–676/A.D. 1233–1277). *Al-tibyān* is available in several printed editions (Cairo, 1977, *inter alia*). For a discussion of al-Nawawī's ideas regarding the correct procedures for Qur'an reciters, see Frederick M. Denny, "The Adab of Qur'an Recitation: Text and Context," in A. H. Johns and S. H. M. Jafri, eds., *International Congress for the Study of the Qur'an*, Series 1 (Canberra: Australian National University Press, 1982), pp. 143–160. Present-day practices are analysed and compared with al-Nawawī's ideal requirements.

39. Waardenburg, "Official and Popular Religion," p. 357ff., counsels using the term "normative" rather than "official" Islam, because of the absence of any single official body or hierarchy. See also Fazlur Rahman's contribution to Part V of this volume. Normative Islam is rooted in the Shariʿa, which is itself subject to a wide range of interpretation and application, although Rahman, again, has some interesting things to say about this. Another term which Waardenburg uses is "alternative" Islam, a relational concept which applies to schools and sects. Significantly, the common denominator in all three—normative, alternative, and folk—is *Islam* itself.

Chapter 5. Pilgrimage and the History of Religions

1. Wilfred Cantwell Smith, "History of Religions—Whither and Why?," *The History of Religions: Essays in Methodology* ed. Mircea Eliade and J. M. Kitagawa (Chicago: University of Chicago Press, 1959), p. 43.

2. Smith, "History of Religions," p. 53.

3. Jacques Waardenburg, "The Academic Study of Islam: An Historian of Religions' Point of View," (paper delivered at the symposium on Islam and the History of Religions, Arizona State University, Tempe, Arizona, January 1980).

4. Arnold van Gennep, *The Rites of Passage*, trans. Monika B. Vizedom and Solon T. Kimball, (Chicago: University of Chicago Press, 1960), p. 15, (first pub. 1908).

5. Cf. Harry B. Partin, "The Muslim Pilgrimage: Journey to the Center" (Ph.D. diss., University of Chicago, 1967), pp. 4, 157.

6. See, e.g., M. Gaudefroy-Demombynes (*Le Pélerinage à la Mekke. Étude d'Histoire Religieuse* (Paris: Paul Geuthner, 1923), p. 179; and Richard F. Burton. *Personal Narrative of a Pilgrimage to Al-Madinah and Meccah* (London: G. Bell and Sons, 1913), vol. 1:123 (first pub. 1855).

7. Edward Westermarck, *Ritual and Belief in Morocco* (London: Macmillan and Co., 1926), pp. 296–97; and Muhammad Rafiqi, "Pelayaran ke Mekka al-Mashrafa" [Journey to Mecca the Noble], *Jasa* (Muar) 3, no. 7 (May 1930):176.

8. Clifford Geertz, *The Religion of Java* (Glencoe, Ill.: Free Press, 1960), p. 11.

9. Burton, *Personal Narrative*, vol. 1:143.

10. Gaudefroy-Demombynes, *Le Pélerinage*, pp. 155–56.

11. Ahmad Kamal, *The Sacred Journey: Being the Pilgrimage to Makkah* (London: Allen and Unwin, 1964), p. 13.

12. Muhammad Hamidullah, "Le pélerinage à la Mecque," in *Les Pélerinages: Sources Orientales* (Paris: Editions du Seuil, 1960), vol. 3:117.

13. Al-Bukhārī *Sharḥ Saḥīḥ al-Bukhārī* (Penang: Persama Press, 1949), vol. 12:22; and A. J. Wensinck, *A Handbook of Early Muslim Tradition* (Leiden: E. J. Brill, 1927), p. 185.

14. Victor Turner, "Pilgrimage as Social Process," in *Dramas, Fields and Metaphors: Symbolic Action in Human Society* (Ithaca, N.Y.: Cornell University Press, 1974), p. 96.

15. Turner, *Dramas*, pp. 182–83.

16. 'Umar al-Naqar, *The Pilgrimage Tradition in West Africa: An Historical Study with Special Reference to the Nineteenth Century* (Khartoum: Khartoum University Press, 1972), pp. xxii–xxiii, 12–15.

17. Hamka (Hajji Abdul Malek b. Karim Amrullah), *Kenang-kenangan Hidup* [Life's Memories] (Jakarta: Gapura, 1951), vol. 1:82–84.

18. Al-Bukhārī, *Saḥiḥ*, vol. 12:21.

19. Turner, *Dramas*, p. 202.

20. Partin, "Muslim Pilgrimage," pp. 163–64.

21. Kamal, *Sacred Journey*, p. 35.

22. The telescoping of the noon (*ẓuhr*) and afternoon (*'aṣr*) prayers, the latter brought forward for the purpose, is further suggestive of the "liminal time" that characterizes the central moments of the Hajj.

23. Malcolm X, *The Autobiography of Malcolm X* (New York: Grove Press, 1966), p. 340, [emphasis in the original].

24. Van Gennep, *Rites of Passage*, p. 3.

25. Victor Turner, *The Forest of Symbols: Aspects of Ndembu Ritual* (Ithaca, N.Y.: Cornell University Press, 1967), p. 94.

26. See, e.g., Vincent Crapanzano, "Rite of Return: Circumcision in Morocco," *The Psychoanalytical Study of Society* 9 (1980); and Barbara Nimri Aziz, "New Perspective on Pilgrimage," (Paper delivered at the 10th International Congress of Anthropological and Ethnological Sciences, Delhi, 1978).

27. Victor Turner, *Image and Pilgrimage in Christian Culture: Anthropological Perspectives* (New York: Columbia University Press, 1978).

28. Al-Hujwīrī, ʿAlī b. ʿUthmān al-Jullābī, *Kashf al-Maḥjūb of Al-Hujwīrī*, trans. R. A. Nicholson (London: Luzac and Co., 1936), p. 327.

Chapter 6. Primitive Mind/Modern Mind

1. See Muhammad Abdul-Rauf, "Outsiders' Interpretations of Islam: A Muslim's Point of View," and Fazlur Rahman, "Approaches to Islam in Religious Studies Review Essay," in Part V of this book.

2. A. F. C. Wallace, "Revitalization Movements," *American Anthropoligist*, 58 (1956): 264–81.

3. Jack Goody, *The Domestication of the Savage Mind* (Cambridge: Cambridge University Press, 1977).

4. Stanley Diamond, *In Search of the Primitive: A Critique of Civilization* (New Brunswick, N.J.: Transaction Books, 1974).

5. Cf. Peter Laslett, *The World We Have Lost* (2d ed.; New York: Scribner's, 1971); and Philip Slater, *Earthwalk* (Garden City, N.Y.: Anchor Books, 1974).

6. Eric Wolf, "Foreword," in *In Search of the Primitive*, p. xiii.

7. Diamond, *In Search*, p. 44.

8. Robin Horton, "Levy-Bruhl, Durkheim and the Scientific Revolution," in *Modes of Thought: Essays on Thinking in Western and Non-Western Societies*, Ruth Finnegan and Robin Horton ed., (London: Faber and Faber, 1973).

9. For the critique, see Goody, *Domestication*, p. 38.

10. Clifford Geertz, "Religion as a Cultural System," in *The Interpretation of Cultures* (New York: Basic Books, 1973), pp. 87–125.

11. Geertz, "Religion," p. 90.

12. Robert Blair Kaiser, "Black Catholic Congregation Ignores Vatican Formalism," *New York Times*, May 26, 1980, p. A10.

13. Marshall Hodgson, "The Impact of the Great Western Transmutation: The Generation of 1789," in *The Venture of Islam: Conscience and History in a World Civilization*, 3 vols. (Chicago: University of Chicago Press, 1974), vol. 3, pp. 176–222. In an article published earlier, Hodgson had shown the inappropriateness of some of these cognitive features to the reading of pre-modern texts. See "Two Pre-Modern Muslim Historians: Pitfalls and Opportunities in Presenting Them to Moderns," in *Towards World Community*, ed. John Nef, Publications of the World Academy of Art and Science, 5 (The Hague: Dr. W. Junk, 1968), pp. 53–68.

14. James Burke, "Faith in Numbers," (New York: Time Life Films, 1978; "Connections," Episode 4).

15. Edward Hall, *Beyond Culture* (New York: Doubleday, 1976), pp. 24–25. Hall also points out that some mental processes, such as morality, can be internalized rather than externalized.

16. Hall, *Beyond Culture*, pp. 24–26.

17. Hall, *Beyond Culture*, p. 28. In this work, Hall draws on Whorf and Sapir's linguistic theories, which he feels have been passed off too lightly. It is interesting that Hall, *Beyond Culture*, and Goody, *Domestication*, dwell upon the effects of this cross-

categorization in the social sciences. Goody shows how even a tabular or charted presentation of a nonliterate belief system totally misrepresents that system through its static and discontinuous form. See also, Gregory Bateson, *Steps to an Ecology of Mind* (New York: Ballantine Books, 1975), pp. 3–8, 38–47; and Michel Foucault, *Order of Things: An Archaeology of Human Sciences* (New York: Pantheon, 1970), pp. xv–xxiv.

18. Goody, *Domestication*, pp. 37, 108–9, and 109–10, respectively. Compare Hall, *Beyond Culture*, pp. 24–25.

19. Goody, *Domestication*, p. 153.

20. Earl W. Waugh, "The Popular Muhammad: Models in the Interpretation of an Islamic Paradigm," Chapter 3 of this book; Mervyn Hiskett, *The Sword of Truth: The Life and Times of Shehu Usuman dan Fadio* (New York: Oxford University Press, 1973), Chapter 2; Marilyn R. Waldman, "The Popular Appeal of the Prophetic Paradigm in Africa," in *Islam in Local Contexts* (*Contribution to Asian Studies*, 17), ed. Richard C. Martin (Leiden: E. J. Brill, 1982) pp. 110–14.

21. Marshall Hodgson, "How did the Early Shiʿa Become Sectarian?" *Journal of the American Oriental Society* 75 (1955):1–13.

22. Goody would also raise questions about whether linear written genealogical lists—a product of literacy—distort our understanding of kinship among nonliterate peoples. According to Goody, the list's features—discontinuity and linearity—are inimical to an understanding of many nonliterate belief systems.

23. William Graham, *Divine Word and Prophetic Word in Early Islam*, Religion and Society, 7 (The Hague: Mouton, 1977). In this connection, we must question Wansbrough's assumption that "Canonization and stabilization of the text of the Qur'ān goes hand in hand with the formation of the community. . . . A fixed text of scripture was not required, nor was it feasible, before political power was firmly controlled. . . ." See Andrew Rippin's "Literary Analysis of *Qur'ān*, *Tafsīr* and *Sīra:* The Methodologies of John Wansbrough," Chapter 9, for an appreciative analysis of John Wansbrough's *Quranic Studies*.

24. Frederick M. Denny, "Islamic Ritual: Perspectives and Theories," Chapter 4 of this book.

25. When I was in Iran, I talked with the village head of Malyan, a place 42 kilometers north of Shiraz, about what the Qur'ān meant to him. He brought his copy down from a niche to read it to or with me, and explained its contents to me in the following way: "It tells us not to lie or steal or cheat or do bad things to our neighbors"—apparently those behaviors deemed most unacceptable in Malyan. For him its contents were fluid, not fixed and ordered. When a reader I edited was used with students in Ghana, they deemed my Qur'ānic selections from the mundane portions of Sūrat al-Nūr less important and representative than ones they preferred from other chapters (oral communication from William Hutchins, November, 1979).

26. Compare Richard M. Eaton, "Approaches to the Study of Conversion to Islam in India," Chapter 7 in this book.

27. Joseph Schacht, *Origins of Muhammadan Jurisprudence* (Oxford: Oxford University Press, 1950); Nabia Abbott, *Quranic Commentary and Tradition: Studies in Arabic Literary Papyri*, vol. 2, Oriental Institute Publications Series 76 (Chicago: University of Chicago Press, 1967).

28. See Michael M. J. Fischer, "On Changing the Concept and Position of Persian

Women," *Women in the Muslim World*, ed. Lois Beck and Nikki Keddie (Cambridge, Mass.: Harvard University Press, 1978), pp. 189–215.

29. Ibid. See also Mahmoud Ayoub, *Redemptive Suffering in Islam: A Study of the Devotional Aspects of 'Ashūrā' in Twelver Shīism* (The Hague: Mouton, 1978).

30. Mujahid al-Sawwaf, "Cultural Aspects of Islamic Pilgrimage," public lecture at The Ohio State University, May 25, 1977.

31. Compare Dale F. Eickelman, "The Art of Memory: Islamic Education and Its Social Reproduction," *Comparative Studies in Society and History*, 20 (1978):485–516. Eickelman shows the parallelism between techniques for teaching religious sciences and for teaching craft skills in the wider society.

32. Fazlur Rahman, "Islam and the Study of Religion," Chapter 12 of this book.

33. Arnold Toynbee, *A Study of History*, vol. 3, quoted in Ronald H. Nash, *Ideas of History* (New York: E. P. Dutton and Co., Inc., 1969), vol. 1, pp. 202–3.

Chapter 7. Approaches to the Study of Conversion to Islam in India

1. Peter Hardy, "Modern European and Muslim Explanation of Conversion to Islam in South Asia: A Preliminary Survey of the Literature," in *Conversion to Islam*, ed. Nehemia Levtzion (New York: Holmes and Meier, 1979), p. 78.

2. In these accounts one frequently meets with such ambiguous phrases as *itaʿat-i islam numudand* or *dar itaʿat-i islam amadand* ("they submitted to Islam" or "they came under submission to Islam"), in which "Islam" might mean either the religion, the Muslim state, or more crudely, the "army of Islam." A contextual reading of such passages usually favors one of the latter two interpretations. See Y. Friedmann, "A contribution to the early history of Islam in India," in *Studies in Memory of Gaston Wiet*, ed. Myrian Rosen-Ayalon (Jerusalem: Institute of Asian and African Studies, 1977), p. 322.

3. The first accurate census reports, those of the late nineteenth century, put the Muslims of East Bengal and West Punjab at between 70 percent and 90 percent of the total, and of the upper Gangetic Plain at around 10 to 15 percent. Regarding the lack of conversions in the heartland, two sociologists have argued that Mughal persecution of the Meo community of Rajasthan, far from strengthening the Islamic identity of that nominally converted community, reinforced their resistance to Islamic influence. See S. L. Sharma and R. N. Srivastava, "Institutional Resistance to Induced Islamization in a Convert Community—an Empiric Study in Sociology of Religion," *Sociological Bulletin* 16/1 (March, 1967):77.

4. Agha Mahdi Husain, ed. and trans., *The Rehla of Ibn Batuta* (Baroda: Oriental Institute, 1953), p. 46.

5. Hardy, "Modern European and Muslim Explanations," pp. 80–81.

6. Aziz Ahmad, *Studies in Islamic Culture in the Indian Environment* (Oxford: Clarendon Press, 1964), p. 105.

7. See Louis Dumont, *Homo Hierarchicus: An Essay on the Caste System*, trans. Mark Sainsbury (Chicago: University of Chicago Press, 1970).

8. Yohanan Friedmann, "Medieval Muslim Views of Indian Religions," *Journal of the American Oriental Society,* 95 (1975):214–21.

9. See, for example, Imtiaz Ahmed, ed., *Caste and Social Stratification among the Muslims* (Delhi: Manohar Book Service, 1973).

10. See Levtzion, *Conversion to Islam*, pp. 21–23, and Arthur Darby Nock, *Conversion: The Old and the New in Religion from Alexander the Great to Augustine of Hippo* (Oxford: Oxford University Press, 1933), p. 8.

11. See Max Weber, *The Sociology of Religion*, trans. Ephraim Fischoff, introd. Talcott Parsons (Boston: Beacon Press, 1963), p. 22.

12. Sharma and Srivstava, "Institutional Resistance," pp. 73–75.

13. See Melford Spiro, "Religion: Problems of Definition and Explanation" in *Anthropological Approaches to the Study of Religion*, ed. M. Banton (New York: Praeger, 1966), p. 96.

14. For a pioneering study of the use of personal names as a correlate of Islamic conversions, see Richard W. Bulliet, *Conversion to Islam in the Medieval Period: An Essay in Quantitative History* (Cambridge, Mass.: Harvard University Press, 1979).

15. Maulavi Nur Muhammad, *Tarikh-i Jhang Sial* (Meerut, 1862), pp. 15–28.

16. Asim Roy, "Islam in the Environment of Medieval Bengal" (Ph.D. diss., Australian National University, 1970), pp. 189–202, *passim.*

17. Ibid., p. 299.

18. Ibid., p. 300.

19. Al-Masʿudi, *Les prairies d'or*, trans. C. Barbier de Meynard and Pavet de Courteille, 9 vols. (Paris, 1891–1917), vol. 2, pp. 85–86.

20. Mahdi Husain, *Rehla*, pp. 176–96.

21. Ibn Battuta observed that although the Muslims of Malabar were the most respected people in the area, "the natives do not dine with them and do not admit them into their houses." *Rehla*, p. 183.

22. See *Gazeteer of Bombay Presidency: Bijapur District*, vol. 23 (Bombay, 1884), pp. 282–305.

23. On the significance of literacy for religious conversion in general, see Jack Goody, "Religion, Social Change and the Sociology of Conversion," in *Changing Social Structure in Ghana*, ed. Jack Goody (London: International African Institute, 1975), pp. 101 ff. See also J. D. Y. Peel, "Syncretism and Religious Change," *Comparative Studies in Society and History* 10 (1967–68):139–40. Marilyn Waldman's paper, Chapter 6 in this volume, discusses the importance of Goody's theory of literacy/nonliteracy for Islamic studies.

24. Thomas Walker Arnold, *The Preaching of Islam* (London: Constable, 1913), pp. 154–93.

25. See my *Sufis of Bijapur: Social Roles of Sufis in Medieval India* (Princeton: Princeton University Press, 1978), especially chapter 6.

26. Mahdi Husain, *Rehla*, p. 20.

27. John Briggs, trans., *History of the Rise of the Mahomedan Power in India*, 3 vols. (Calcutta, 1966), vol. 2, pp. 245–46.

28. Data collected in the early twentieth century illustrate this. Shrines of the first category would include that of Hasan Teli of Lahore for oilmen; that of Shaykh Musa for blacksmiths; that of ʿAli Rangrez for dyers; and that of Pir Badar in Chittagong for sailors. The second category would include the tomb of Shah Sufaid in Jhelum Dis-

trict for lepers; the tomb of Miran Nau Bahar for curing hysterical fits; the tomb of Nizam al-Din in Lahore for warts; that of Pir Bukhari in Quetta for venereal diseases; and that of Shah Mina in Lucknow for legal difficulties. See Thomas Arnold, "Saints and Martyrs [Muhammadans in India]," *Encyclopaedia of Religion and Ethics*, ed. James Hastings, vol. 11:70–71.

29. D. D. Kosambi, "The Basis of Ancient Indian History (I)," *Journal of the American Oriental Society*, 75 (1955):38.

30. See Richard M. Eaton, "The Political and Religious Authority of the Shrine of Baba Farid in Pakpattan, Punjab" in *Moral Conduct and Authority: the Place of Adab in South Asian Islam*, ed. Barbara Metcalf (Berkeley, Calif.: University of California Press, 1983).

31. John P. Thorp, "Masters of Earth: Conceptions of 'Power' among Muslims of Rural Bangladesh," (Ph.D. diss., University of Chicago, 1978), pp. 40–45. This general argument respecting Bengal will be more fully developed in Richard M. Eaton's forthcoming study on Islam in medieval Bengal.

32. Mohammed Mujeeb, *The Indian Muslims* (London: Allen and Unwin, 1967), p. 10.

33. *Census of India*, 1901, vol. 6, p. 176.

34. See, for example, Eaton, *Sufis of Bijapur*, chapter 5.

35. P. M. Holt, et al., eds., *Cambridge History of Islam*, 2 vols. (Cambridge: Cambridge University Press, 1970), vol. 2, p. 77.

36. See Azim Nanji, *The Nizari Isma'ili Tradition in the Indo-Pakistan Subcontinent* (Delmar, N.Y.: Caravan Books, 1978).

37. Clifford Geertz, "Religion as a Cultural System," in *Anthropoligical Approaches to the Study of Religion*, ed. M. Banton (New York: Praeger, 1966), p. 40.

38. This actually occurred in the case of the shrine at Kallar Kahar in Jhelam District, Punjab, an apparently Buddhist shrine which the historical saint Makhdum Jahanian is said to have more or less redefined as the tomb of a Muslim *faqir* or holyman. See *Punjab District Gazetteers: Jhelam District* (Lahore, 1883–84), p. 63.

39. Geertz, "Religion as a Cultural System," pp. 35–36.

Chapter 8. The Hermeneutics of Henry Corbin

1. *Mélanges offerts à Henry Corbin*, ed. Seyyed Hussein Nasr (Teheran: Teheran Branch, Institute of Islamic Studies, McGill University, 1977) Wisdom of Persia, vol. 9:iii ff.

2. *En Islam Iranien*, 4 vols., Bibliothèque des idées (Paris: Editions Gallimard, 1971), vol. 1:xi–xii.

3. *Anthologie des philosophes Iraniens*, vol. 1, Sayyed Jalāloddīn Ashtiyānī with analytical introduction by Henry Corbin (Teheran and Paris, 1972), Bibliothèque Iranienne, vol. 18.

4. For a slightly different analysis see Hamid Algar "The Study of Islam: the Work of Henry Corbin," *Religious Studies Review* 6/2 (April, 1980):1ff.

5. First published in Paris in 1960 and in a revised edition in 1979. The English translation is called *Spiritual Body and Celestial Earth*, trans. N. Pearson, Bollingen Series, no. 91 (Princeton: Princeton University Press, 1977).

6. Fazlur Rahman, *The Philosophy of Mullā Sadrā* (Ṣadr al-Dīn al-Shīrāzī), (Albany, State University of New York Press: 1975).

7. Among Corbin's earliest publications were translations of Martin Heidegger and Karl Jaspers, the German philosophers. For many years he was best known for this contribution to twentieth-century philosophical thought.

8. *En Islam Iranien*, vol. 1:xxvii.

9. Ibid., 1:xix.

10. Ibid., 1:xix–xx.

11. Ibid., 1:xiv.

12. Ibid., 1:4.

13. Ibid., 1:xix.

14. Ibid., 1:33.

15. Cf. "Mundus imaginalis ou l'imaginaire et l'imaginal," *Cahiers internationaux du symbolisme*, Brussels, 6 (1964):3–26. Published in English translation in *Spring* (1972):1–19.

16. *En Islam Iranien*, 1:5.

17. Ibid., 1:9.

18. Ibid., 1:xvi.

19. Ibid., 1:xviii.

20. Ibid., 1:37.

21. In the article cited above Hamid Algar argues that Corbin has defied the historical evidence by treating a variety of Sunni thinkers, eg., Ibn Sīnā, Ibn ʿArabī, even Suhrawardī, as Shiʿa.

Chapter 9: Literary Analysis of Qur'ān, Tafsīr, *and* Sīra

1. John Wansbrough, *The Sectarian Milieu: Content and Composition of Islamic Salvation History* (Oxford: Oxford University Press, 1978), pp. 116–17; also see his review of Patricia Crone and Michael Cook, *Hagarism: the Making of the Islamic World* (Cambridge: Cambridge University Press, 1977) in *Bulletin of the School of Oriental and African Studies* [hereafter, *BSOAS*] 41 (1978):155–56. Other interesting reviews of *Hagarism* are J. van Ess in *The Times Literary Supplement* Sept. 8, 1978, pp. 997–98 and N. Daniels in *Journal of Semitic Studies* [hereafter, *JSS*] 24 (1979):296–304. Cf. M. A. Cook, "The Origins of *Kalam*," *BSOAS* 43 (1980):32–43 for a good example of what *can* be demonstrated by external sources. Also see Patricia Crone, *Slaves on Horses: The Evolution of the Islamic Polity* (Cambridge: Cambridge University Press, 1980) especially ch. 1; Michael Cook, *Early Muslim Dogma: A source-critical study* (Cambridge: Cambridge University Press, 1981), and his *Muhammad* (Oxford: Oxford University Press, 1983).

2. This *sabab*, the author admits (see note 3 below), is not found in al-Ṭabarī's *Ta'rīkh;* this fact should have raised the curiosity of the author about the literary qualities of the material with which he was dealing. It should be noted in this regard that al-Ṭabarī indeed recognized the difference between exegesis and history.

3. Fred McGraw Donner, "Mecca's Food Supply and Muhammad's Boycott," *Journal of the Economic and Social History of the Orient* 20 (1977):249–66; another, slightly different example is found in Uri Rubin, "Abū Lahab and Sūra CXI," *BSOAS* 42

(1979):13–28, esp. pp. 13–15. On the *asbāb al-nuzūl* see A. Rippin, "The exegetical genre *asbāb al-nuzūl*: a bibliographical and terminological survey," *BSOAS* 48/1 (1985).

4. *Quranic Studies: Sources and Methods of Scriptural Interpretation* (Oxford: Oxford University Press, 1977). Reviews of *QS* are as follows: *Bibliotheca Orientalis* [hereafter *BO*] 35 (1978):349–53 (van Ess); *BSOAS* 40 (1977):609–612 (Ullendorf); *Der Islam* 55 (1978):354–56 (Paret); *Journal of the American Oriental Society* [*JAOS*] 100 (1980):137–41 (Graham); *Jewish Quarterly Review* [*JQR*] 68 (1978):182–84 (Nemoy); *Journal of the Royal Asiatic Society* [*JRAS*] (1978):76–78 (Serjeant); *JSS* 24 (1979):293–96 (Juynboll); *Muslim World* [*MW*] 47 (1977):306–307 (Boullata); *Zeitschrift der deutschen morganländischen Gesellschaft* [*ZDMG*] 128 (1978):411 (Wagner); *Theologische Literaturzeitung* 105 (1980):1–19 (Rudolph).

5. Major reviews of *SM* are as follows: *BSOAS* 43 (1980):137–39 (van Ess); *Journal of the American Academy of Religion* [*JAAR*] 47 (1979): 459–60 (Martin); *JSS* 26 (1980): 121–23 (Rippin); *Der Islam* 57 (1980): 354–55 (Madelung); *BO* 37 (1981):97–98 (Juynboll); *JRAS* (1980):180–82 (Cook); *ZDMG* 130 (1980):178 (Nagel).

6. See esp. his review of Josef van Ess, *Anfänge muslimischer Theologie*, *BSOAS* 43 (1980):361–63.

7. See *SM* 58–59; Crone and Cook, *Hagarism*, pp. 17–18.

8. An example would be the *tafsīr*s ascribed to al-Kalbī and Muqātil; for a variety of reasons which he outlines in *QS*, Wansbrough concludes that the form in which the texts are found today probably stems from a period later than the date of the supposed authors.

9. Examples would be *Fiqh Akbar I*, and the *Risāla* of al-Ḥasan al-Baṣrī; see *QS*, 160–63.

10. See Wansbrough's review of Nabia Abbott, *Studies in Arabic Literary Papyri, II, Qur'ānic Commentary and Tradition*, in *BSOAS* 31 (1968):613–16; cf. A. Grohmann, "The Problem of Dating Early Qur'āns," *Der Islam* 33 (1957):213–31; Grohmann's whole point, of course, is to emphasize the difficulty involved in dating Qur'ānic manuscripts.

11. John Burton, *The Collection of the Qur'ān* (Cambridge: Cambridge University Press, 1977). See Wansbrough's review in *BSOAS* 41 (1978):370–71.

12. Thomas L. Thompson, *The Historicity of the Patriarchal Narratives: The Quest for the Historical Abraham* (Berlin and New York: Walter de Gruyter, 1974), p. 328.

13. H. W. F. Saggs, *The Encounter with the Divine in Mesopotamia and Israel* (London: Athlone Press, 1978), pp. 65–66.

14. See Wansbrough's review of Neusner's work *BSOAS* 39 (1976):438–39 and 43 (1980):591–92 and of Neusner's students, *BSOAS* 41 (1978):368–69 (Zahavy); 42 (1979):140–41 (Green); 43 (1980):592–93 (Gereboff). The most important work of Rudolf Bultmann is *The History of the Synoptic Tradition*, trans. John Marsh, 2d ed. (Oxford: Blackwell, 1968). Neusner has published so much it is virtually impossible to select any one writing; his paper, "The Study of Religion as the Study of Tradition in Judaism," in *Methodological Issues in Religious Studies*, ed. Robert D. Baird (Chico, Calif.: New Horizons Press, 1975), pp. 31–48, is most useful.

15. Neusner's work, on the other hand, seems to imply that a certain amount of historical information is extricable. Implicitly the debate is over basic concerns of interpretational theory, e.g., H. G. Gadamer, *Truth and Method* (New York: Seabury,

1978) *vs.* E. D. Hirsch, Jr., *Validity in Interpretation* (New Haven: Yale University Press, 1967).

16. Joseph Schacht, "The Present State of Studies in Islamic Law," *Atti del terzo Congresso di Studi Arabi e Islamici* (Naples: Instituto Universitario Orientale, 1967), p. 622. Schacht concludes: "I have too strong a confidence in the scholarly competence of the workers in the field of Islamic law, both lawyers and orientalists, to regard this as anything but a passing aberration." If only that were true!

17. Also out of the common desire (need?) to provide "endings," i.e., to eliminate ambiguity; see F. Kermode, *The Genesis of Secrecy* (Cambridge, Mass.: Harvard University Press, 1979), chapter 3; idem, *The Sense of an Ending* (New York: Oxford University Press, 1967).

18. W. M. Watt, "The Materials Used by Ibn Isḥāq," in *Historians of the Middle East*, ed. Bernard Lewis and P. M. Holt (London and New York: Oxford University Press, 1962), pp. 23–24. Watt quotes C. H. Becker (agreeing with Lammens), ". . . the *Sīra* is not an independent historical source. It is merely *ḥadīth*—material arranged in biographical order," (p. 23) to which Watt retorts: "Since Becker wrote, there has been the important work of Joseph Schacht on legal *ḥadīth*. . . . Professor Schacht holds that it was not until the time of al-Shāfiʿī (d. 820) that it became the regular practice for legal rules to be justified by a *ḥadīth* reporting a saying or action of Muḥammad. . . . If this theory is correct . . . then *ḥadīth* as they are found in the canonical collections were not in existence in the time of Ibn Isḥāq (d. 768)" (pp. 23–24). Thus, for Watt, the historical validity of Ibn Isḥāq's material is proven since it was written before the fabrication of legal *ḥadīth!* Cf. P. Crone, *Slaves on Horses*, p. 211, nt. 88: "Watt disposes of Schacht by casuistry."

19. Fuat Sezgin, *Geschichte des arabischen Schriftums*, (Leiden: E. J. Brill, 1967), vol. 1.

20. Nabia Abbott, *Studies in Arabic Literary Papyri*, II, *Qur'ānic Commentary and Tradition* (Chicago: University of Chicago Press, 1967); cf. Wansbrough's review (nt. 10 above).

21. See Sezgin, *GAS* 1:32; cf. A. Rippin, "Ibn ʿAbbās's *Al-Lughāt fī'l-Qur'ān*," *BSOAS* 44 (1981):15–25; also "Al-Zuhrī, *naskh al-Qur'ān* and the problem of early *tafsir* texts," *BSOAS* 47 (1984):22–43, and Wansbrough, *QS*, chapter 4.

22. An example of such "additional evidence" appears in *QS* and *SM* in the notion of "terminological transfer."

23. Harry Austryn Wolfson, *The Philosophy of the Kalam* (Cambridge, Mass.: Harvard University Press, 1976), p. 72; see Wansbrough's review of the work, *BSOAS* 41 (1978):156–57.

24. "Islamic Religious Tradition" in *The Study of the Middle East*, ed. L. Binder (New York: Wiley, 1976), p. 61.

25. Specifically *The Qur'ān, Translated*, 2 vols. (Edinburgh: T. & T. Clark, 1937–39), and *Introduction to the Qur'ān* (Edinburgh: University Press, 1963 [1953]).

26. Cf. Serjeant's review of *QS* in *JRAS* (1978):78, and also van Ess's review in *BO* 35 (1978):349.

27. The term is not meant as one of derision but rather as one descriptive of textual method; see James Barr, *Fundamentalism* (Philadelphia: Westminster Press, 1978), esp. pp. 11–89. Modern scholarship on the Qur'ān treats that book as textually (if not

theologically) inerrant and, more basically, lacking in contradiction. The latter point is nowhere more clearly illustrated than in attempts to understand prayer and almsgiving in the Qur'ān in terms of a (reconstructable!) historical progression; the alternative view that the various passages on these topics represent variant traditions of different localized communities which have been brought into conjunction seems far more plausible in light of our knowledge of Judeo-Christian tradition and its establishment. But to assert this is to contradict the typical Western approach to the Qur'ān.

28. See the well-phrased statements of Franz Rosenthal in the introduction to the reprint of Charles C. Torrey, *The Jewish Foundation of Islam* (New York: KTAV, 1967 [1933]).

29. M. Hodgson's emphasis on the Irano-Semitic background of Islamic culture may prove an honorable exception to this general statement; see Marshall G. S. Hodgson, *The Venture of Islam*, 3 vols. (Chicago: University of Chicago Press, 1974), esp. vol. 1.

30. For modern studies of South Arabia, see, for example, the following recent works: Jacques Ryckmans, *Les inscriptions anciennes de l'Arabie du Sud: Points de vue et problèmes actuels* (Leiden: E. J. Brill, 1973); and J. Pirenne, "La religion des Arabes préislamiques d'après trois sites rupestres et leurs inscriptions" in *Al-Bahit: Festschrift Joseph Henninger zum 70. Geburtstag am 12. Mai 1976* (St. Augustin bei Bonn: Anthropos-Instituts, 1976), pp. 177–217 and cf. the use Serjeant makes of such works in his review of *QS*, *JRAS* (1978):76–77.

31. Adams, "Islamic Religious Tradition," in *The Study of the Middle East* (see nt. 24 above), p. 38.

32. Adams, p. 40, in reference to the "irenic" approach to Islamic studies advocated by W. C. Smith.

33. Jane Smith, in "Islamic Understanding of the Afterlife" [paper presented at the symposium on Islam and the History of Religions (see preface to the present volume)], points directly to the problem very explicitly but seems not to see the solution: "Does the asking of 'wrong' questions necessarily mean that answers will be unrelated to the truths about actual Muslim faith and practice?" If the study of Islam continues to be confronted in terms of "actual Muslim faith and practice" then the problem will continue to exist. The question must be asked: "Is that what we are after?" "Are we studying sociology or intellectual history?" We can do either, and both are without a doubt important, but one cannot ask intellectual-historical questions of sociological data.

34. See *SM* 24–25; *QS* 1, 40–43, 47–48, 51–52, 57–58 as well as the analysis of haggadic *tafsīr* in chapter 4 of *QS* which Wansbrough conceives of as illustrating the point (see *SM* 24).

35. Geza Vermes, "Redemption and Genesis xxii—The Binding of Isaac and the Sacrifice of Jesus," in his *Scripture and Tradition in Judaism: Haggadic Studies*, 2d rev. ed. (Leiden: E. J. Brill, 1973), pp. 193–227. Also see P. R. Davies and B. D. Chilton, "The Aqedah: A Revised Tradition History," *Catholic Biblical Quarterly* 40 (1978): 514–46.

36. And this would include those who attempt to postulate some sort of aberrant Judaism and/or Christianity known specifically to Arabia.

37. This procedure within Qumran is perhaps most clearly enunciated in Bleddyn J. Roberts, "Biblical Exegesis and Fulfillment in Qumran," in *Words and Meaning:*

Essays Presented to David Winton Thomas, ed. Peter R. Akroyd and Barnabas Lindars (Cambridge: Cambridge University Press, 1968), pp. 195–207, although such an interpretation goes against the mainstream of Qumranic scholarship where the trend to try to identify characters such as the Wicked Priest and Teacher of Righteousness predominate as in, e.g., Vermes (see nt. 35 above). Also see *SM* esp. 52–54.

38. See *QS* 49; *SM* 58, 139, where the notion of the lack of eschatology in the *Sīra* indicates a secure political position.

39. "An historical circumstance so public [as the emergence of the Qur'ān] cannot have been invented": see Serjeant's review of *QS* in *JRAS* (1978):77. The notion that a "conspiracy" (!) is involved in such a historical reconstruction becomes a rallying point for many objections; see N. Daniel's review of *Hagarism* in *JSS* 24 (1979):296–304. Contrary to Daniel (p. 298), one could claim that one hundred years *is* a long time, especially when one is dealing not with newspaper headlines and printing presses but the gradual emergence of a text at first within a select circle, then into ever widening circles. One could point to similar instances of "conspiracies" in the canonization of other scriptures, for example the identification of John the disciple with the Gospel of John in well less than a century after the emergence of the text. Besides, as in so many things, it all depends on which conspiracies one likes or does not like; Serjeant says of John Burton [*The Collection of the Qur'ān* (Cambridge: Cambridge University Press, 1977)] that he "argues vastly more cogently than Wansbrough's unsubstantiable assertions, that the consonantal text of the Qur'ān before us is the Prophet's own recension," but involved in Burton's book—if one bothers to read it carefully and not get carried away by its conclusion—is a "conspiracy" to which Serjeant's objection to Wansbrough's theory should apply as well. But obviously the conclusions are what count for Serjeant, not the method by which they are reached. (See his review of *QS*, *JRAS* [1978]:76). Cf. also Angelika Neuwirth, *Studien zur Komposition der mekkanischen Suren* (Berlin and New York: Walter de Gruyter, 1981) and my review *BSOAS* 45 (1982):149–50.

40. See, for example, Raphael Loewe, "Divine Frustration Exegetically Frustrated—Numbers 14:34 *tenū'ātī*," in *Words and Meanings*, ed. Lindars and Akroyd, esp. pp. 137–38; G. Vermes, *Scripture and Tradition*, introduction.

41. The historical appearance of exegetical "lists" of scriptural passages, whether of (apparent) scriptural contradiction, semantic aspects, or legal rulings (see *QS*, chapter 4 for these types of lists) indicate the emergence of a fixed text of scripture. Note M. R. Waldman's observation in Chapter 6 of this book: "As the Qur'ān itself became 'listed,' i.e., arranged in fixed order according to some fixed criteria of listing, further listing of the contents of the Qur'ān according to other principles of listing followed naturally." Precisely, Wansbrough would perhaps say; the earliest evidence of "listing" according to other criteria indicates the likely historical moment of the emergence of the fixed Qur'ānic canon.

42. See my review of *SM*, *JSS* 26 (1981):121–23.

43. See his review of van Ess, *Anfänge muslimischer Theologie*, in *BSOAS* 43 (1980): 361–63.

44. *MW* 67 (1977):307; the quote from *QS* is somewhat out of context, although cf. Wansbrough's review of van Ess, *Anfänge* in *BSOAS* 43 (1980):361.

45. Fazlur Rahman, *Major Themes of the Qur'ān* (Chicago: Bibliotheca Islamica, 1980), p. xiv; see my review in *BSOAS* 44 (1981):360–63. Rahman incorrectly quotes

QS; it should read ". . . the kind . . ."; there is also no explanation point (!) in Wansbrough's text. The possibility that there could be a difference of opinion over the value of literary analysis *per se* cannot be overlooked but Rahman's statements hardly are sufficient to urge such a position; cf. however, van Ess's review of *SM*, *BSOAS* 43 (1980):137–39, where precisely that argument is attempted; one needs to look no further than, for example, Frank Kermode, *The Genesis of Secrecy* (see nt. 17 above) to see the continued vitality of literary analysis, however.

46. G. H. A. Juynboll, in his review of *QS* in *JSS* 24 (1979):293–96, expresses this inability perfectly: "What makes W.'s theories so hard to swallow is the obvious disparity in style and contents of Meccan and Medinan *sūras*" (p. 294). Similar to this are Rahman's comments in Chapter 12, and in *Major Themes*, p. xvi, about chronological "necessity" due to the doctrine of *naskh* (which he conceives of as "removal" of verses alone, not as legal abrogation). The possibility that *naskh* refers to replaced Jewish practices (Burton) or to abrogated earlier dispensation (Wansbrough) is not even entertained by Rahman; both these alternate solutions obviate the chronological "necessity."

Chapter 10. Towards a Hermeneutic of Qur'ānic and Other Narratives in Isma'ili Thought

1. See in particular his early article, "How Did the Early Shī'a become Sectarian?," *Journal of the American Oriental Society* 75 (1955):1–13, and *The Venture of Islam*, 3 vols. (Chicago: University of Chicago Press, 1974) vol. 1, pp. 256–67 and 372–84.

2. This is particularly evident in his treatment of "popular" esoteric material. See, for instance, his article "Satpanth" in *Collectanea*, vol. 1 (Bombay: Ismaili Society, 1948), pp. 1–8.

3. The literature on literary theory is enormous. For the purposes of this volume, however, several fairly recent works reflect some ongoing concerns and controversies: Roland Barthes, *Critique et verité*, (Paris: Seuil, 1966); *Essays on the Language of Literature*, ed. S. B. Chatman and S. R. Levin (Boston: Houghton Mifflin, 1967); Northrop Frye, *Anatomy of Criticism. Four Essays by Northrop Frye* (New York: Atheneum, 1966); E. D. Hirsch, *Validity in Interpretation* (New Haven: Yale University Press, 1967); Paul Ricoeur, *La metaphore vive* (Paris: Seuil, 1975) and a series of works on literature written and/or edited by Joseph Strelka, published since 1968, including *Problems of Literary Evaluation*, ed. J. Strelka (University Park, Pa.: Pennsylvania State University Press, 1969). Each of Strelka's works contains extensive references and bibliographies.

4. Quoted by Eugene Vance, "Pas de trois: Narrative, Hermeneutics and Structure in Medieval Poetics," in *Interpretation of Narrative*, ed. Mario J. Valdes and Owen J. Miller (Toronto: University of Toronto Press, 1978) p. 122. Other papers in the book, based on an international colloquium on the subject held at the University of Toronto, represent some of the effort and ongoing debate in the field of narrative interpretation.

5. Quoted in Henry Corbin, *Histoire de la philosophie islamique* (Paris: Gaillimard, 1964) p. 17.

6. *Daʿā'im al-Islām*, 2 vols. ed. A. A. A. Fyzee (Cairo: Dār al-Maʿārif, 1951–60) *Ta'wīl al-Daʿā'im*, 2 vols. ed. M. al-Azami (Cairo: Dār al-Maʿārif, 1968–72). For the latter, see also Ismail K. Poonawala, *Bibliography of Ismaʿili Literature* (Malibu, Calif.: Undena Publications, 1977), p. 64.

7. For al-Shīrāzī, see Poonawala, *Ismaʿili Literature*, pp. 103–4. The interpretation is to be found in his *al-Majālis al-Mu'ayyadiyyah*, as yet not fully edited. Some *majālis* are summarized in J. Muscati and M. Movelvi, *Life and Lectures of al-Mu'ayyad* (Karachi: Ismailia Association of Pakistan, 1956). A recent, partial edition is Hamid al Din Hatim, ed., *al-Majālis* (Bombay: Published by the author, 1975), the first of eight volumes.

8. The source is discussed and an account of the story provided by Bernard Lewis in "An Ismaʿili Interpretation of the Fall of Adam," *Bulletin of the School of Oriental and African Studies* 9 (1938):691–704.

9. For the background to their history and the Ginan tradition, see Azim Nanji, *The Nizari Ismaʿili Tradition in the Indo-Pakistani Subcontinent*, Monographs in Islamic Religion and Theology (New York: Caravan Books, 1978).

10. Claude Lévi-Strauss, *The Savage Mind* (London: Widenfeld and Nicolson, 1962), pp. 16–22, where the idea is fully developed.

11. See Nanji, *Nizari Ismaʿili Tradition*, pp. 114ff. from which the following account is drawn.

12. Muḥammad, ʿAli, Ḥasan, Ḥusayn and Faṭima. The Shiʿi emphasis is based on their interpretation of Qur'ān 33:33 and 3:61.

13. Sukumari Bhattacharji, *Hindu Theogony* (Cambridge: Cambridge University Press, 1970), p. 358.

14. The Hindu concept and the list is given in Alain Daniélou, *Hindu Polytheism* (New York: Pantheon Books, 1964) pp. 116–81. For the understanding of this concept (and its use in doctrine) in the Ginans, see Nanji, *Nizari Ismaʿili Tradition*, pp. 110–13.

Chapter 12: Islam and the Study of Religion

1. Jacques Waardenburg, "Islam and the History of Religions: A Historian of Religions' Perspective," paper presented at the symposium on Islam and the History of Religions, Arizona State University, January 1980.

2. John Wisdom, *Other Minds* (Oxford: Blackwell, 1956).

3. Jane I. Smith, "Islamic Understanding of the Afterlife," paper presented at the symposium on Islam and the History of Religions, Arizona State University, January 1980.

4. Edward W. Said, *Orientalism* (New York: Pantheon Books, 1978).

5. Robert King Merton, *The Sociology of Science: Theoretical and Empirical Investigations* (Chicago: University of Chicago Press, 1973), chapter 5, "The Perspectives of Insiders and Outsiders," pp. 99–136.

6. Fazlur Rahman, *Islam and Modernity: Transformation of an Intellectual Tradition* (London and Chicago: University of Chicago Press, 1982).

7. John Wansbrough, *Quranic Studies: Sources and Methods of Scriptural Interpretation* (Oxford: Oxford University Press, 1977); and idem, *The Sectarian Milieu: Content and Composition of Islamic Salvation History* (Oxford: Oxford University Press, 1978).

8. Fazlur Rahman, *Islamic Methodology of History* (Karachi: Central Institute of Islamic Research, 1965).

9. I have given some examples to illustrate my critique of Wansbrough in the Introduction to *Major Themes of the Qur'ān* (Chicago: Bibliotheca Islamica, 1980) and in a review of recent books on the Qur'ān by Western authors, in *The Journal of Religion* 64/1(1984):86–89.

10. All reviews have either rejected or denounced utterly Wansbrough's two books, which this author does not view as coincidence. The most sympathetic reviews are those of Josef van Ess, who does not accept Wansbrough's conclusions but, nonetheless, thinks the method may be useful; note, however, that in his review of *Sectarian Milieu*, van Ess advocates a return to the philological method. It may be that Wansbrough's is the call of a true genius whom nobody has yet understood except Andrew Rippin. If so, then we expect to hear much more that makes sense than we have so far; for what we *have* heard so far is hardly encouraging, I am afraid. [For a list of reviews of Wansbrough's works, see notes 4 & 5 of chapter nine. Editor's note.]

11. Jean Jacques Waardenburg, *L'Islam dans le miroir de l'occident* (Paris: Mouton, 1963).

12. Edward W. Said, *Orientalism* (New York: Pantheon Books, 1978).

About the Contributors

MUHAMMAD ABDUL-RAUF is Rector of the International Islamic University in Kuala Lumpur, Malaysia, and former Director of the Islamic Center, Washington, D.C. His Ph.D. in Islamic studies is from the University of London. He has lectured widely in this country and abroad and he is the author of several books on Islamic religion.

CHARLES J. ADAMS is professor of Islamic studies and former Director of the Institute of Islamic studies at McGill University. His Ph.D. in history of religions is from the University of Chicago. He has held visiting lectureships in North America and the Middle East. Professor Adams has written extensively about Islam and the study of Islamic religion, including *A Reader's Guide to the Great Religions*, which he edited and to which he contributed the chapter on Islam.

FREDERICK M. DENNY is associate professor of religious studies, University of Colorado at Boulder. His Ph.D. in Islamic studies and history of religions is from the University of Chicago. Much of his research and published writings focus on the Qur'ān in Muslim religious life. He has done field work in Egypt and Indonesia and is the author of *An Introduction to Islam* (Macmillan, 1985).

RICHARD M. EATON is associate professor of oriental studies at the University of Arizona at Tucson. His Ph.D. in history is from the University of

Wisconsin. He is the author of *Sufis of Bijapur, 1300–1700: Social Roles of Sufis in Medieval India* (Princeton University Press, 1978) and of numerous articles on conversion to Islam in India.

WILLIAM A. GRAHAM is associate professor of Islamic religion, Harvard University. He is a member of the Harvard Committee on the Study of Religion, and his Ph.D. is from Harvard in history and comparative study of religion. He is the author of *Divine Word and Prophetic Word in Early Islam* (Mouton, 1977) and of several articles on the concept of scripture in Islam and in other religious traditions.

RICHARD C. MARTIN is associate professor and chair of religious studies at Arizona State University. His Ph.D. in Near Eastern languages and literatures is from New York University. He is the author of *Islam: A Cultural Perspective* (Prentice-Hall, 1982) and has written several articles on understanding the Qur'ān and on history of religions' approaches to Islamic studies.

AZIM NANJI is professor of religious studies, chair of the Department of Humanities/Religious Studies, and Director of the Global Studies program at Oklahoma State University, Stillwater. His Ph.D. is from Harvard University, and he is the author of *The Nizari Ismaʿili Tradition in the Indo-Pakistani Subcontinent* (Caravan Books, 1978) and coauthor of *The Religious World: Communities of Faith* (Macmillan, 1981).

FAZLUR RAHMAN is professor of Islamic thought in the Department of Near Eastern Languages and Civilizations, University of Chicago. His Ph.D. is from Oxford University. He is the author of several books and articles on Islamic philosophy, history, and religion, including *Islam* (2nd Ed.; University of Chicago Press, 1979) and *Major Themes of the Qur'an* (Bibliotheca Islamica, 1981).

ANDREW RIPPIN is associate professor of religious studies at the University of Calgary. His Ph.D. is from McGill University, 1981. Professor Rippin has published articles on the Qur'ān in *BSOAS*, *Arabica*, *Muslim World*, among others.

WILLIAM R. ROFF is professor of history at Columbia University. His Ph.D. is from Australian National University. His publications include *The Origins of Malay Nationalism* (Yale University Press, 1967), *Kelantan: Religion, Society and Politics in a Malay State* (Oxford University Press, 1974), and numerous articles and edited works on Islam in the Malay Peninsula.

MARILYN R. WALDMAN is associate professor of history and chair of the Division of Comparative Studies, The Ohio State University. Her Ph.D. in history at the University of Chicago focused on Islamic studies and included work in history of religions. Among her publications is *Toward a Theory of*

Historical Narrative: A Case Study in Perso-Islamicate Historiography (Ohio State University Press, 1980).

EARLE H. WAUGH is professor of Islam and the history of religions, Department of Religious Studies at the University of Alberta. His Ph.D. is from the University of Chicago in history of religions. His writings on approaches to the study of Islamic religion include "Following the Beloved: Muhammad as Model in the Sufi Tradition," in *The Biographical Process*, eds. Capps and Reynolds (The Hague: Mouton, 1976).

Index

ʿAbbās, Mahmūd al-ʿAqqād, 54
Abbot, Nabia, 102, 157
Abdul-Rauf, Muhammad, 92, 176, 189, 193, 197
Abū Bakr Ibn Mujāhid, 34
Abū Jaʿfar al-Ṭūsī, 139
Abū Yazīd of Bistām, 86
Adam, 167–68
Adams, Charles J., 3, 126, 158, 159
Ahmad, Aziz, 109
Al-Azhar University, 180, 184
ʿAlā al-Dawlah al-Semnānī, 133
ʿAlī Ibn Abī Ṭālib, 52, 169, 170, 171
Ali Reza, 114
Ali, Ameer, 122
Allah, *Allāh*, 111, 114
Allah Yagat Iśvar, 114
Amils, 109
Andrae, Tor, 63, 65
Ansar, *anṣār*, 51
Arkan, *arkān*, 64
Arnold, Thomas, 117
Asbab al-Nuzul, *asbāb al-nuzūl*, 153, 187
Ashʿaris, Ashʿarite, 197
Ashtiyānī, S. J., 132

Baba Farid of Pakpattan, 117, 119
Baha al-Haqq Zakaria, 119
Bahamani Sultanate, 113
Baird, Robert, 44
Baluchistan, 110
Bandanawaz, Sayyid Muhammad Husayni Gisudaraz, 117, 118
Baraka, *barakah*, 76, 117
Batin, *bāṭin*, 138, 148, 169
Bauer, Walter, 49
Baur, F. C., 25
Bell, Richard, 158
Beltromi, Eugeneo, 44
Bengal, 107, 110, 113–15, 119, 120–22
Bible, Judeo-Christian, 24–25, 28–29, 161
Binder, Leonard, 12–13
Black, Max, 44–45

Boehme, Jacob, 141
Boullata, I. J., 162
Bousquet, G. H., 63, 65
Bukka, 109
Bultmann, Rudolph, 155
Burton, John, 154
Burton, Richard, 60, 66

Calendar, Islamic, 71–72
Chandal, 110
Chao, Yuen Ren, 44
-Chotomous Thinking, 94–100
Cline, Felix, 44
Conversion: by accretion and reform, 111–22; general, 89, 106–23; liberation theory, 109–11; by patronage, 108–9
Cook, Michael, 152
Corbin, Henry, 126, 129–50, 164
Coromandel, 115
Cousins, Ewart, 46
Creation, 166–72
Crone, Patricia, 152

Daʿwa, *daʿwa*, 68
Dar al-Harb, *dār al-hārb*, 70
Dar al-Islam, *dār al-islām*, 70
Dawla, 88
De Chardin, Teilhard, 46
Deccan, the, 113, 119
Delhi Doab, 112, 119
Delhi Sultanate, 109, 119
Denny, Frederick M., 35, 39, 61, 102, 189
Dhikr, 31, 38, 103
Diamond, Stanley, 94–95
Dilthey, Wilhelm, 8
Din, *dīn*, 88
Douglas, Mary, 70–71
Dumont, Louis, 110
Durga Puja, 121
Durkheim, Emile, 69, 95, 122

Eaton, Richard M., 89
Eliade, Mircea, 43, 48
Encyclopedia of Religion and Ethics, 6
Extension Transference, 97–98

Fārābī, al-, 196
Fatiha, the, *fātiḥa*, 37, 39
Fatima, *Faṭima*, 114, 170, 171
Fiqh, *fiqh*, 63–64
Firishta, 117
Foucault, Michel, 14
Frege, Gottlob, 44
Furqān, 31
Furūʿ, 97

Gadamer, Hans-Georg, 126
Ganges, Gangetic Plain, 108, 109, 120, 122
Gaster, Theodor, 73–74
Gaudefroy-Demombynes, M., 82
Geertz, Clifford, 10, 60, 65, 66, 88, 95, 122, 126
Ghazālī, Abū Ḥāmid Muḥammad al-, 40, 82
Ghusl, *ghusl*, 84
Gibb, H. A. R., 193
Ginans, 165, 169–73
Gnosticism, Shiʿi, 139
Goldziher, Ignaz, 156, 199
Goody, Jack, 89, 94, 98–104
Gosain, 114
Graham, William A., 20–21, 101–2
Gujarat, 115, 119

Hadith, *ḥadīth*, 32, 33, 57, 64, 97, 101, 102, 103, 139, 140, 150, 185, 199
Ḥafiẓ, 38
Haji Muhammad, 114
Hajj, *ḥajj*, 64, 68, 69, 77, 78–86, 103
Hall, Edward, 97
Haqiqa, *ḥaqīqa*, 138, 139, 144, 167, 169
Haram, 70
Ḥarām, 69–70
Hardy, Peter, 107
Harihari, 109
Ḥasan, 170, 171
Ḥassān b. Thābit, 32
Ḥaydar Āmulī, 132, 133
Hegel, G. W. F., 142, 147

Heidegger, Martin, 126
Hindu elites, conversion of, 122
History of religions, vii–x, 1–10, 19–21, 41–49, 59–61, 91–94, 104–5, 125–26
Hockett, Charles F., 44
Hodgson, Marshall G. S., 96, 101, 164
Horton, Robin, 95
Hujwīrī, Al-, 86
Ḥusayn, 170
Ḥusayn, Ṭāhā, 52–55
Husserl, Edmund, 13

ʿIbāda, 38, 63–64, 69
Iblīs, 168
Ibn ʿAbbās, 157
Ibn al-ʿArabī, 137
Ibn Babūyā, 139
Ibn Baṭṭuṭa, 108, 116, 117
Ibn Isḥāq, 48–52, 156
Ibn Khaldūn, 37
Ibn Rushd, 133, 142
Ibn Sīnā, 196
Ibn Taymiyya, 64, 74, 97
Ibrāhīm (Abraham), 167, 201
Ibrahim Adham, 82
ʿĪd al-Fiṭr, 69
ʿĪd of Sacrifice, 69
Iḥrām, 84
Imām Jaʿfar al-Ṣādiq, 53–54
Imams, 101, 139, 172
Iman, *īman*, 69
India, conversion to Islam in, 106–23
Iran, 134–37
ʿIsā, 167
Ishmael, 201
Islam: Judeo-Christian background of, 157–62, 185–86; normative, 65, 77, 104; popular, ix, 65, 77; rituals of, ix, 59–86
Islamic studies, vii–x, 1–5, 10–16, 179–202; Muslim response to, vii, 179–88, 189–202
Ismaʿili Shiʿa, 127
Isphahan, School of, 134, 135
Iśvara, 114
Ithna-ʿAshari Shiʿa, 129–50
Ivanow, Vladimir A., 164

Jahiliyya, *jāhiliyya*, 48, 71–72, 92
Jats, 110, 113, 119
Jinn, 111

Kaʿba, 71
Kashmir, 119, 201
Kayasthas, 109
Kemal, Namik, 193
Khadīja, 186
Khalaji Sultans of Delhi, 109
Khālid, Khālid M., 56–57
Khatris, 109
Khizr, 111
Khuda, 114
Khusrau Khan, 109
Kitāb al-Mabānī, 36
Kitagawa, Joseph, 42
Koch, 110
Konkan, 115
Kosambi, D. D., 119
Krishna, 112
Kulaynī, al-, 139

Lambert, Richard, 12
Landolt, Hermann, 132
Lévi-Strauss, Claude, 10, 60–61, 170, 194
Levtzion, Nehemiah, 111
Lewis, Bernard, 11–12, 79–80
Literacy, 98–100
Loewe, Raphael, 161

Maharashtra, 109
Malabar, 115
Malcolm X, 85
Maqra', 38, 39
Martin, Richard C., 143, 197, 202
Marx, Karl, 87
Maṣāḥif, muṣḥaf, 30, 33, 34
Massignon, Louis, 130
Maturidis, 197
Mawlid, 74
Mawsim ḥajj, 81
Meo, 112
Merton, Robert, 194

Middle East Studies. (*See* Islamic studies)
Mina, 73, 84
Mīqāt, 83
Mīr Dāmād, 134
Model Theory, 42–49
Morenz, Siegfried, 40
Mosque construction, 114–15
Mu'ayyad fī-Dīn al-Shīrāzī, 167
Muʿtazila, 47
Mughal Empire, 113, 119
Muḥammad, 19–21, 30, 32, 34, 41, 58, 60, 118, 139, 144, 169, 170–72, 180–81, 185; modern views of, 52–57; traditional image of, 49–52
Muḥammad Muḥyī al-Dīn, 53–54
Mujeeb, Mohammad, 120–21
Mukrī, Muḥammad, 132
Mullā Ṣadrā Shīrāzī, 132, 134, 140
Müller, Friederich Max, 5, 6, 25, 43
Mūsā, 167
Muwaḥḥidūn, 97

Nadel, S. F., 65
Nadwa, 39
Names, Muslim, 113–14
Nanji, Azim, 127
Nāṣir-i Khusraw, 132, 166
Nasr, Seyyed Hossein, 76, 132, 133
Naṣṣ, 101, 103
Nawawī, al-, 76
Nelson, Kristina, 35, 39
Neusner, Jacob, 16–17, 155
Niranjan, 114
Nizari Ismaʿlis, 165, 172
Nock, A. D., 111
Northwest Frontier, 110
Nupe, 65, 74
Nuṭaqā', 167

Oriental studies. *See* Islamic studies
Orientalism, 13–16. *See also* Islamic studies
Ottoman empire, 136

Pakistan, 121, 183
Parasnis, 109
Partin, Harry, 84
Pepper, Stephen, 44
Persian wheel, 120, 122
Personalist approach, 9
Phenomenology, 7–9, 13–14, 23, 41, 104, 125–26, 129–30, 142–50
Plato, 135
Pod, 110
Prabhu, 114
Punjab, 107, 110, 113–15, 119–121

Qadi, *qāḍī*, 113, 116–18
Qāḍī al-Nuʿmān, 167
Qirā'a, 33–36
Qubba, 74
Qummī, al-, 139
Qur'ān, 19, 23–40, 71, 93, 97, 101, 103, 104, 114, 128, 138, 145, 153–63, 167, 173, 176, 181, 182, 184–87, 196–202; recitation of the, ix, 29–40, 75–76
Quraysh, 50–51, 186

Rahman, Fazlur, 67, 92, 104, 127, 140, 143, 163, 176
Rajasthan, 112
Rajbansi, 110
Rakshya Kali, 121
Ramsey, Ian, 45–47
Religion in Geschicte und Gegenwart, 6
Religions in History, 151–52, 198–200
Ricouer, Paul, 126
Rippin, Andrew, 126, 127, 176, 189, 198–201
Roff, William R., 61, 193
Russell, Bertrand, 44
Ruzbehān-i Baqlī, 132, 133

Saʿy, *saʿy*, 84
Sacred Books of the East, 6, 25
Safavid Empire, 136
Saggs, H. W. F., 155
Said, Edward W., 14–15, 193, 202
Saʿīd, Labīb al-, 35
Salat, *ṣalāt*, 32, 37, 64, 69, 72, 77, 102
Saljuke, Salah, 179–80
Salvation History, 153–58
Satpanth, 169

Sawm, *ṣawm*, 64, 69, 73, 77
Sawwaf, Mujahid al-, 103
Sayyid Murtaza, 114
Sayyid Sultan, 114
Schacht, Joseph, 102, 156–57, 199
Schweitzer, Albert, 43
Scripture, 20, 21–29
Serjeant, R. B., 74, 159
Sezgin, Fuad (Fuat), 157
Shāfiʿī *madhhab*, 116
Shariʿa, *sharīʿa*, 47, 68, 88, 138, 144, 145, 148, 167, 197
Shaykh Aḥmad Aḥsāʾī, 134
Shaykh Mansur, 114
Shaykhis, 134
Shiʿa Islam, 47, 101, 126, 127, 129–50, 164–73
Shuʿayb, 200
Sials, 113
Sīdī Aḥmad al-Badawī, 74
Silsila, *silsila*, 75
Sind, 109, 119–20
Sira, *sīrā*, 41–58, 126, 154, 160
Sitala, 121
Smith, Wilfred Cantwell, 9, 63, 78–79, 190, 193, 197
Snouck-Hurgronje, Christiaan, 60, 63, 66, 68, 79
Structuralism, 10, 16
Sufis: and conversion, 117–18, 122
Sufism, 136, 195
Suhrawardi, Shihab al-Din al-, 130, 131, 133, 135
Sunna, 68, 102, 104, 156, 181, 182, 185, 197
Sunni Islam, 135–36, 140
Swedenborg, Emmanuel, 141

Ta'wil, *ta'wīl*, 145, 165–69, 170, 172, 173
Taʿziya, 73
Tafsir, *tafsīr*, 33, 102, 126, 154, 160
Ṭahāra, 64
Tajwid, *tajwīd*, 33, 38
Talbīya, 84, 85
Tālib, Aḥmad, 55–56, 58
Ṭanzil, *tanzīl*, 166
Tariqa, *ṭarīqa*, 74–75, 103
Tawaf, *ṭawāf*, 84, 85
Tawhid, *tawḥīd*, 64, 70, 171
Theology, 1–3, 91
Tilawa, *tilāwa*, 38–40
Toynbee, Arnold, 105
Turner, Victor, 10, 60, 83

Ulama, *ʿulamāʾ ʿālim*, 38, 195
ʿUthmān, 30, 34

Van Gennep, Arnold, 61, 74, 80, 86
Van der Leeuw, Gerardus, 26, 142
Vermes, Geza, 160, 161
Vijaynagar Empire, 109
Von Grunebaum, Gustav E., 11

Waardenburg, Jacques, 79, 190, 202
Wach, Joachaim, 3, 42
Wahhabis, 64, 74, 189
Waldman, Marilyn R., 89
Wallace, A. F. C., 92
Wansbrough, John, 49, 126–27, 151–63, 176, 198–201
Watt, W. Montgomery, 74–75, 156
Waugh, Earle H., 21, 189, 197
Weber, Max, 42, 87, 111
Wellhausen, Julius, 25, 49
Wensinck, A. J., 79
Westermark, Edward, 60
Wisdom, John, 176, 191
Wolfson, Harry A., 157
Wuquf, *wuqūf*, 84

Yaḥya, ʿUthmān, 132
Yamani Arabs, 50–52

Zahir, *ẓahīr*, 138, 148
Zakat, *zakāt*, 64, 76–77, 169
Zamzam, well of, 81
Ziyara, *ziyāra*, 103
Zoroaster, Zoroastrianism, 135